GW01605122

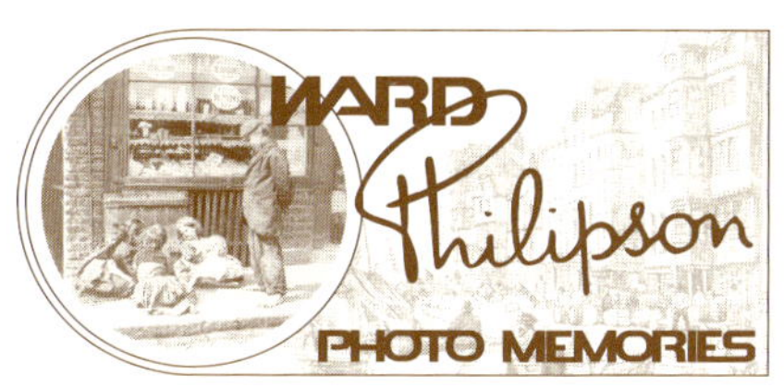

~ FIRST SELECTION OF WORK ~

Featuring over a century of photographs, views, etchings and engravings.

The North of England as seen by a family of photographers who were founders in the development of photographic art.

compiled by

John A. Moreels

WARD Philipson Gallery,
Blandford Square, Newcastle upon Tyne NE1 4HZ
Tel: 0191 232 7281 Fax: 0191 222 1548
e-mail: gallery@wardphilipson.co.uk

First Published 1998.

Publishing and Copyright 1998 by:
WARD Philipson Group Ltd.,
Halifax Road, Dunston Industrial Estate,
Gateshead, Tyne & Wear, NE11 9HW.

Tel: 0191 460 5915 Fax: 0191 460 8540
e-mail: inter.imaging@wardphilipson.co.uk

Main Gallery:
WARD Philipson Gallery,
Blandford Square,
Newcastle upon Tyne, NEI 4HZ.
(near The Discovery Museum)

Tel: 0191 232 7281 Fax: 0191 222 1548
e-mail: gallery@wardphilipson.co.uk
Visit our web site at www.wardphilipson.co.uk.

Photographic Printing:
WARD Philipson/Inter~Imaging Colour Lab
Tel: 0191 232 7281

Artwork and Photographic Finishing:
WARD Philipson/Inter~Imaging Design Team
Tel: 0191 232 7281

Scanning and Reproduction:
WARD Philipson Image Production Centre
Tel: 0191 232 7281

Duotone Printing and Finishing:
WARD Philipson Colour Print
Tel: 0191 460 5915

I.S.B.N. 0 9534224 0 2

Introduction

In 1996 two of the oldest family-owned companies in Newcastle upon Tyne amalgamated to form the Ward Philipson Group, incorporating everything from photography to print. During the early years of both companies the relevant families were leaders in their specialist field of technology resulting in the production of many historical prints and publications. Thomas Bewick's son shared workshops with Wards, resulting in a large collection of engravings and early printed material, including printed silk programmes for local theatres including the Theatre Royal in Newcastle, which can now be viewed in the Ward Philipson Gallery.

Ward's family business, established in 1845, is one of the oldest printing companies still existing and growing in the modern environment. Their history includes the production of Wards Directory of Newcastle upon Tyne in 1850 and the first half-penny newspaper ever published in the United Kingdom in 1853. Philipson's, established in 1923, were one of the earliest photographers, film processors and engravers in England and although always based in Newcastle upon Tyne became well known throughout the country.

This first collection is a picture book, a compilation of interesting photographs featuring views, etchings and engravings which introduce a new meaning to the North's history. The book contains an era of images solely to be of factual interest, thought provoking and to take you back in time. Many prints are from the photographers' own elegantly composed and sensitively conceived technique, talent and ability. Other prints are the company's own appreciation of others' talents, recording the unique abilities of the engravers and etchers of the earliest years.

Most of the collection was discovered at the Blandford Square premises. Very little documentation has survived except for a range of company negative registers, but with the will and determination of researchers and colleagues captions have been given to all of the photographs. With the help of others, including Beamish Museum archivers, the researchers are continuing their work, selecting and detailing further negatives and prints. We will continue to gather information which will be available at our Newcastle gallery upon request. All information is given in good faith but no responsibility is accepted for errors or omissions. If you have any information relating to any print which may help our researchers please contact us.

The actual etchings and engravings probably date back to the early 1800's with the photographic recordings of these being prepared after the 1900's. The earliest photographs were probably taken around 1870 when the photographic materials included the wet collodion process with glass plates. Some of the prints in this collection have been reproduced directly from the glass plate, the quality and detail of which remains first class. They are now stored securely and safely with new photographic negatives being utilised for further production.

All of these photographs are now available as re-prints in any size, shape and quantity. Many are now readily available as duotone litho prints and postcards from our gallery and stockists. A full list and details are available on request. The range will also be continually increased as further negatives are discovered. I hope you enjoy this collection and look forward to compiling our second edition.

Many happy recollections!

John A. Moreels

The Lambton Worm

This tune was used in a pantomime at the old Tyne Theatre in 1867.

There are many versions of this old Durham legend of the Lambton Worm in song form. All are taken from the old ballad of that name by J. Watson. How the legend originated and what amount of truth (if any) there is in the old tale is hard to say. Amongst North Country folk however, to question the veracity of the story is looked upon as treason. Is not Lambton Castle still standing by the river Wear? Is not "The Worm Well" into which young Lambton threw the strange looking "fish" still there, also the hill round which the dragon wrapped his tail seven times and known to this day as Worm Hill? Have not our fathers told us this story many a time round the family fireside? I still remember the dreadful anxiety amongst my brothers and myself when the knight went forth to the Mortal Combat, and what a relief it was, when the battle was over and the young heir returned victorious. In olden days this was the tail that was told and sung by the Wandering Minstrels in our old Northern Clime.

In modern days the old dragon has been brought back to life, in pantomime and on the music hall stage and the solemn warning of the ballad, has given place to the quips and jokes of the comedian. This song written in extravagant burlesque is very popular and a great favourite of the Dunelm Singers.

The illustrations are by D. Smith, the well known North Country Cartoonist.

The words and rhyme of 'The Lambton Worm'
as performed in a pantomime at
the Old Tyne Theatre in 1867.
Cat No: A101 Ref: H9185

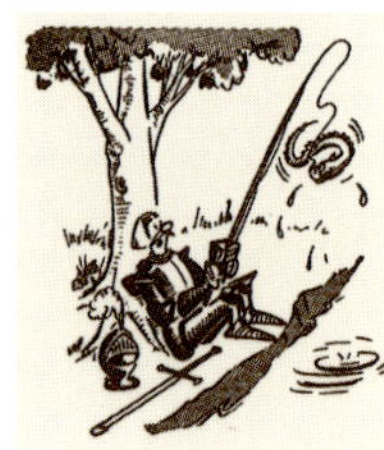

One Sunday mornin' Lambton
went a-fishin'in the Wear;
An' catched a fish upon he's heuk,
He thowt leuk't varry queer,
But whatt'n a kind ov fish it was
Young Lambton cuddent tell
He waddn't fash te carry'd hyem,
So he hoyed it in a well.

Chorus:
Whisht! lads, haad yor gobs
An' Aa'll tell ye sall an aaful story,
Whisht! lads, haad yor gobs
An' Aa'll tell ye 'boot the worm.

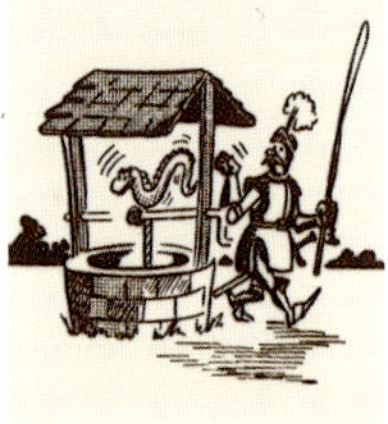

Noo Lambton felt inclined te gan
An' fight i' foreign wars.
He joined a troop o' Knights that cared
For nowther woonds nor scars,
An' off he went te Palestine
Where queer thing him befel,
An varry seun forgat aboot
The queer worm i' the well.

But the worm got fat an' growed an' growed,
An' growed an aaful size;
He'd greet big teeth, a greet big gob,
And greet big goggle eyes.
An' when at neets he craaled aboot
Te pick up bits o' news,
If he felt dry upon the road,
He milked a dozen coos.

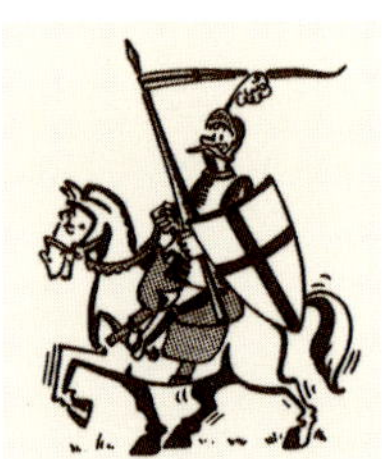

This feorful worm wad often feed
On caalves an' lambs an' sheep,
An swally little bairns alive
When they laid doon te sleep.
An' when he'd eaten aall he cud
An' he had had he's fill,
He craaled away an' lapped he's tail
Seven times roond Pensher Hill.

The news of this myest aaful worm
An' his queer gannins on
Seun crossed the seas, gat te the ears
Ov brave an' bowld Sor John.
So hyem he cam an' catched the beast
An' cut im' in twe haalves,
An' that seun stopped he's eatin' bairns
An' sheep an' lambs and caalves.

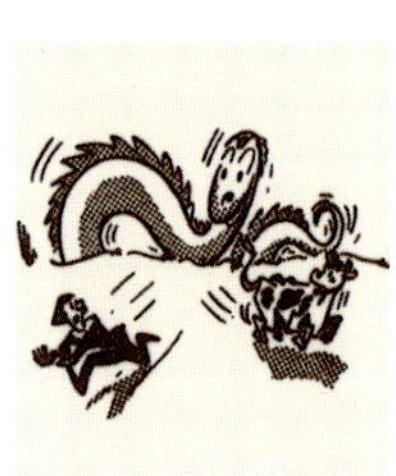

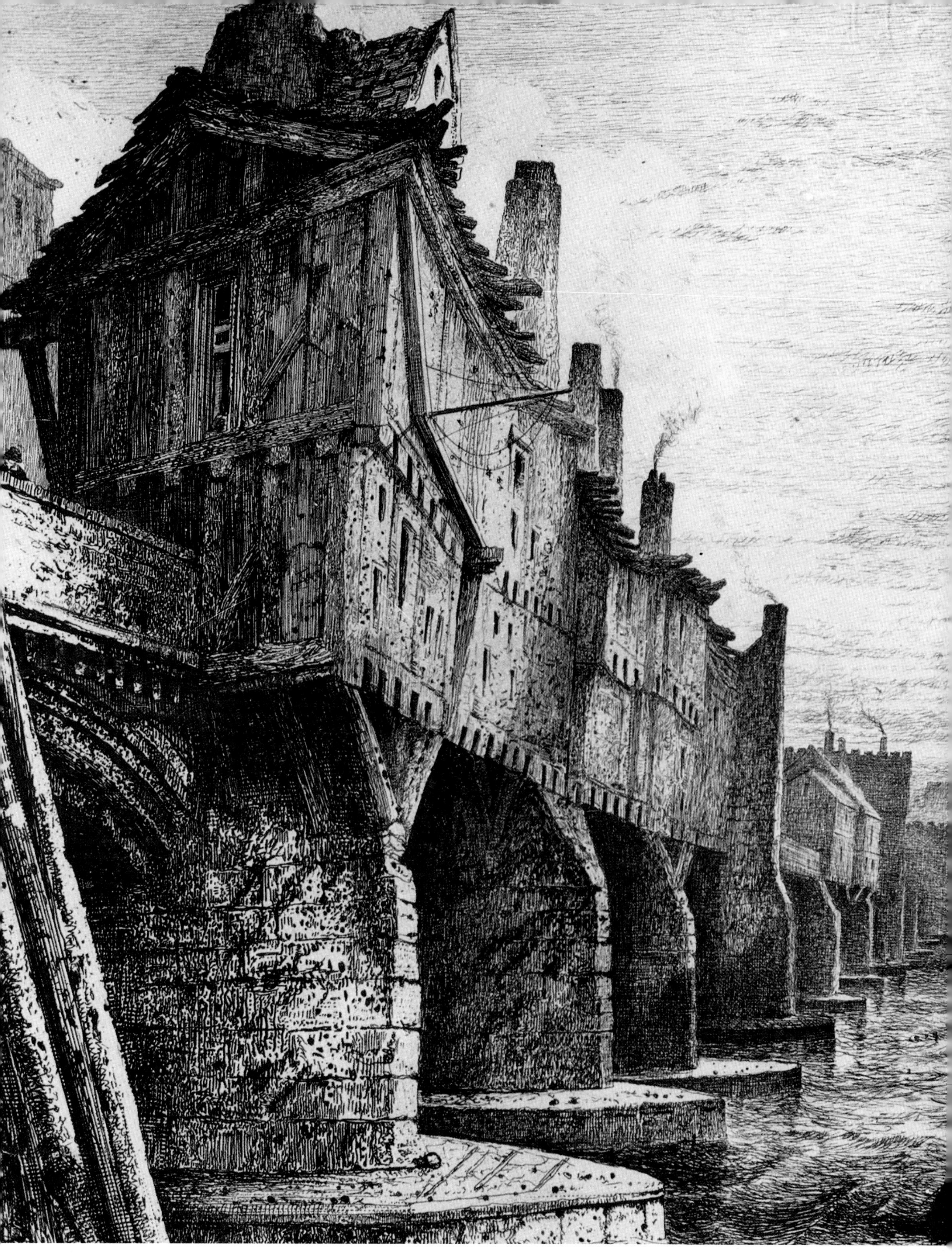

The Great Bridge of Tyne, circa 1700, swept away in 1777.
Drawn by Geo. B. Richardson and etched by T. M. Richardson Snr.
Cat No: WPG001 Ref: T/1408

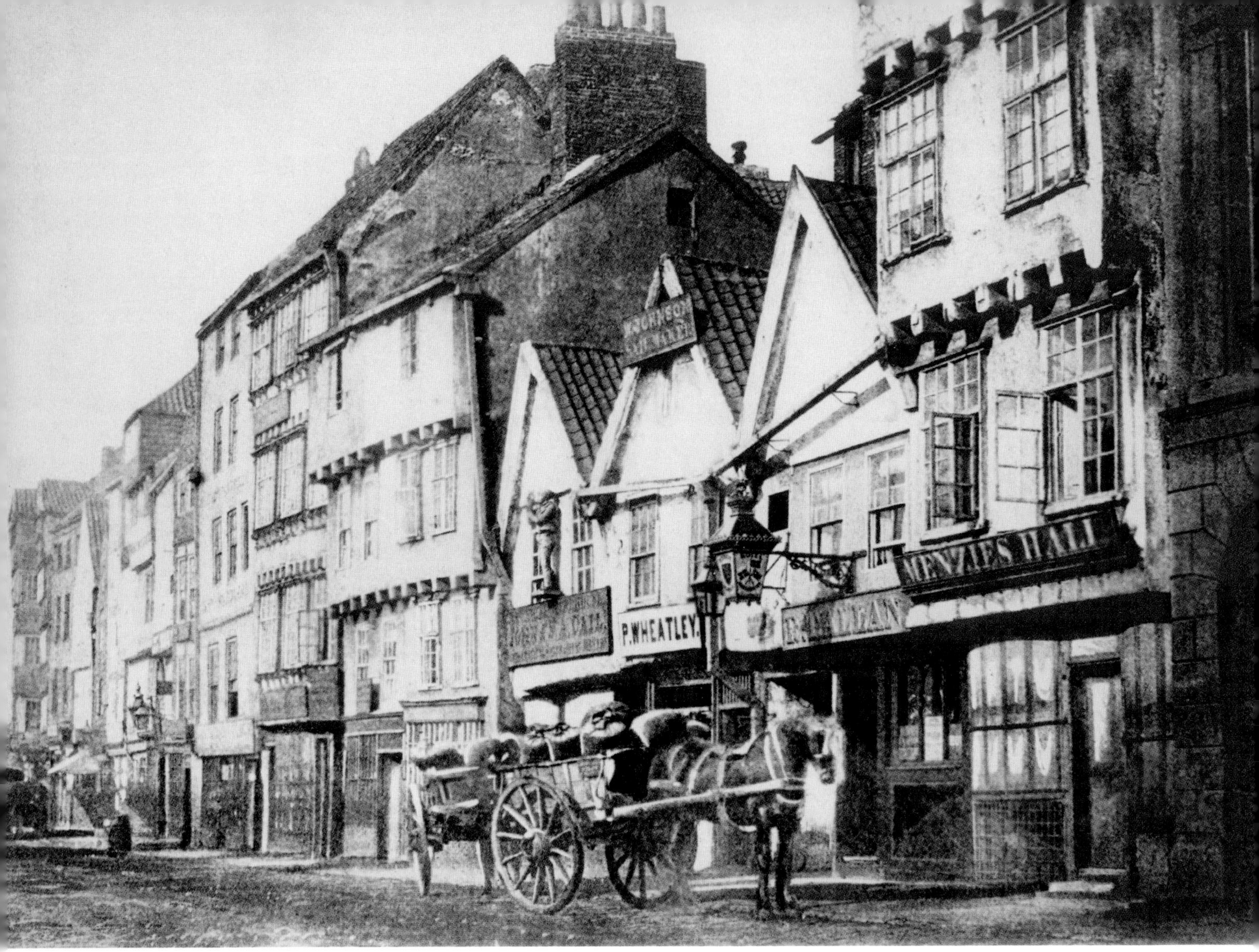

Quayside, Newcastle upon Tyne before the fire of 1854. Printed by W. S. Corder from a paper negative by John Parry made in 1848. The Custom House is the building to the extreme right.
Cat No: A102 Ref: C6872

Newcastle upon Tyne from the south.
Cat No: A103 Ref: D8723

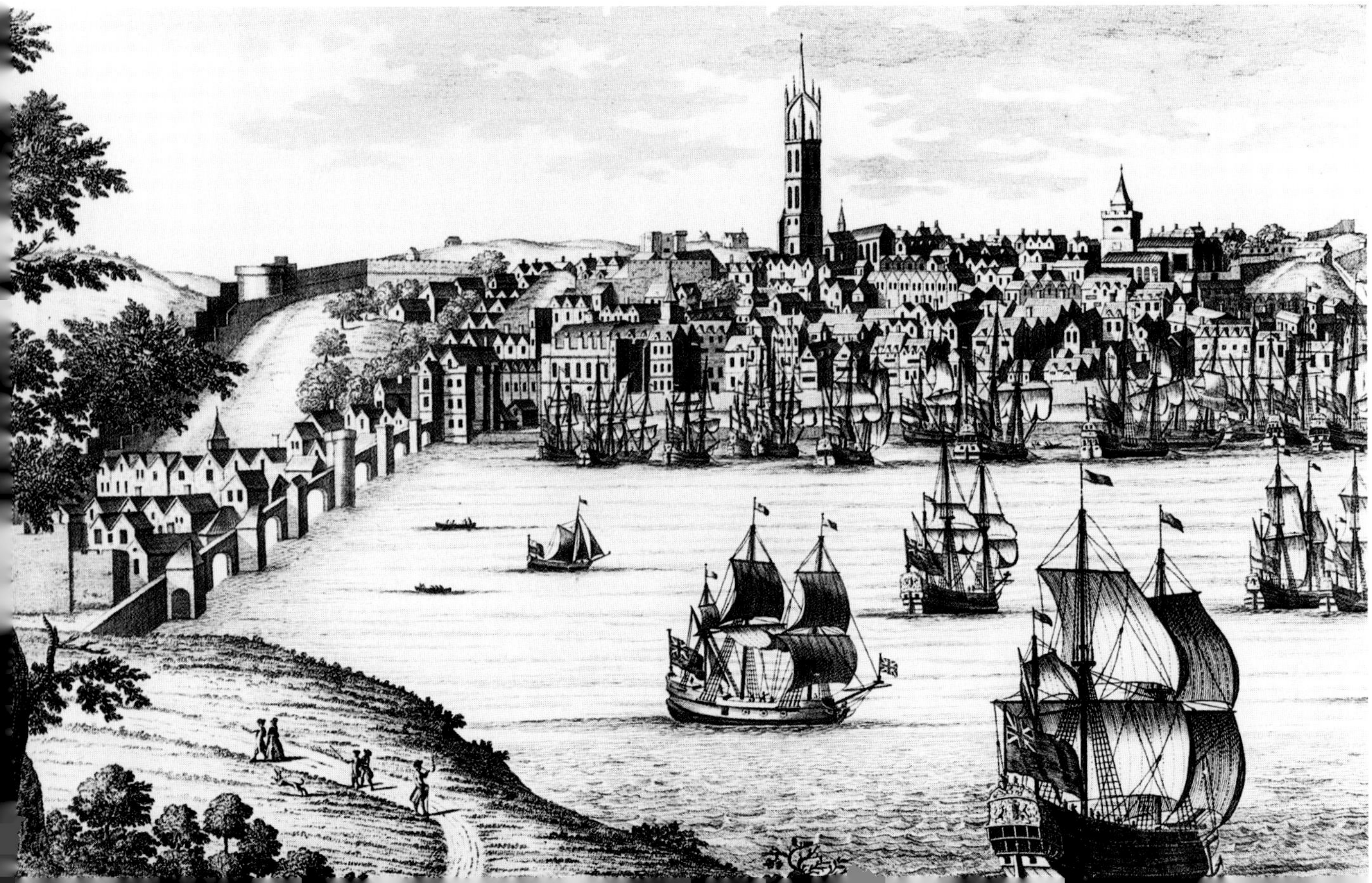

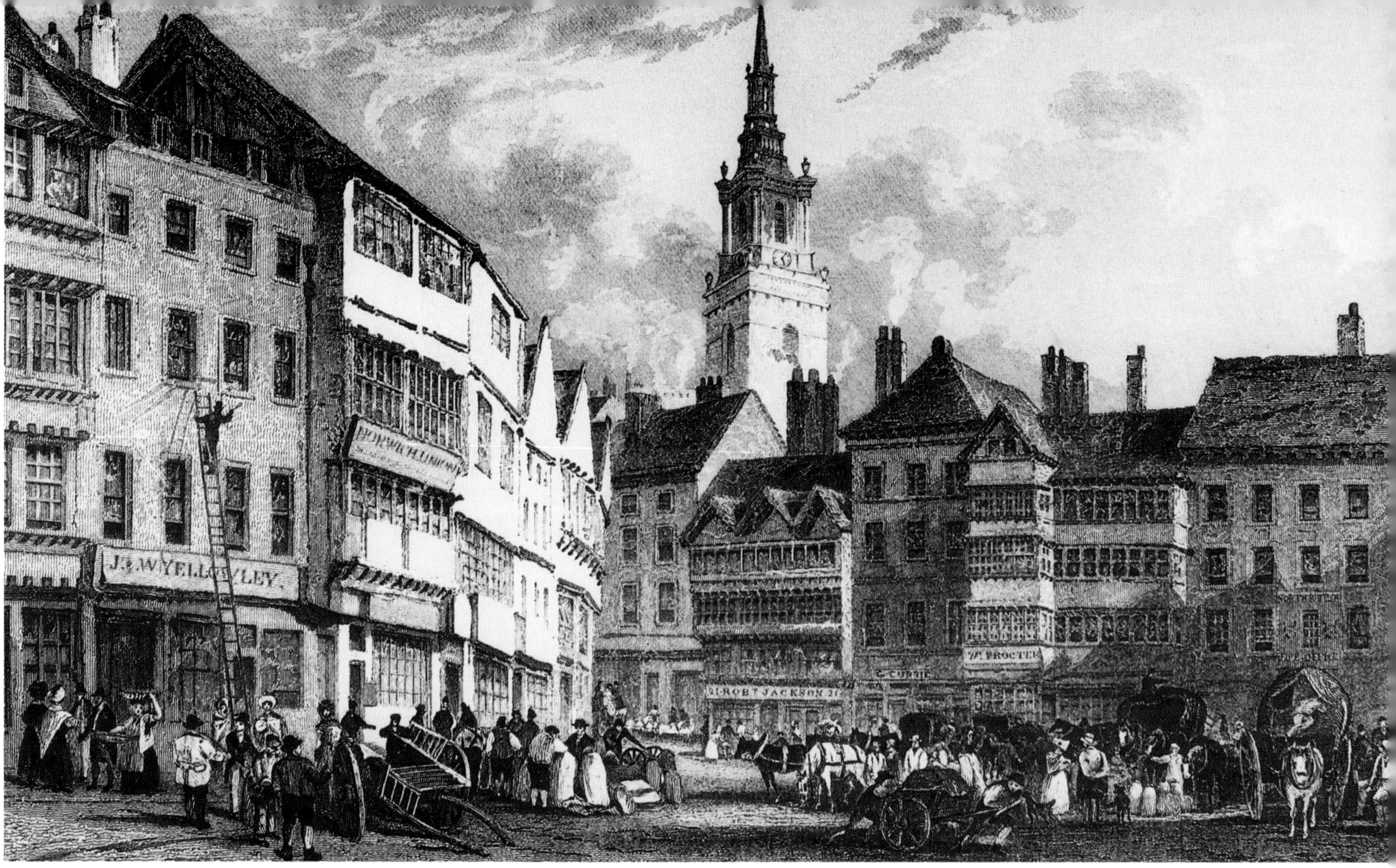

Sand Hill, Newcastle upon Tyne, circa 1833. Lots of activity at J. & W. Yellowley, Robert Jackson at No. 21, with C. Currie and Wm. Procter next door.
Cat No: WPG002 Ref: P4965

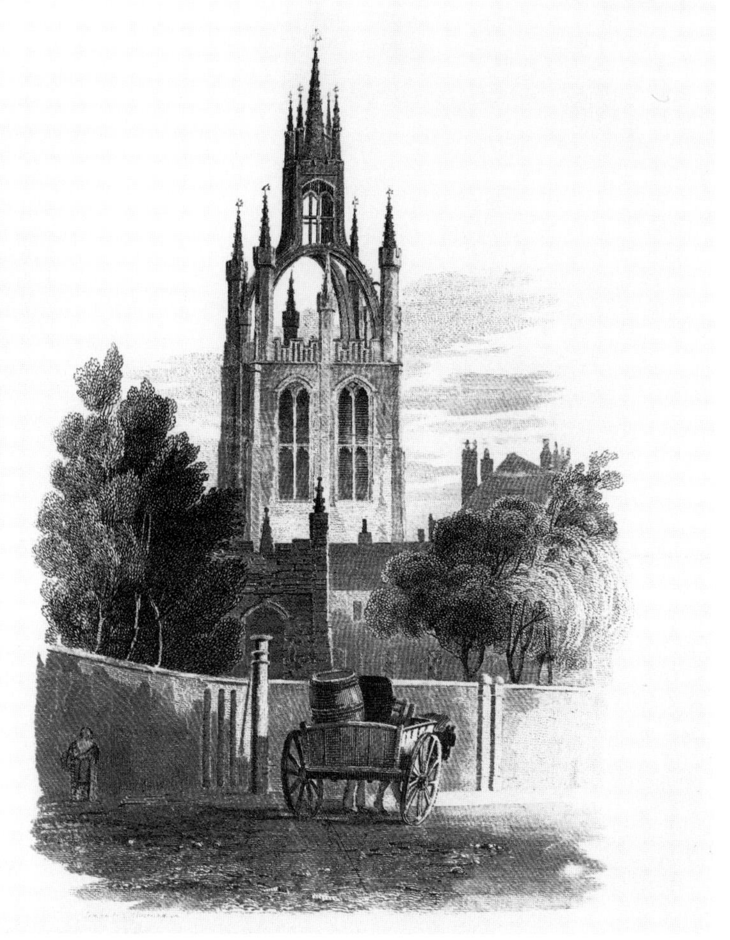

Lantern Tower of St. Nicholas Cathedral, Newcastle upon Tyne.
Cat No: A104 Ref: C2243

Bessie Surtees House, Newcastle upon Tyne.
Cat No: A105 Ref: D739

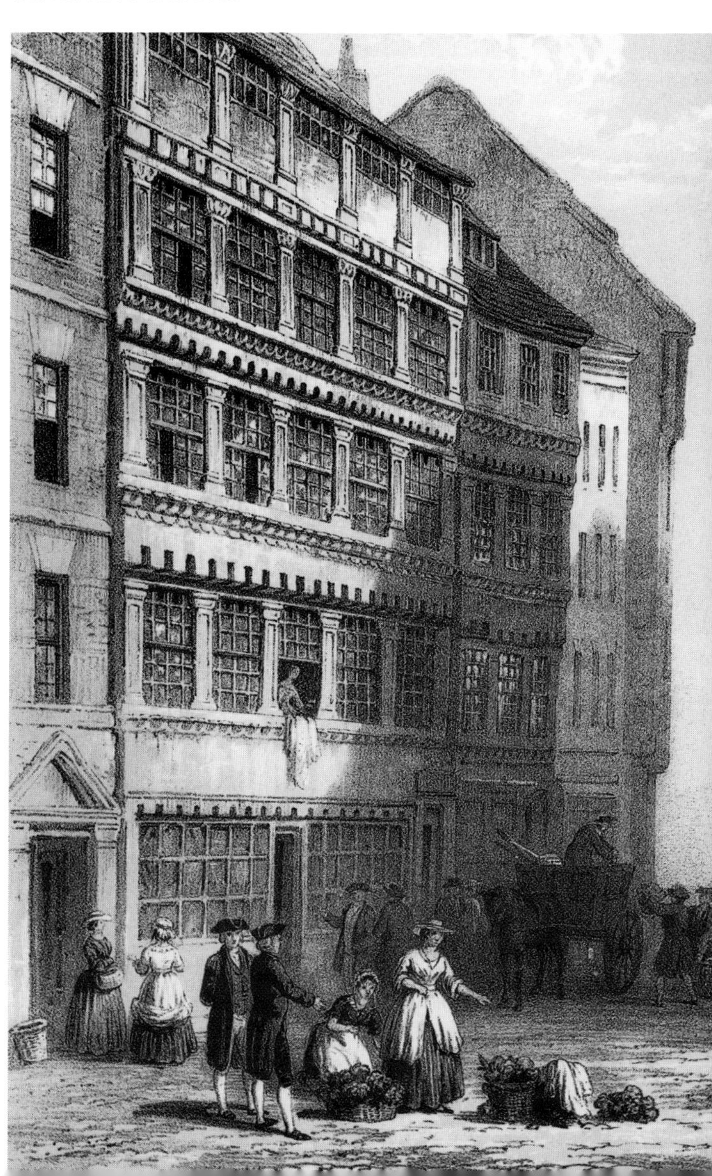

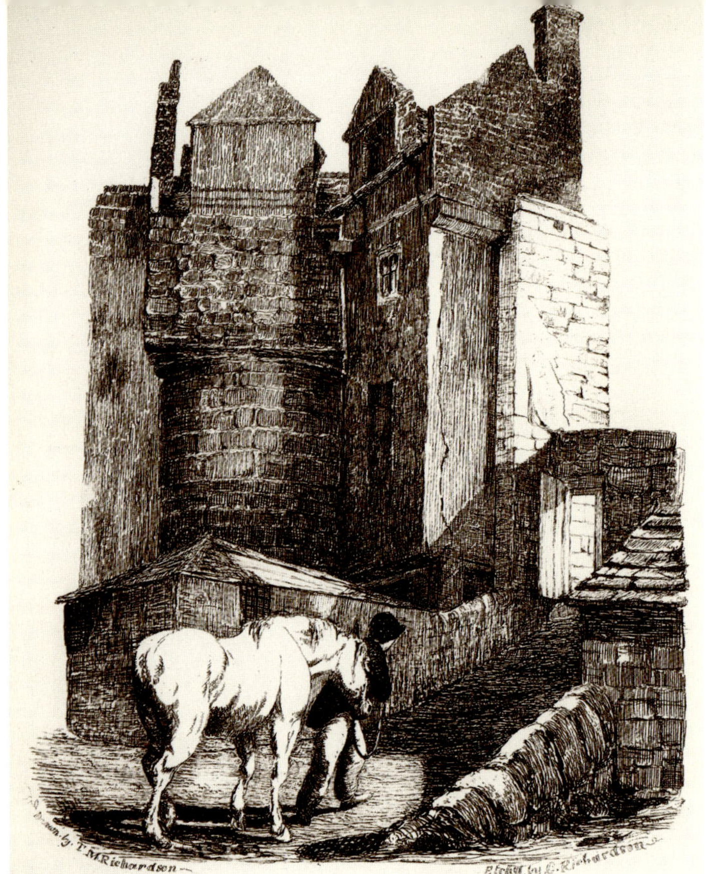

West Spital Tower, Newcastle upon Tyne, drawn by T. M. Richardson, etched by G. Richardson.
Cat No: A106 Ref: C3967

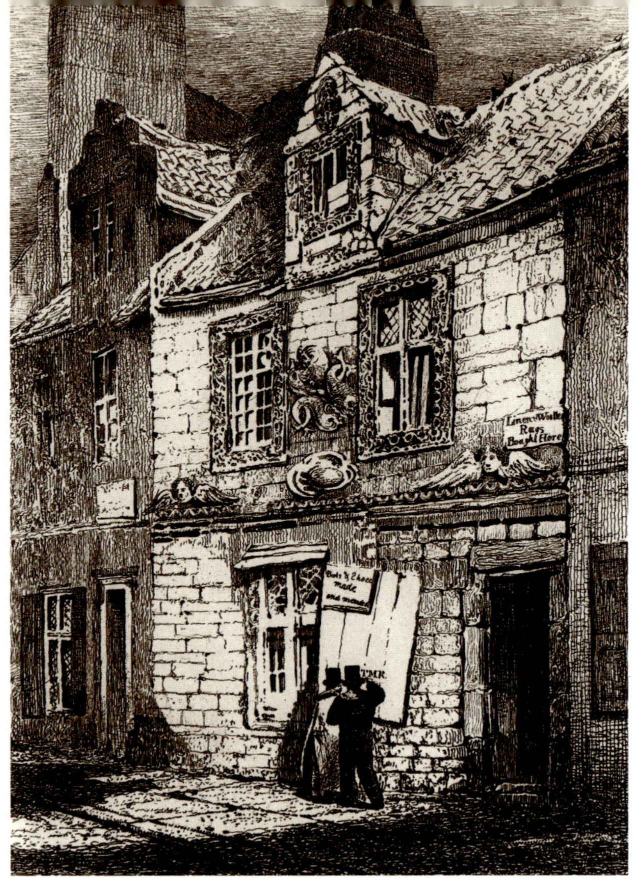

Linen & Woollies, Boots & Shoes - old house in Low Friar Street, Newcastle upon Tyne, drawn and etched by T. M. Richardson Snr.
Cat No: A107 Ref: C3959

Moving the cargo at the Quayside, Newcastle upon Tyne, looking East.
Cat No: WPG003 Ref: 3942

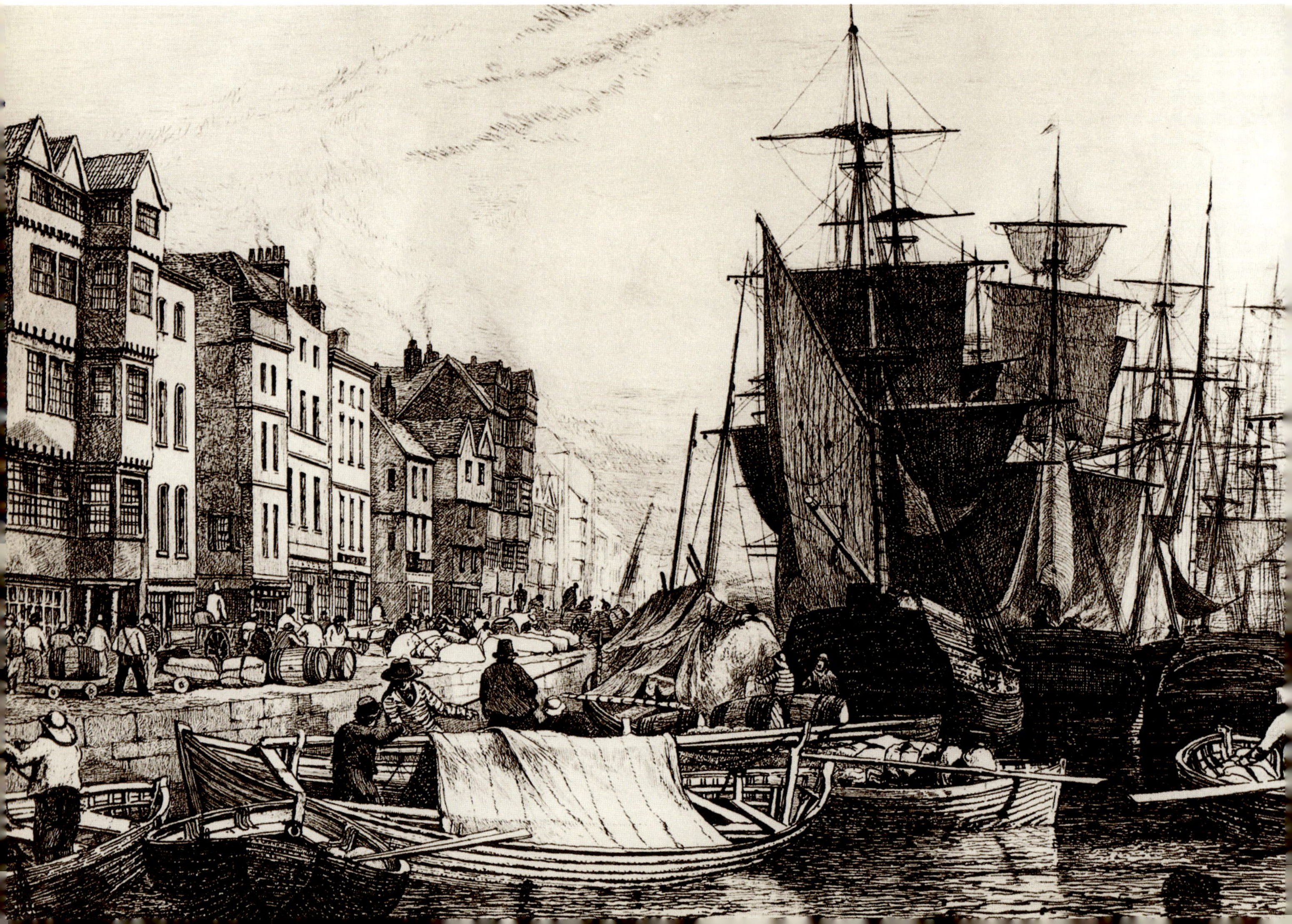

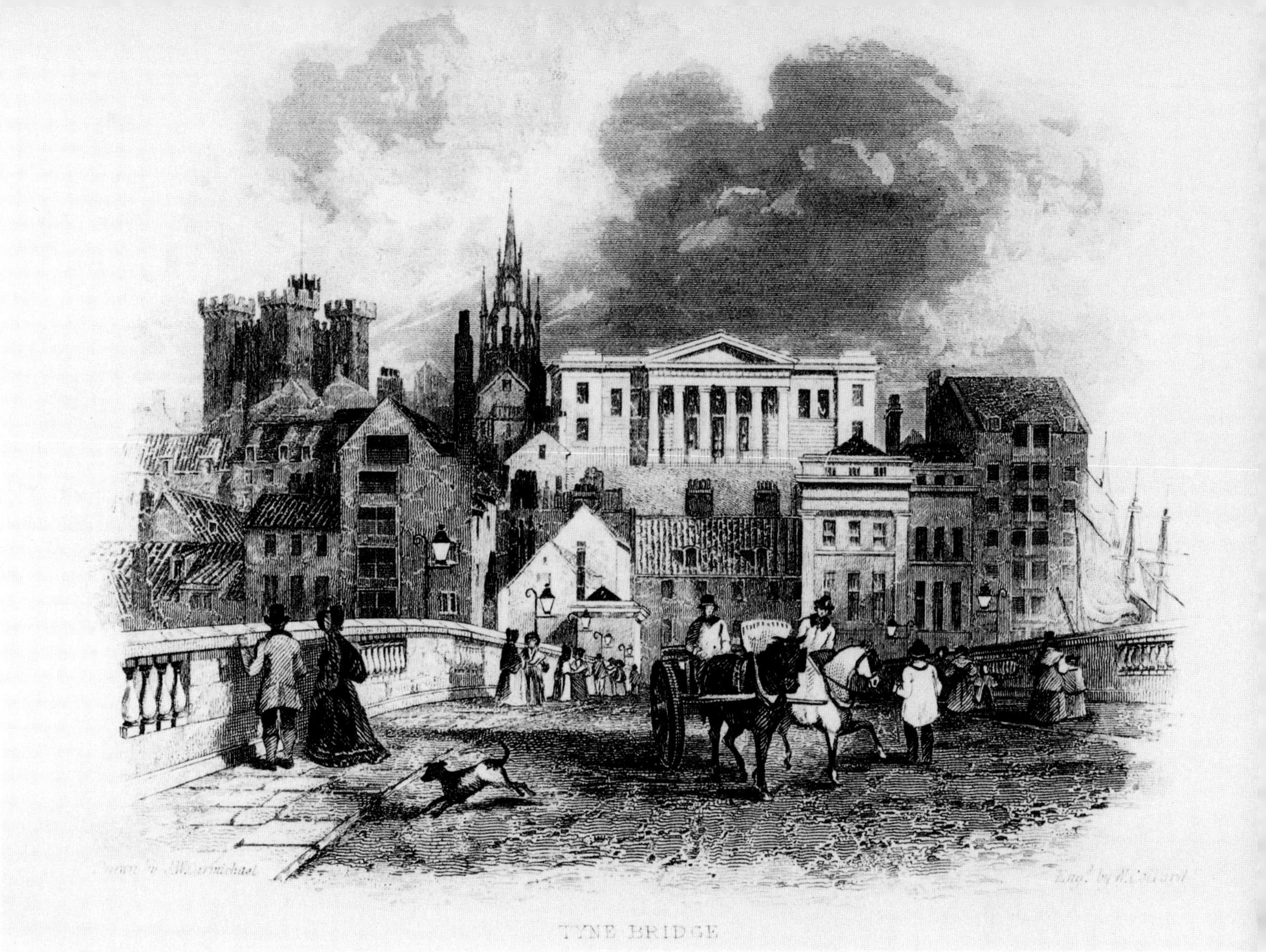

Tyne Bridge, Newcastle upon Tyne, drawn by J. W. Carmichael and engraved by W. Collard.
Cat No: WPG004 Ref: D8487

Custom House, Quayside, Newcastle upon Tyne, drawn by J. W. Carmichael, engraved by W. Collard.
Cat No: A109 Ref: D3168

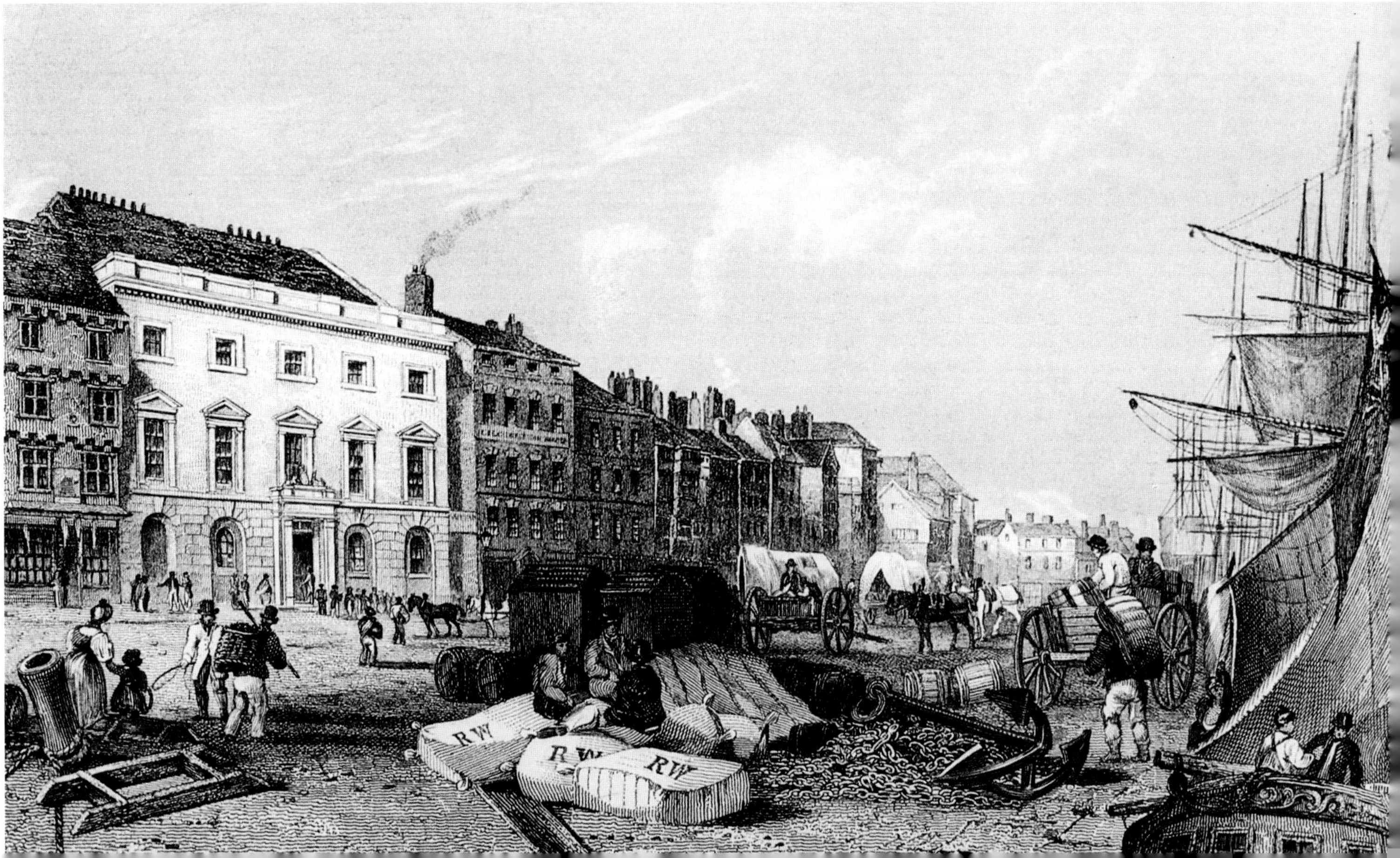

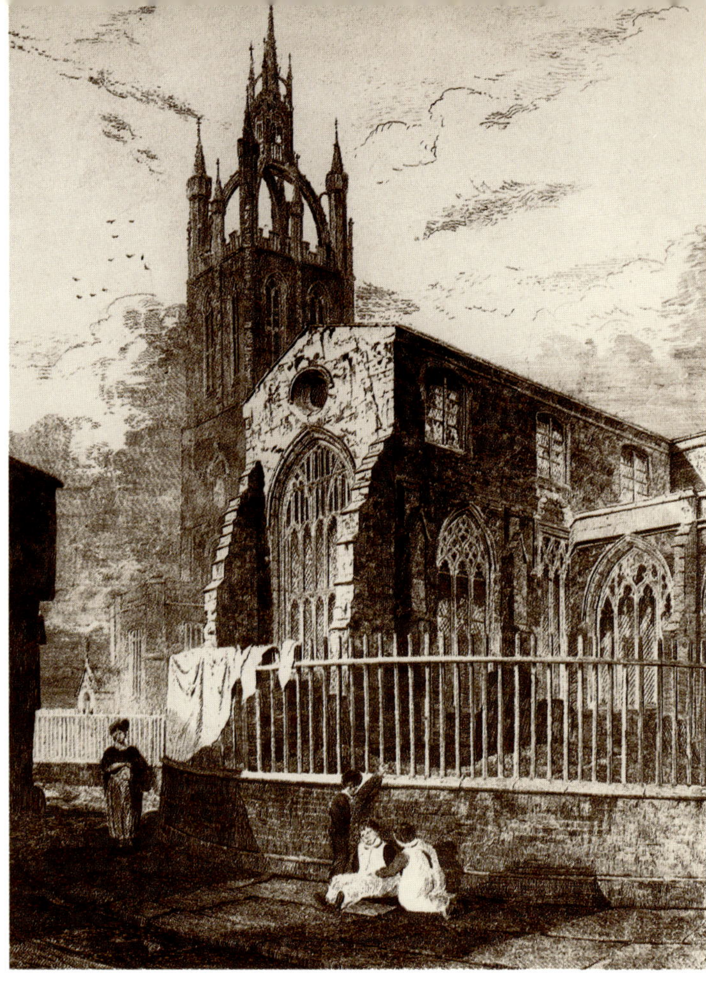

South transept of the
Church of St. Nicholas,
Newcastle upon Tyne.
Cat No: A110 Ref: C3938

A busy day in Grey Street, shopping at 'Atcheson and Yelloly', C. F. Frames and the New Bazaar and Warehouse, with the Theatre Royal and Grey's Monument in the distance.
Cat No: WPG005 Ref: S2137

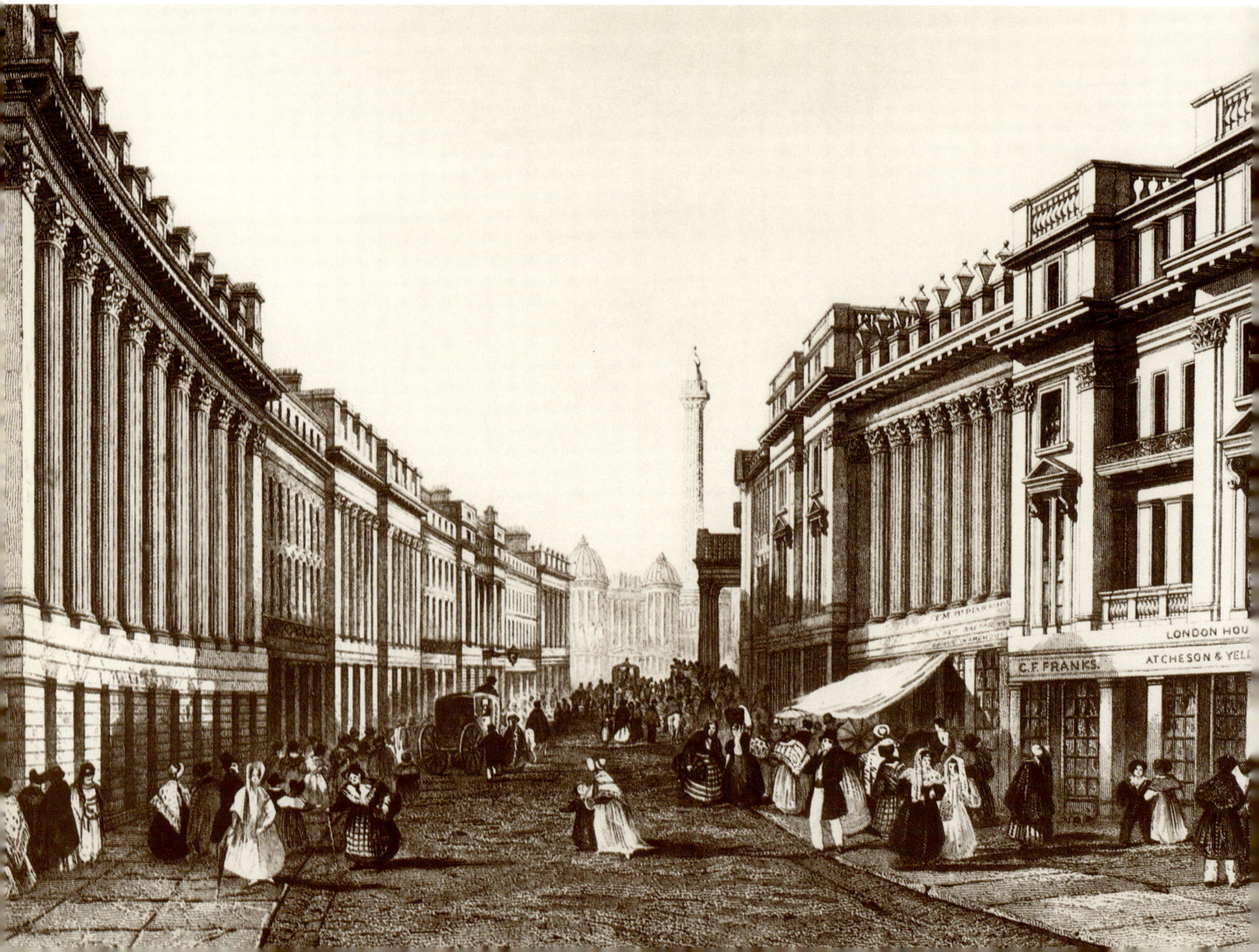

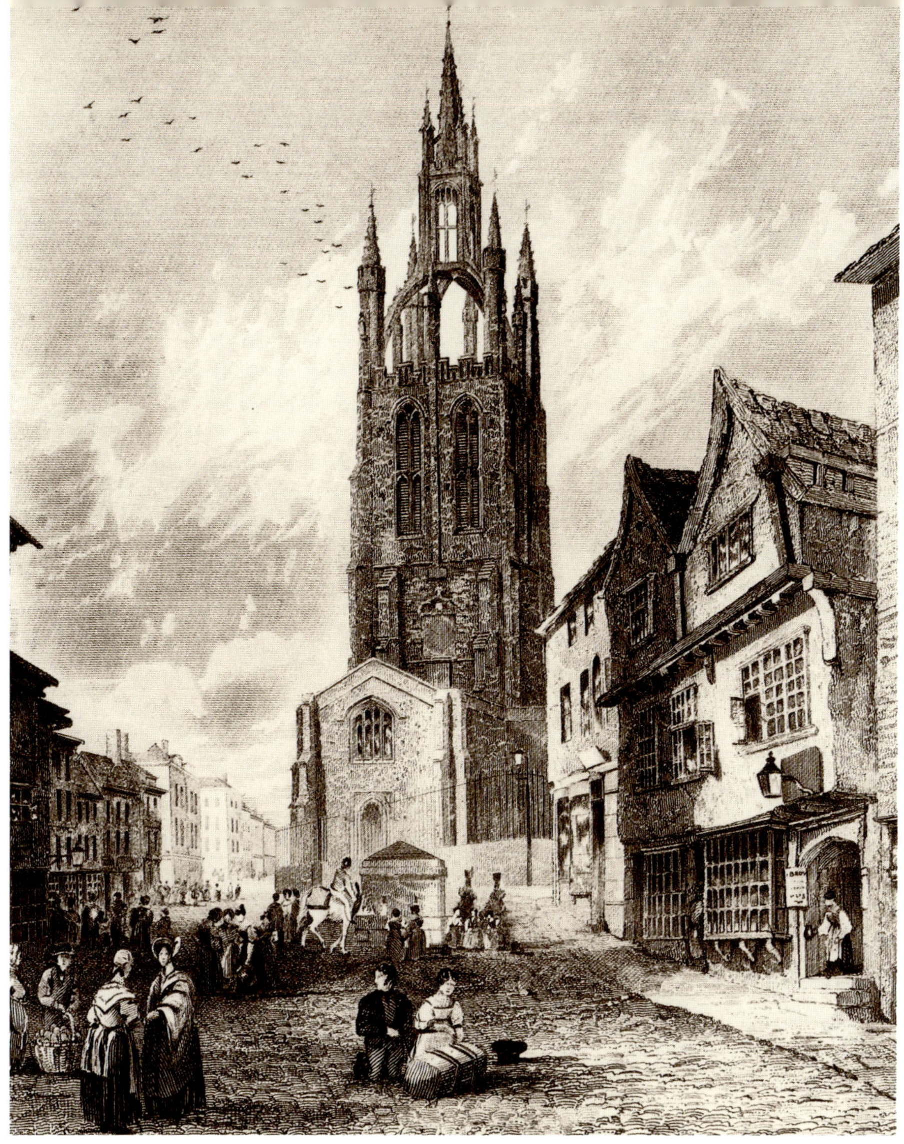

St. Nicholas Cathedral, Newcastle upon Tyne. Notice the sign below the lamp on the right, was it the first sale sign for 'Brown Ale'?
Cat No: WPG006 Ref: D8491

Theatre Royal, Grey Street, Newcastle upon Tyne, drawn by J. W. Carmichael, engraved by M. Collard and published by W. & T. Fordyce.
Cat No: WPG007 Ref: X1225

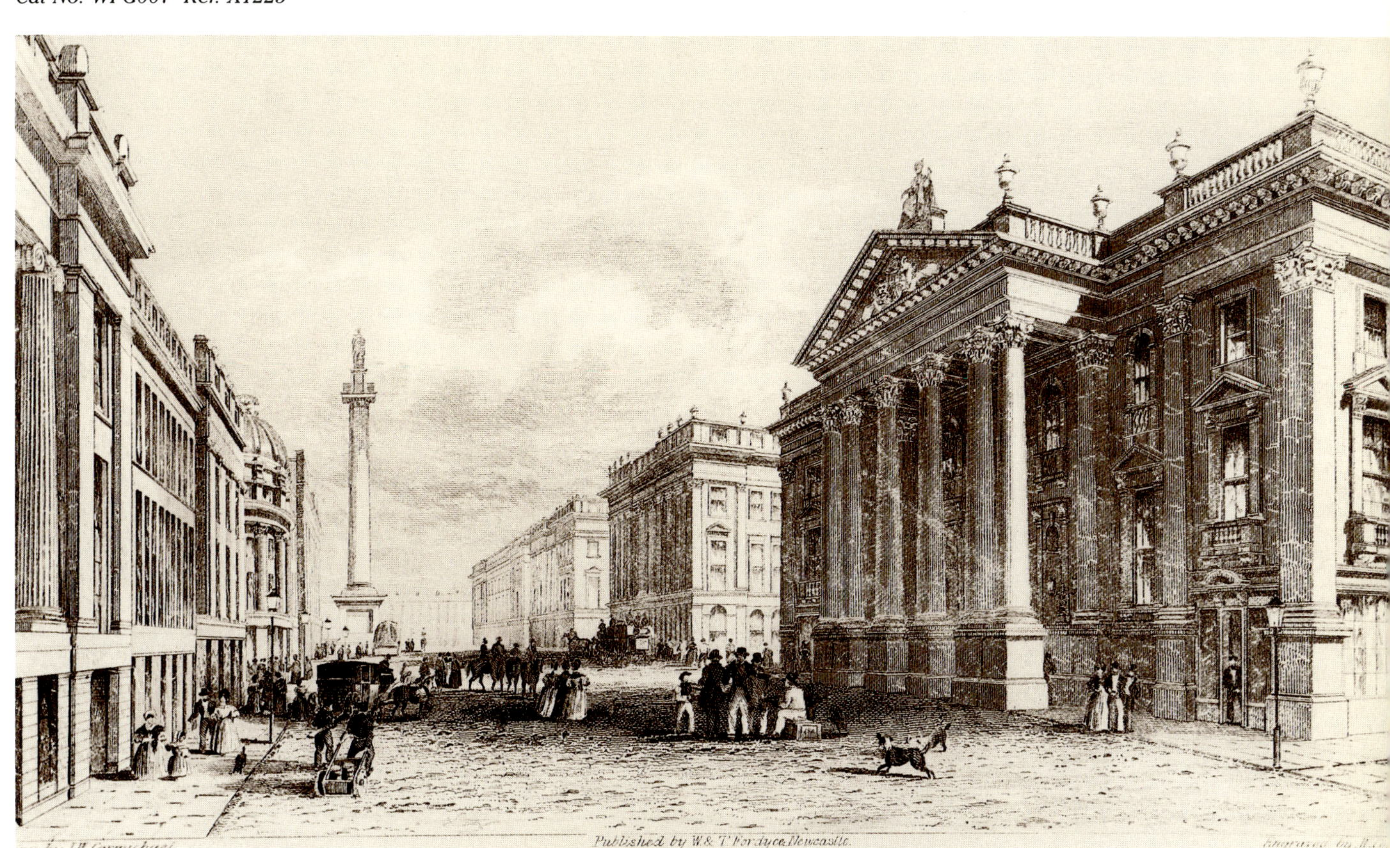

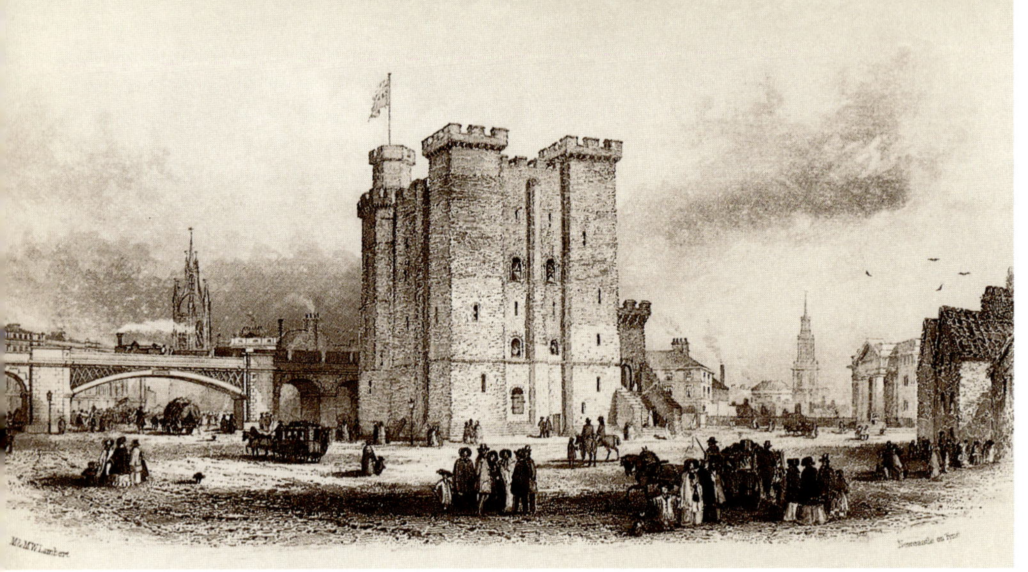

The Castle, Newcastle upon Tyne by M. & M. W. Lambert from the site of the High Level Bridge. From left to right you can view the railway bridge, St. Nicholas Cathedral, Castle, All Hallows Church and Moot Hall.
Cat No: A111 Ref: A488

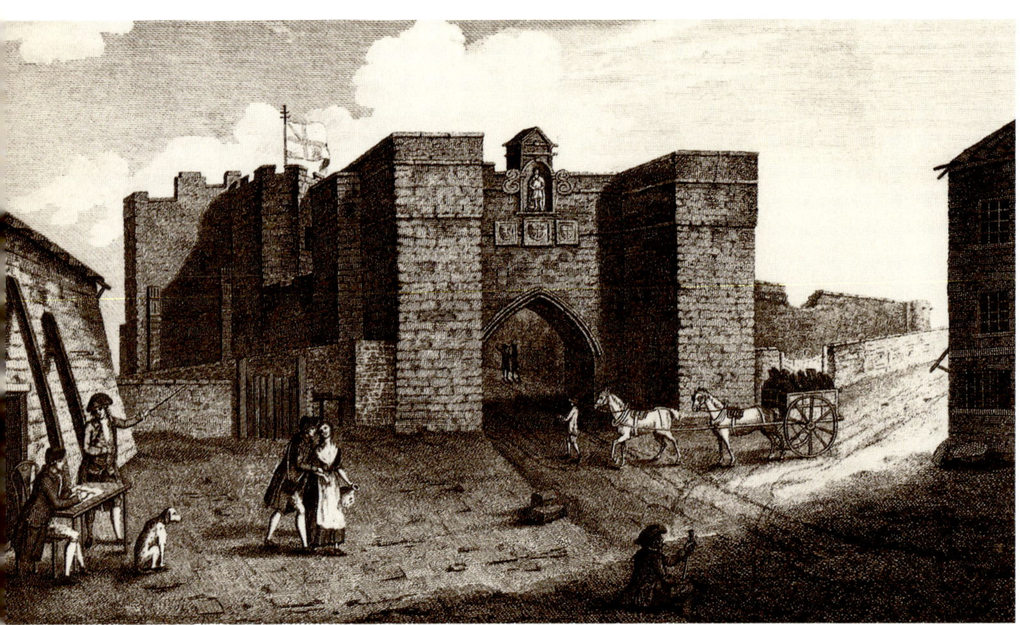

View taken from the North of the Gate of that town called Newgate by John Brand, 1781.
Cat No: A112 Ref: D737

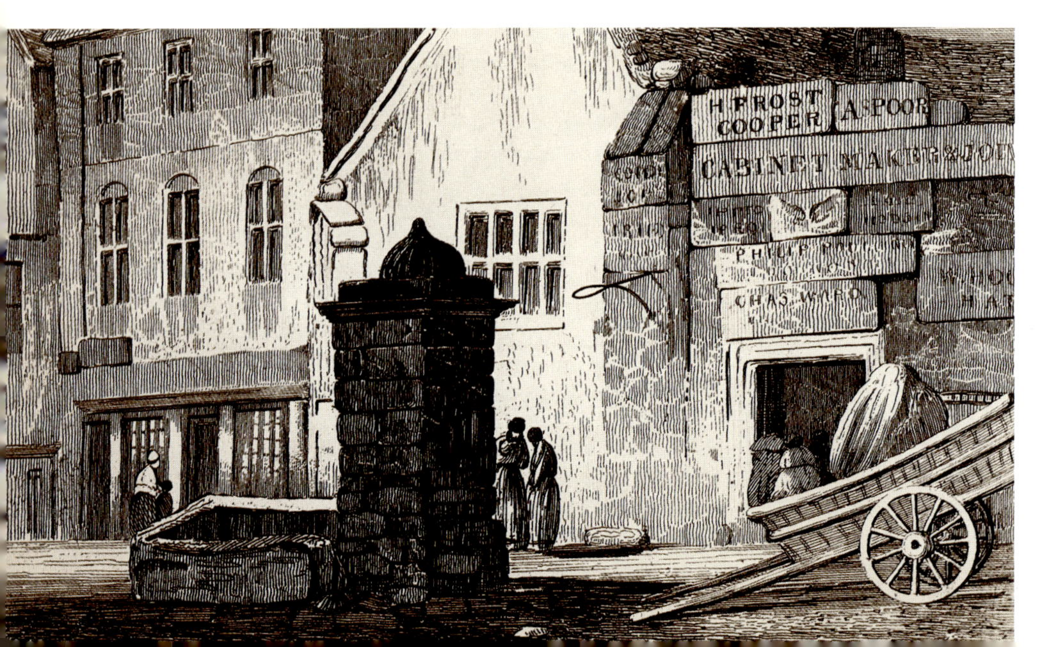

Old Newcastle upon Tyne - Ancient Pant, Bigg Market.
Cat No: A113 Ref: C3958

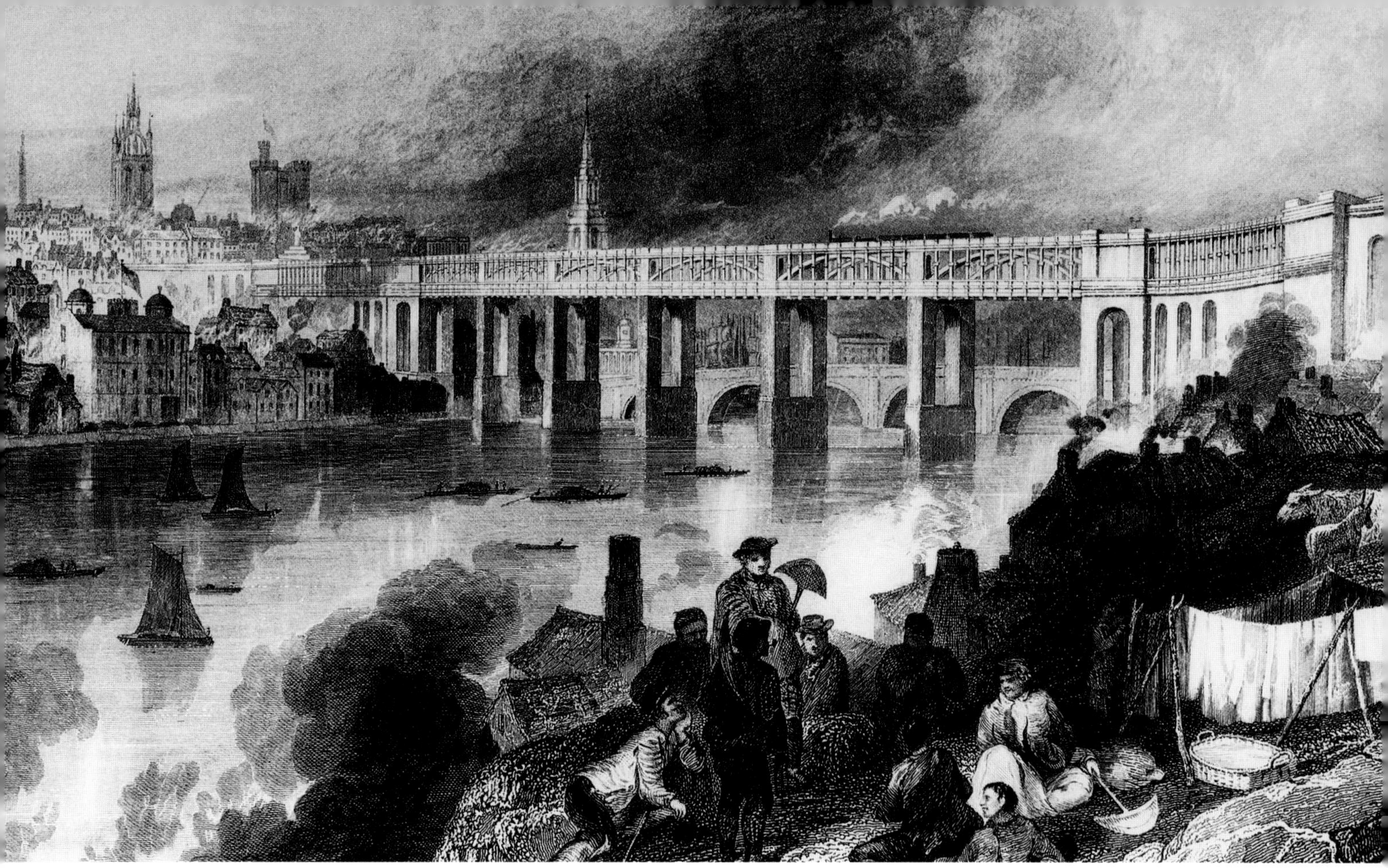

A working family at rest with the High Level Bridge and River Tyne from Gateshead.
Cat No: WPG008 Ref: D740

The Tyne, with Newcastle in the foreground from Teams, Gateshead. Engraved by T. E. Nicholson.
Cat No.: WPG009 Ref: X4073

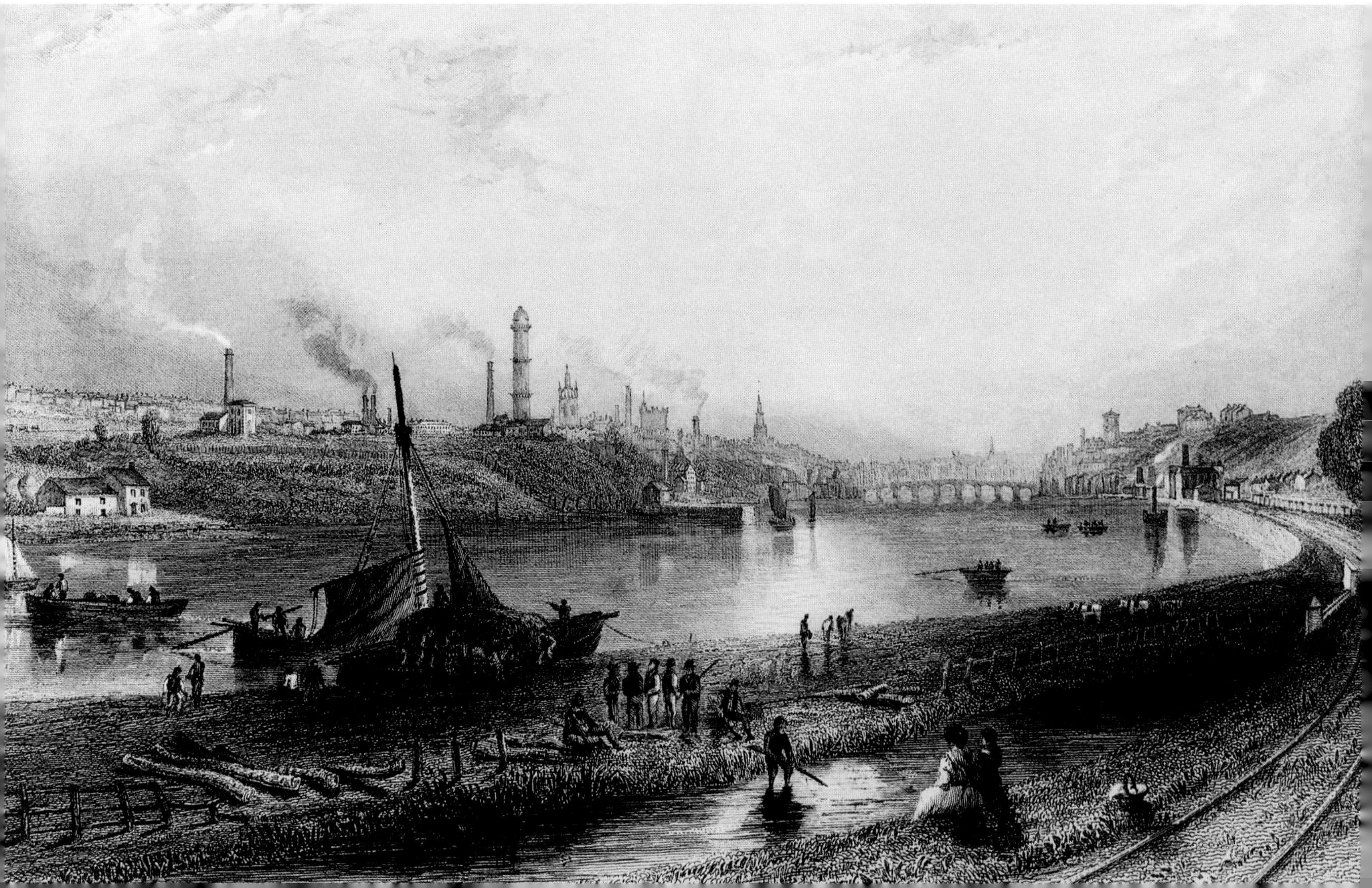

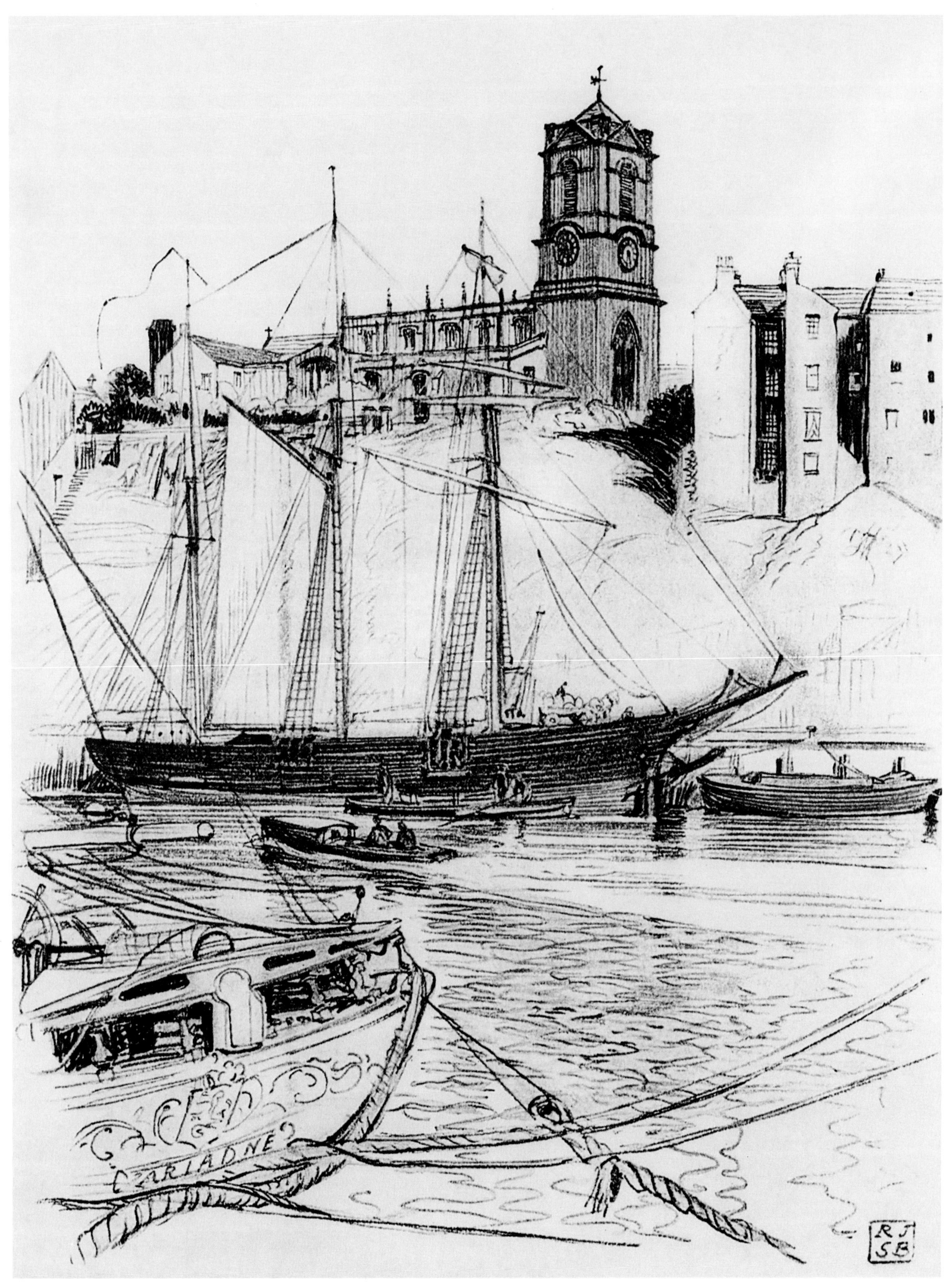

The sailing ships at berth, beneath St. Mary's Church, Gateshead.
Cat No: A114 Ref: X526

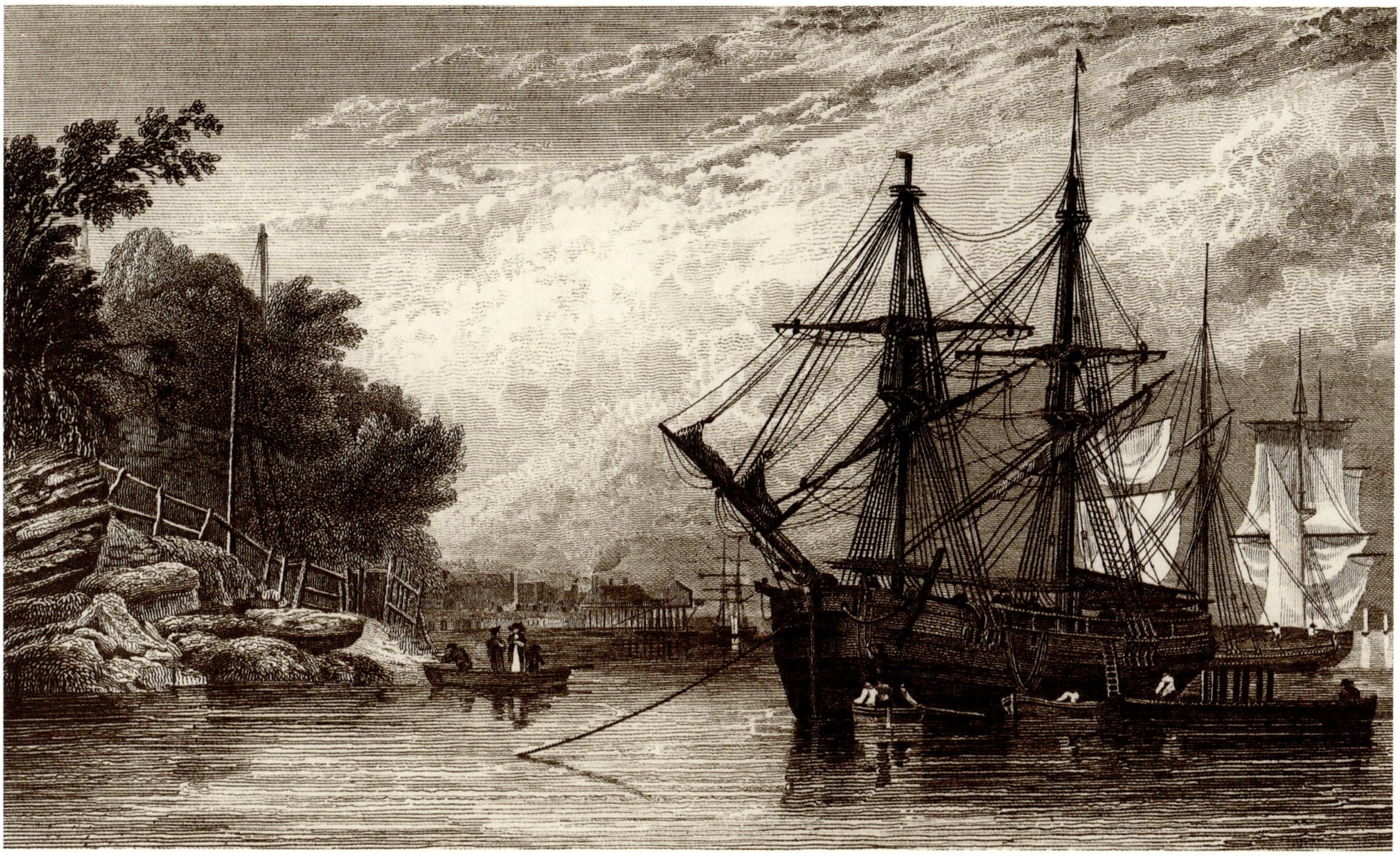

Felling boat landing, Newcastle upon Tyne.
Cat No: WPG010 Ref: T4228

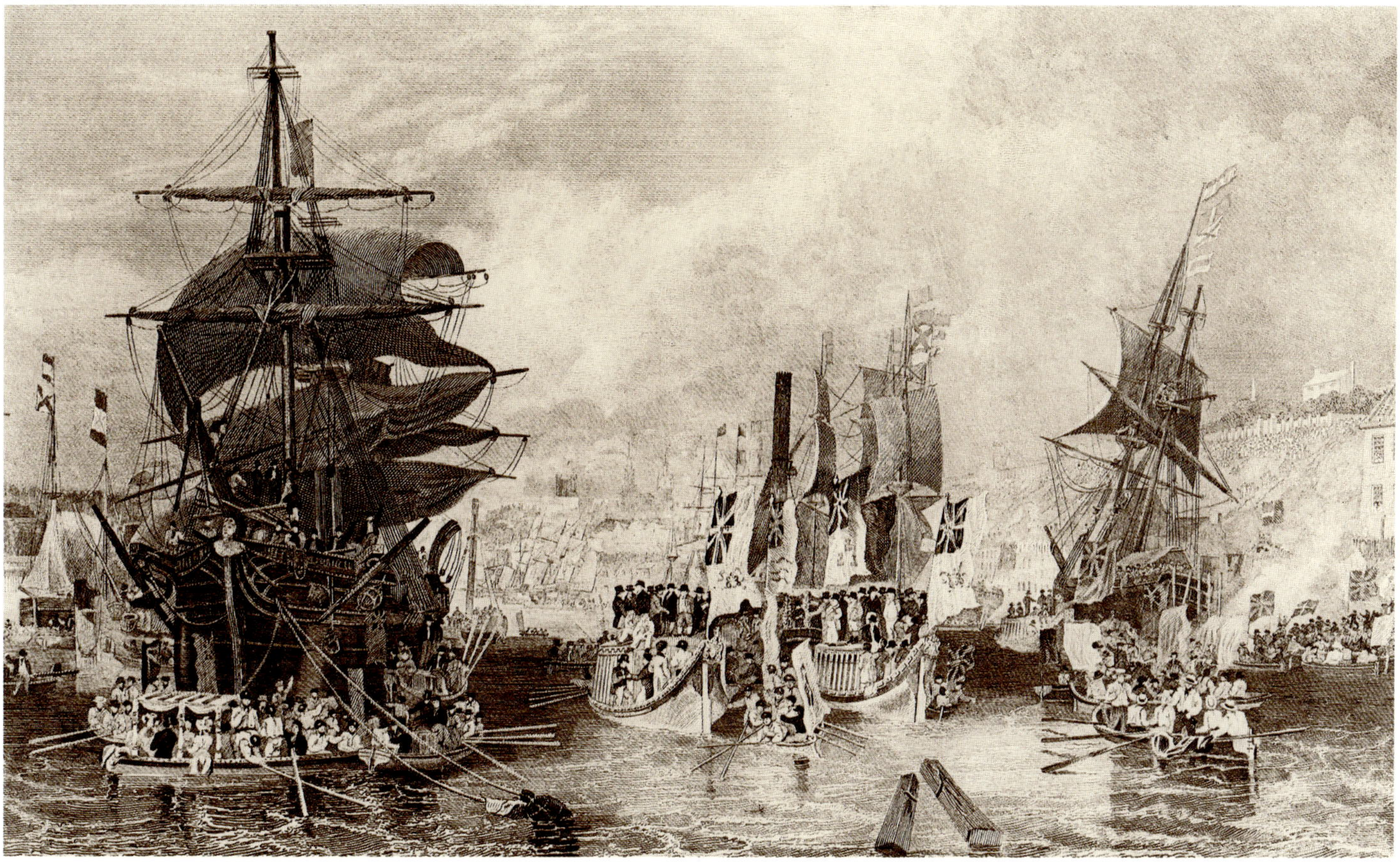

Ascension Day on the Tyne.
Cat No: WPG011 Ref: D5539

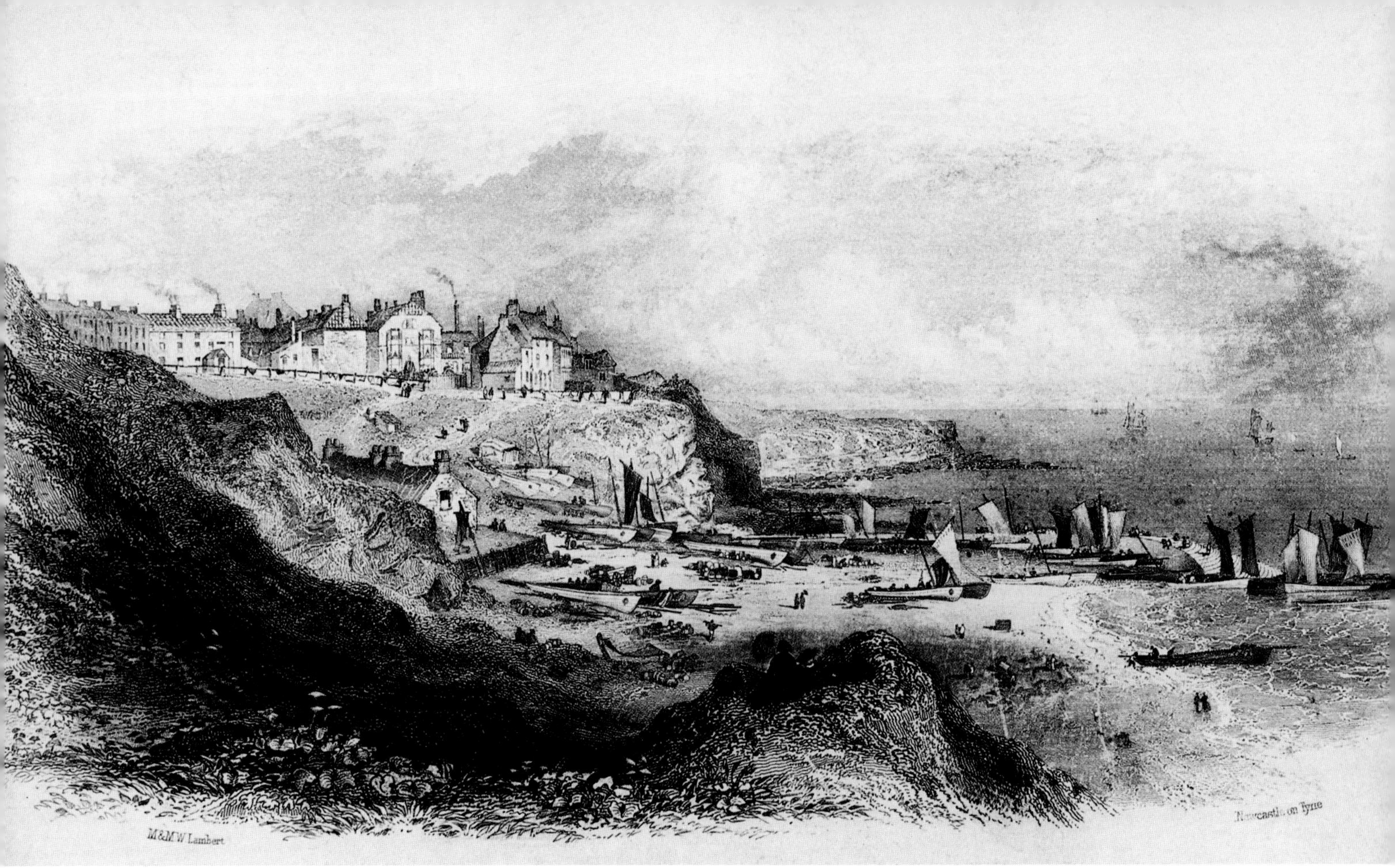

Cullercoats by M. & M. W. Lambert.
Cat No: A115 Ref: A489

Byker Railway Bridge, Newcastle upon Tyne.
Cat No: A116 Ref: D8489

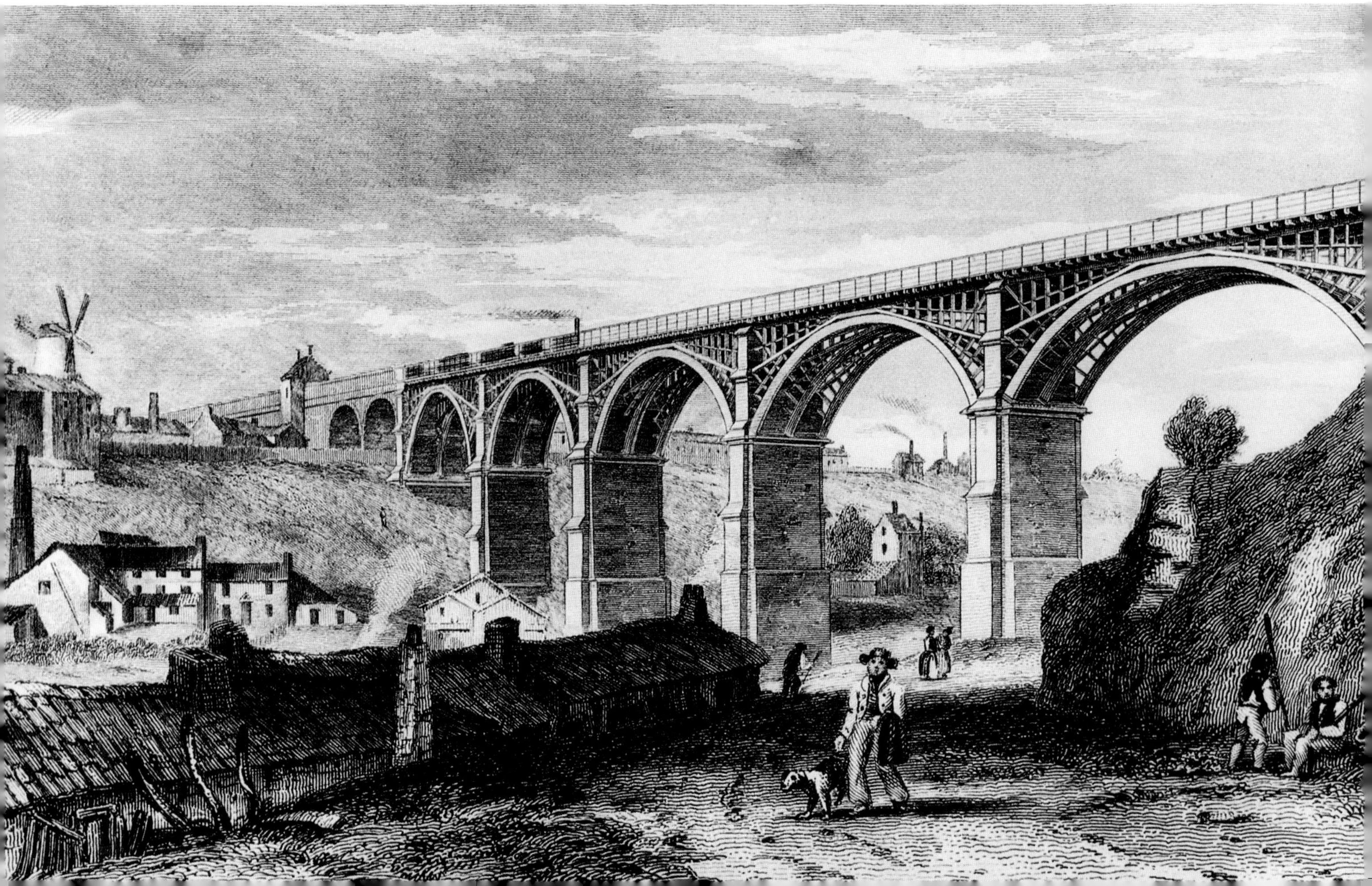

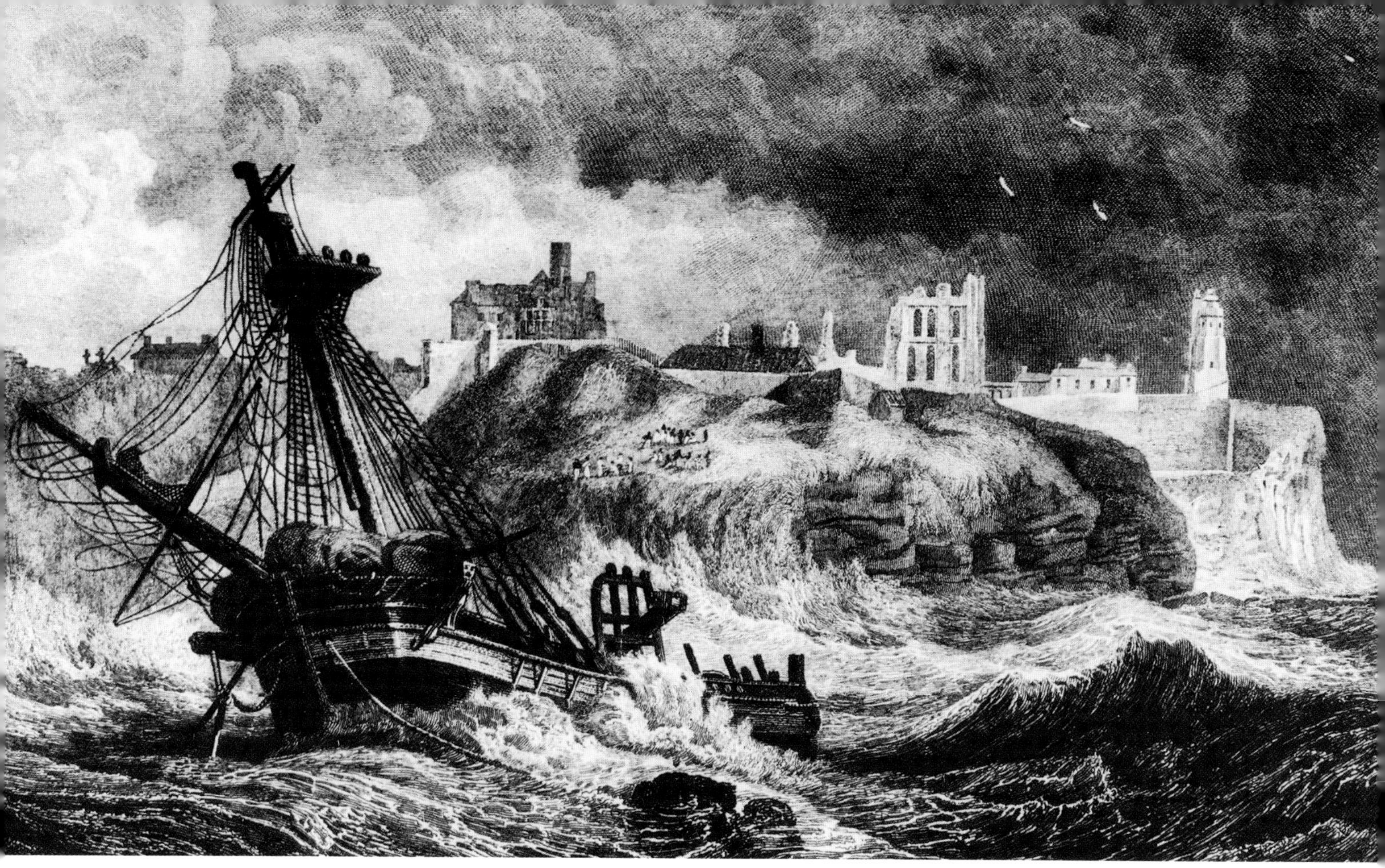

Tynemouth Castle and the wreck of 'The Betsy Cains', 18 February 1827. This Vessel brought William III to England in 1688. Drawn by J. W. Carmichael, engraved by Lambert & Collard.
Cat No: WPG012 Ref: H9152

Shields Harbour - West Entrance.
Cat No: A117 Ref: A2705

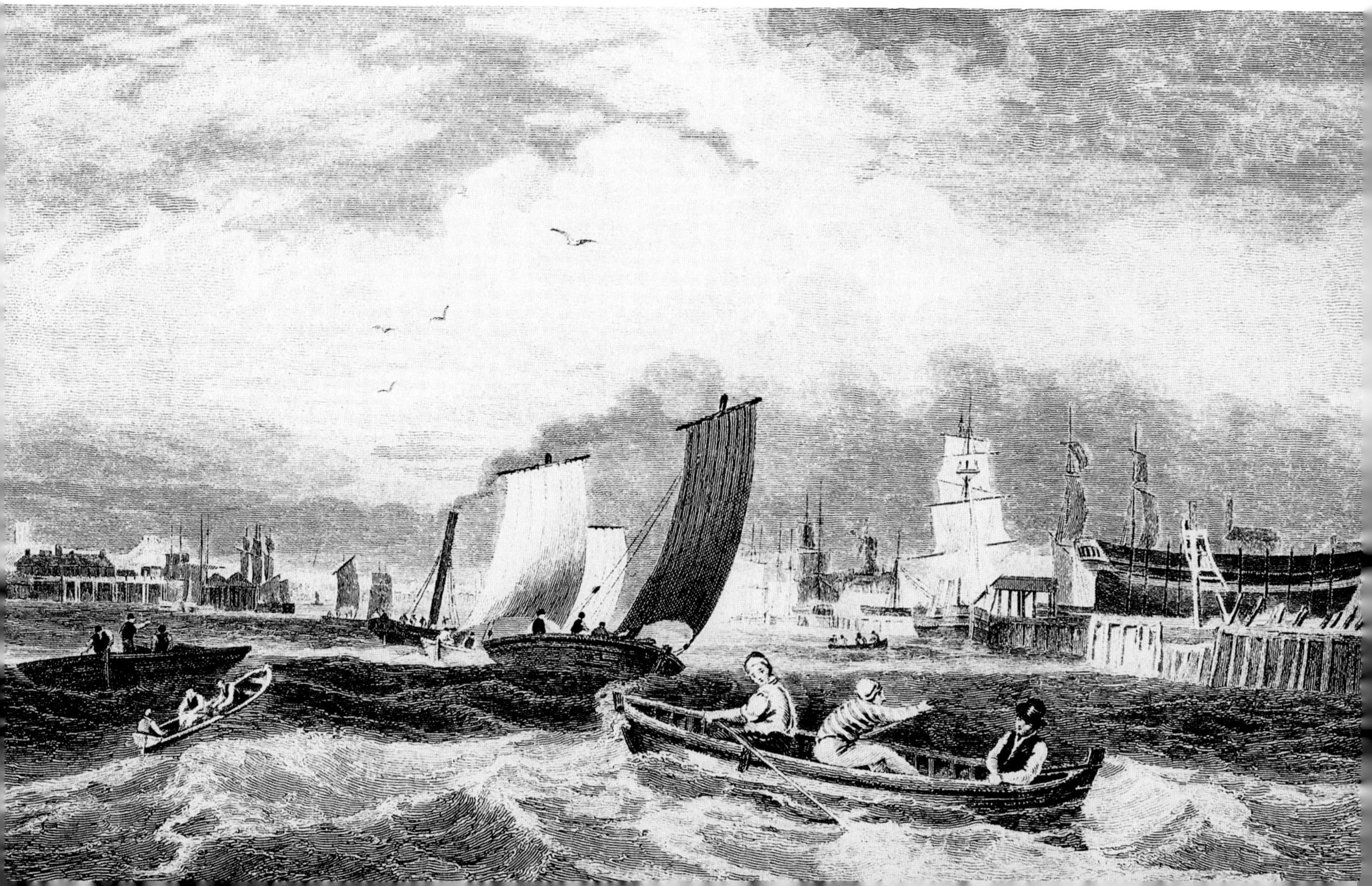

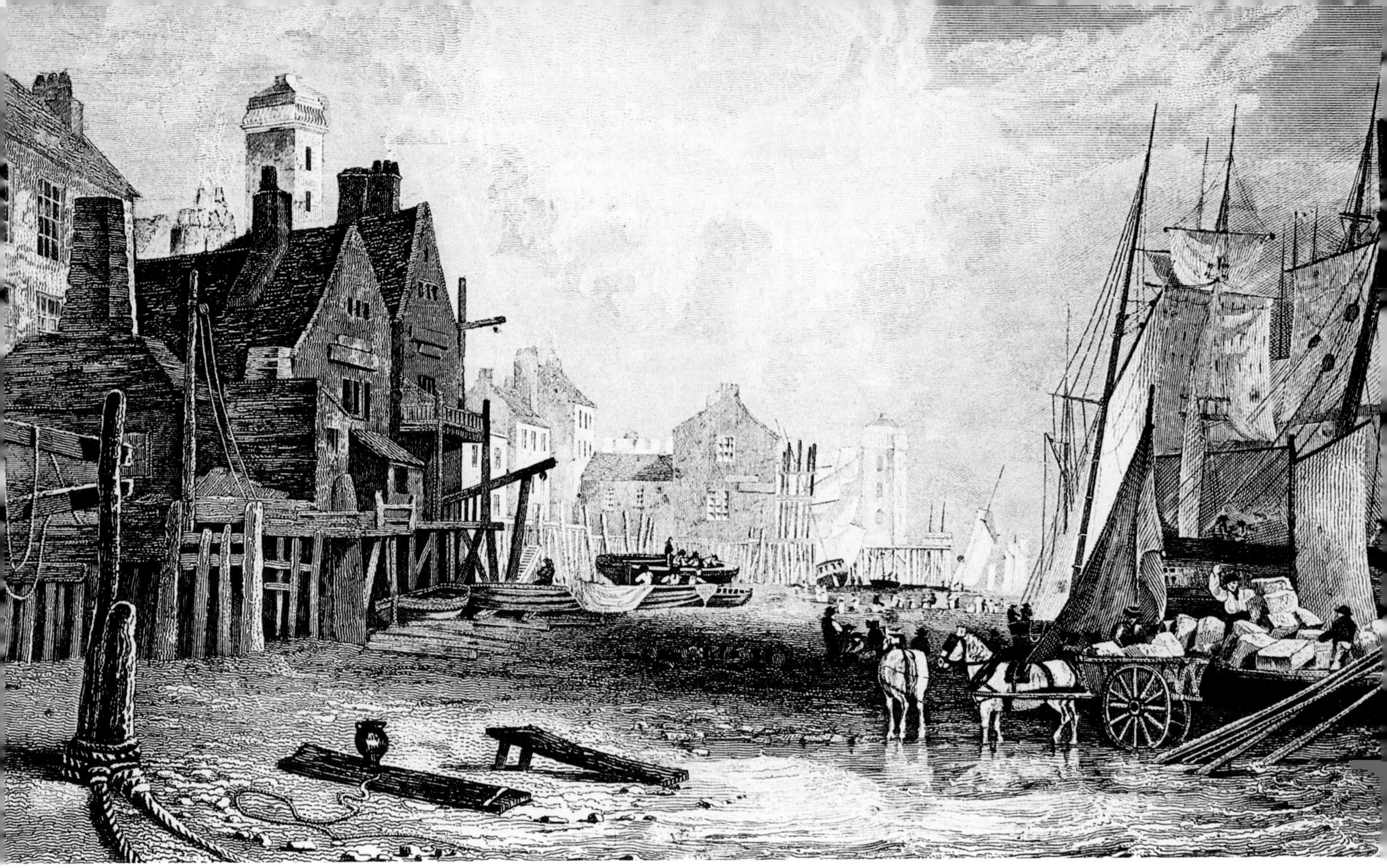

Shields Harbour looking east.
Cat No: WPG013 Ref: A2706

Sailing ships on the Tyne from South Shields, Durham.
Cat No: WPG014 Ref: C1548

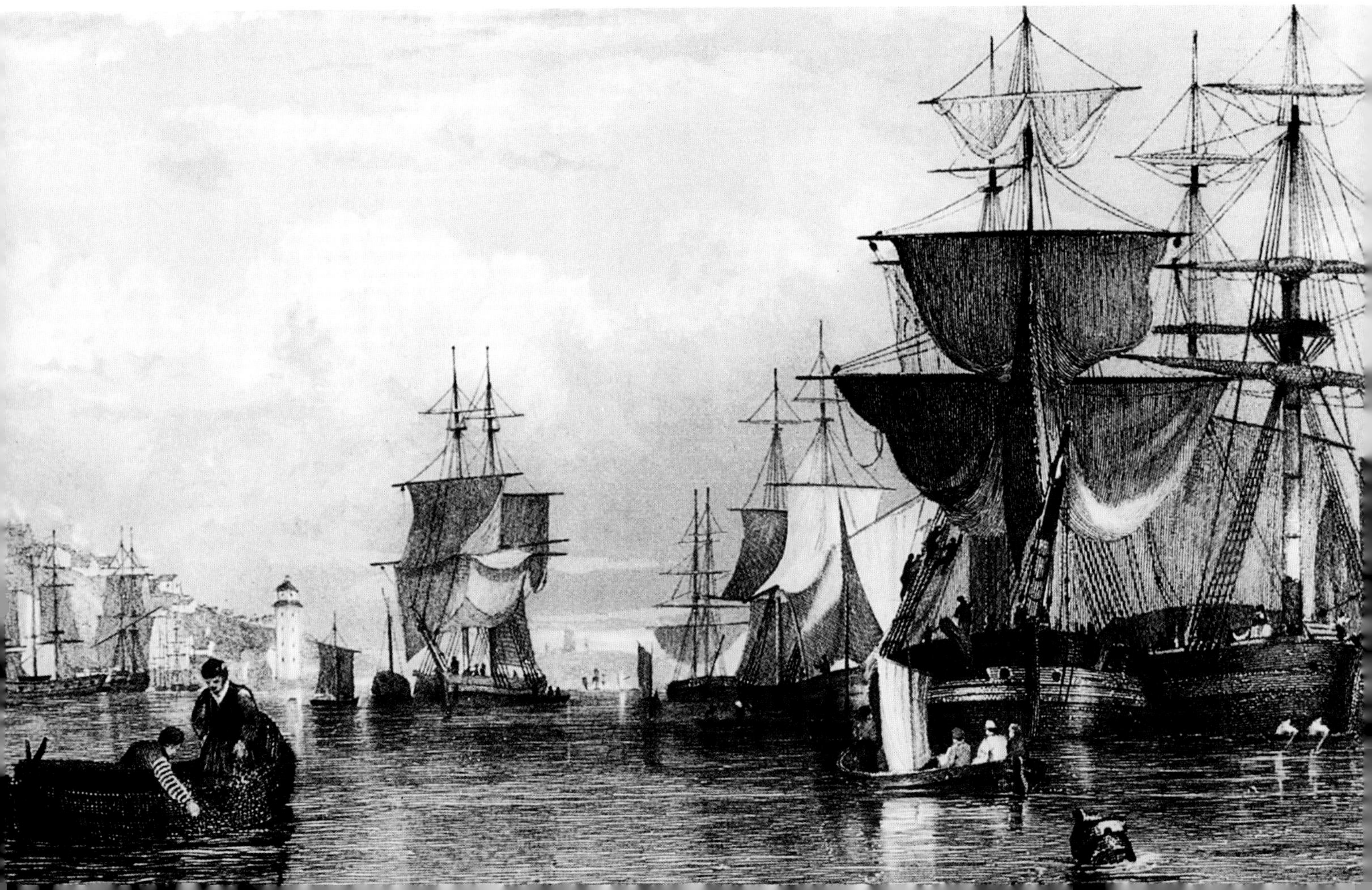

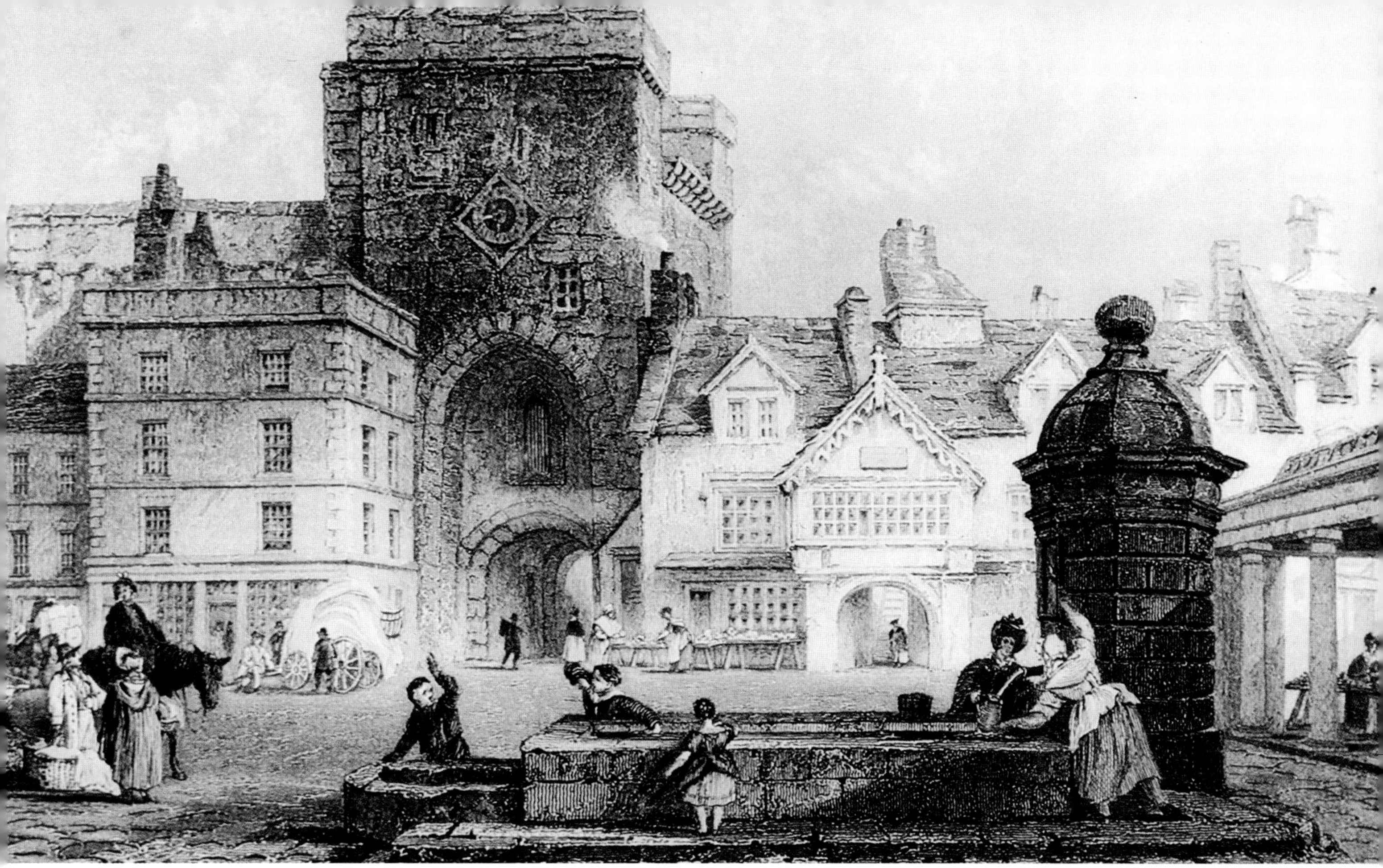

Hexham Market Place, Northumberland.
Cat No: WPG015 Ref: C1536

Prudhoe Castle, south view.
Cat No: A118 Ref: C3086

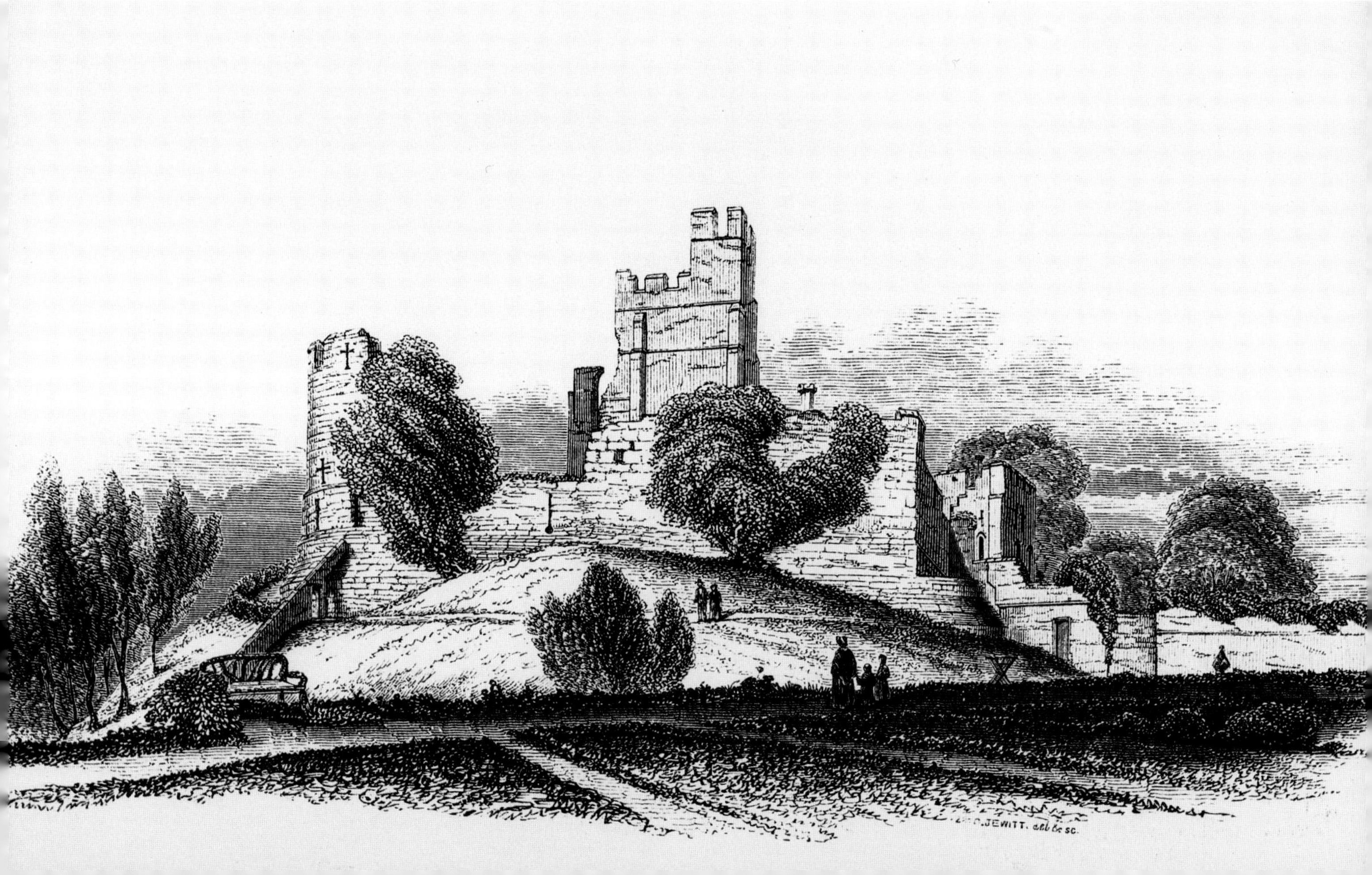

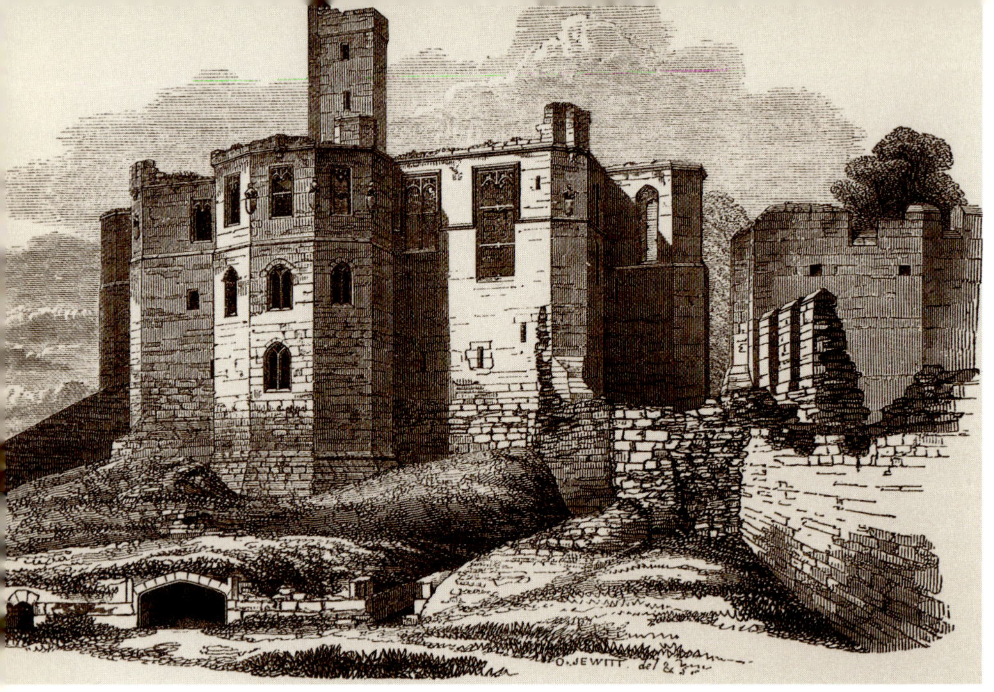

Warkworth Donjon, South Side, Northumberland.
Cat No: A119 Ref: C3080

Warkworth Hermitage by O. Jewitt.
Cat No: A120 Ref: C3083

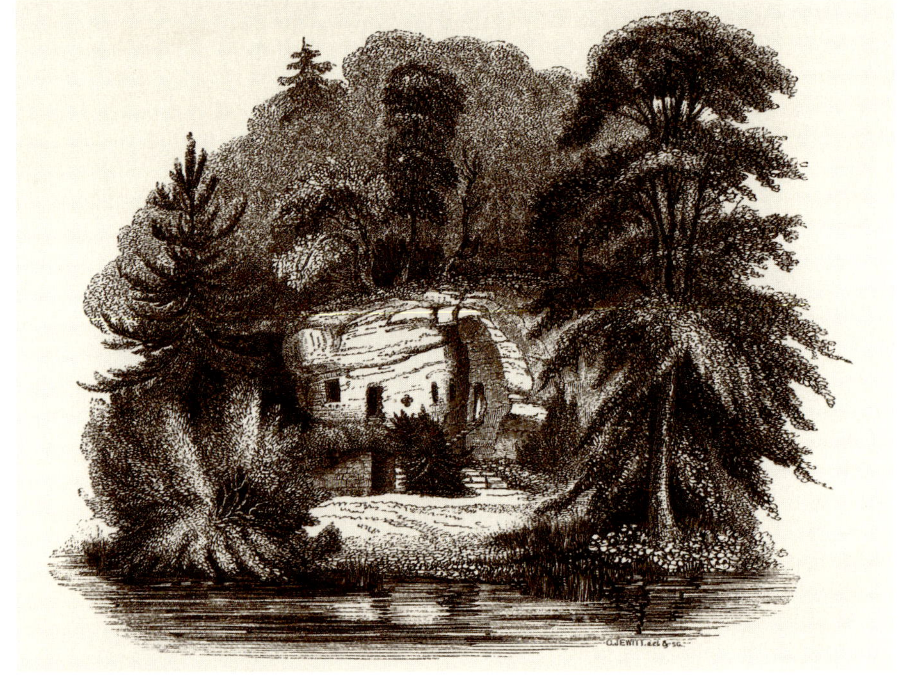

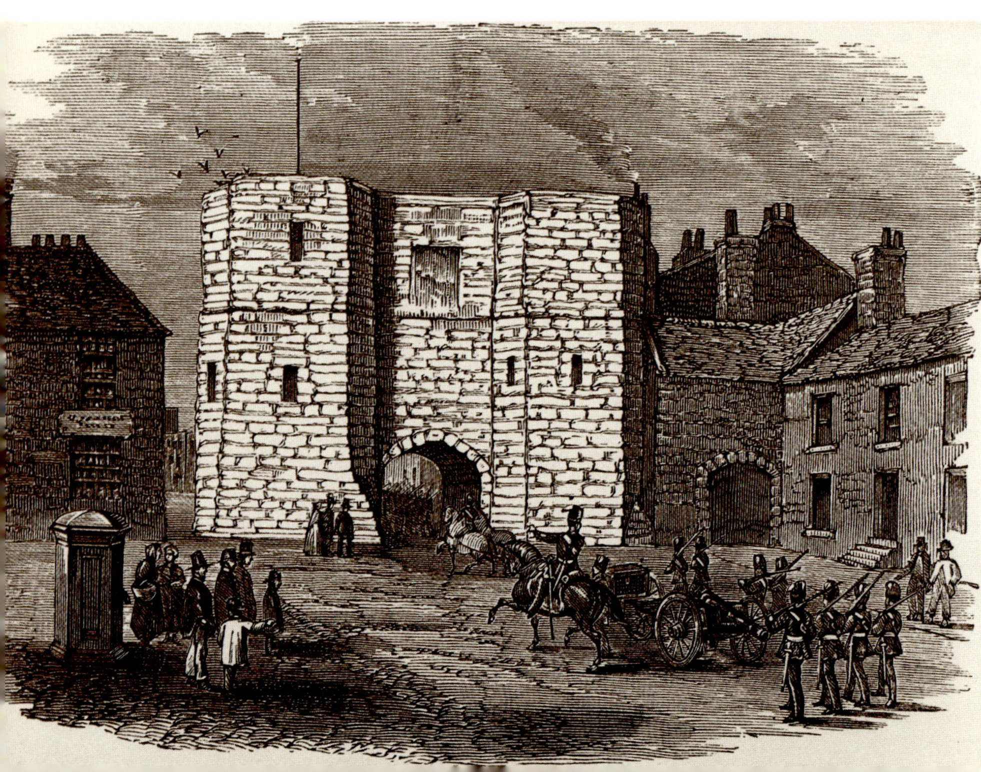

Bondgate Tower, Alnwick.
Cat No: A121 Ref: T3335

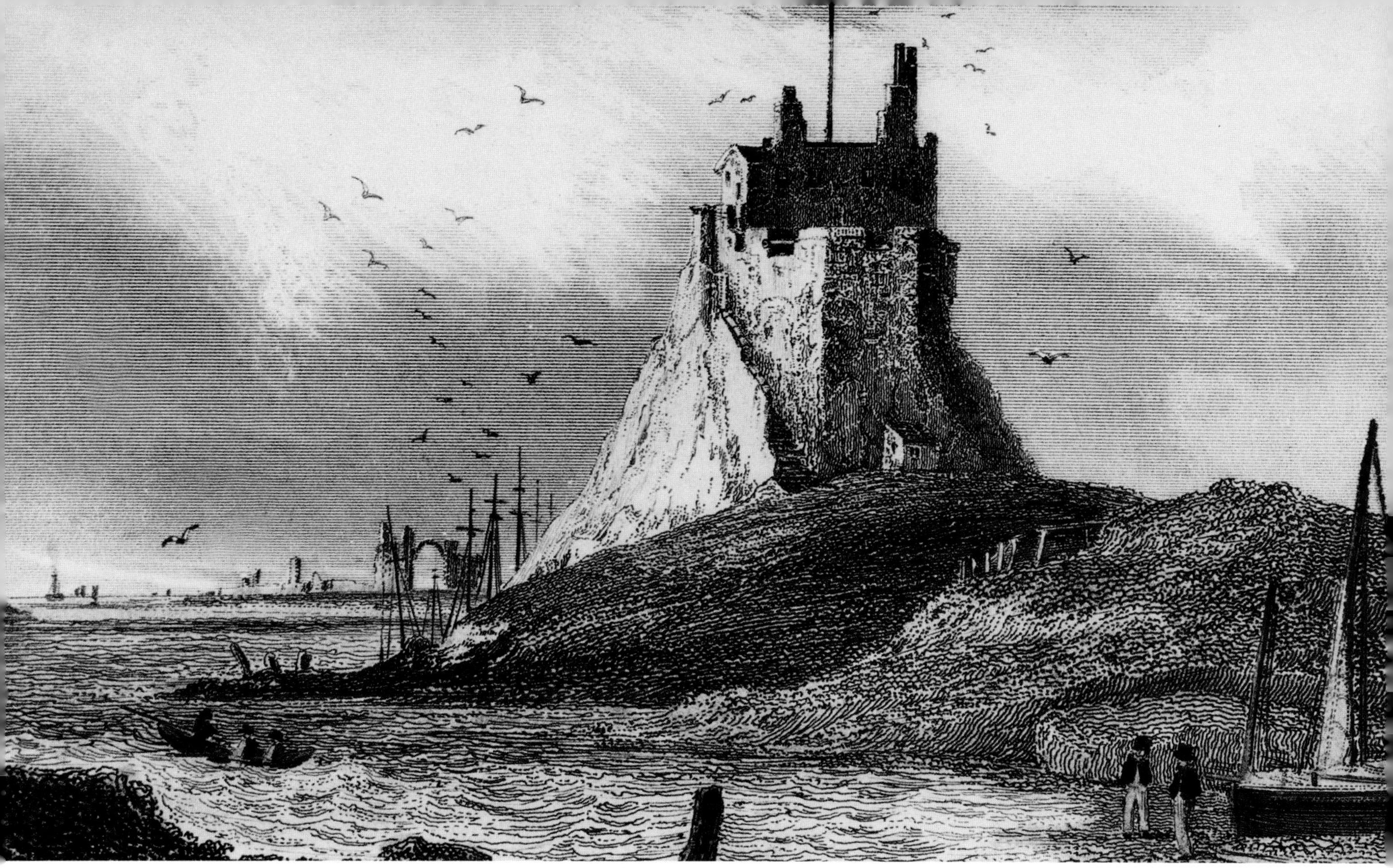

Holy Island Castle.
Cat No: WPG016 Ref: T/4306

Inside Lindisfarne Priory, Holy Island.
Cat No: A122 Ref: R640

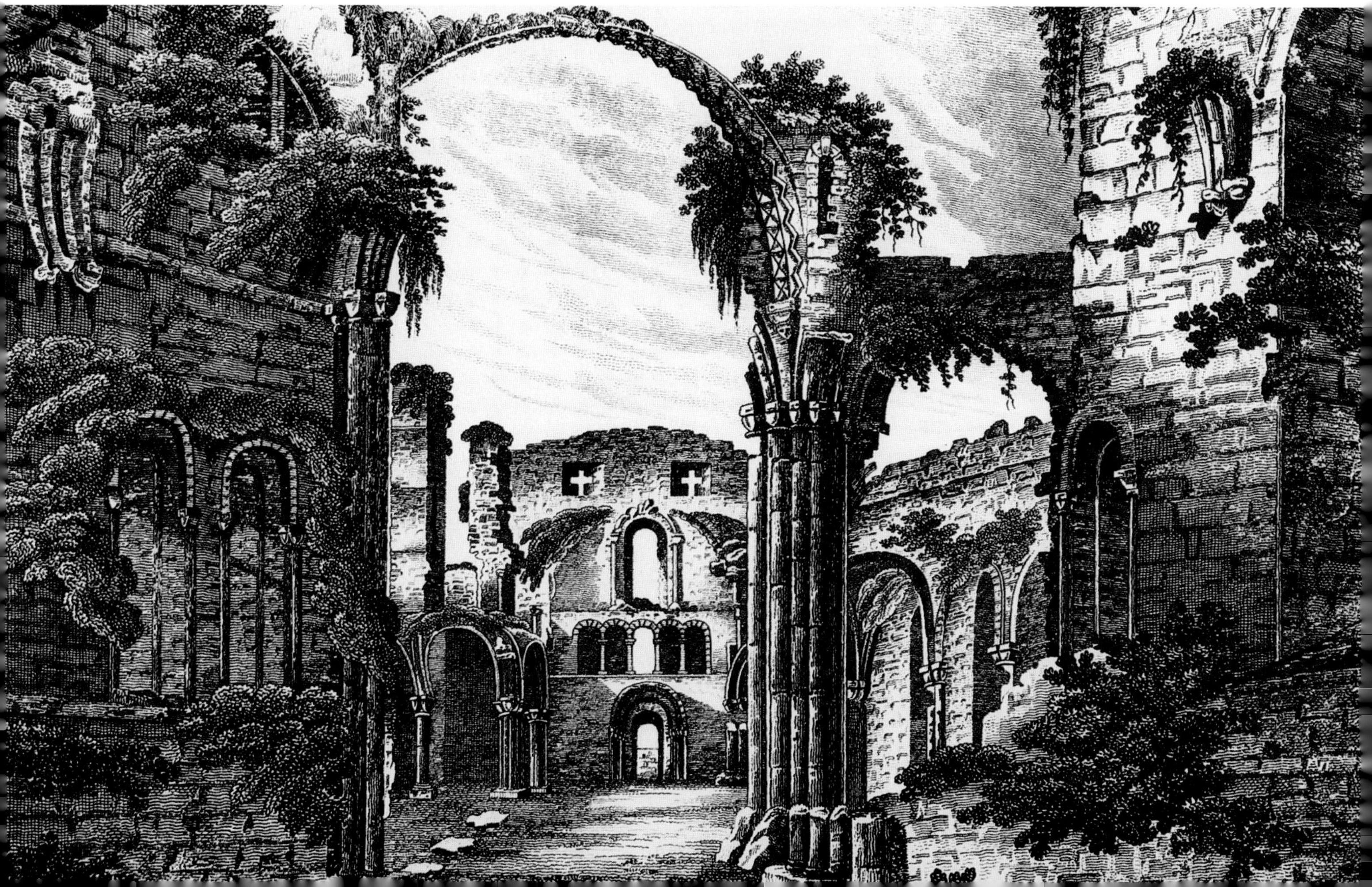

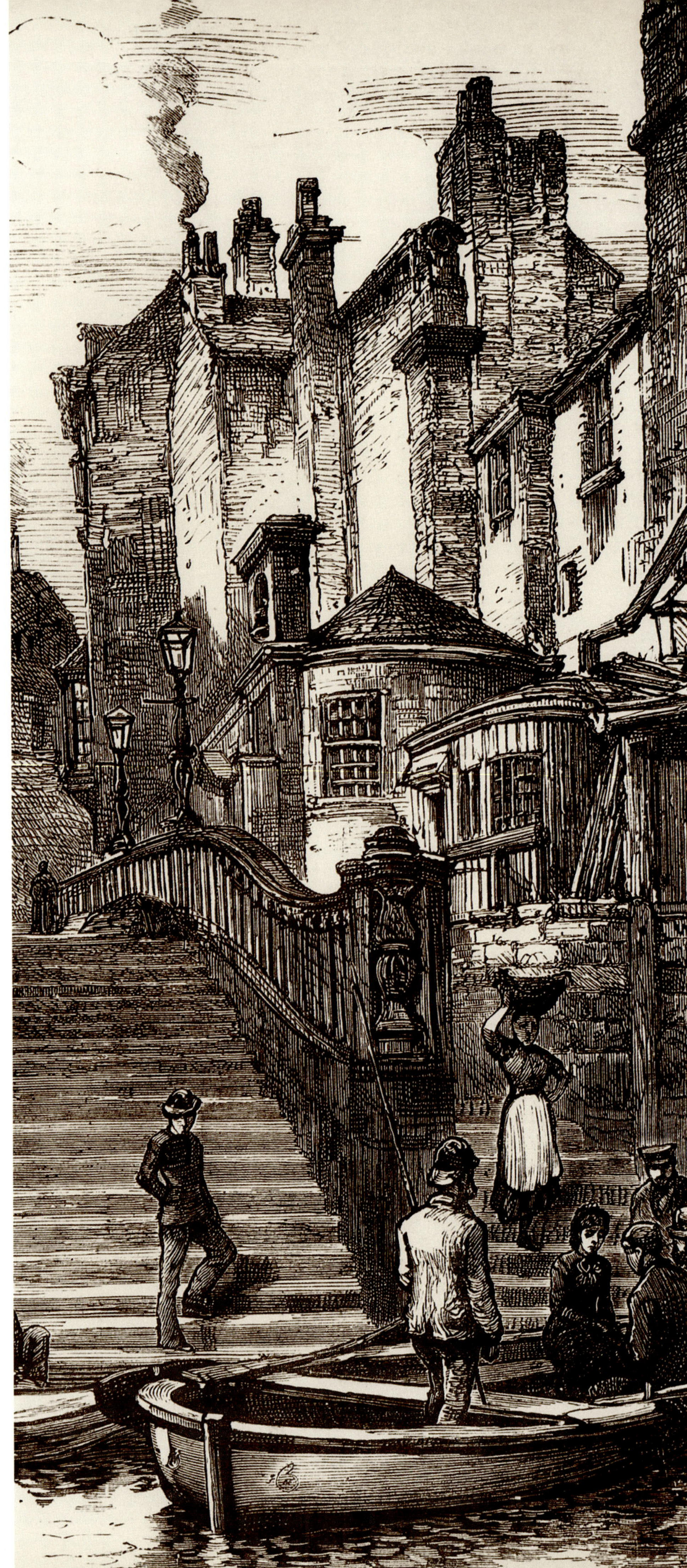

Sunderland Quayside Ferry Landing.
Cat No: WPG017 Ref: T4227

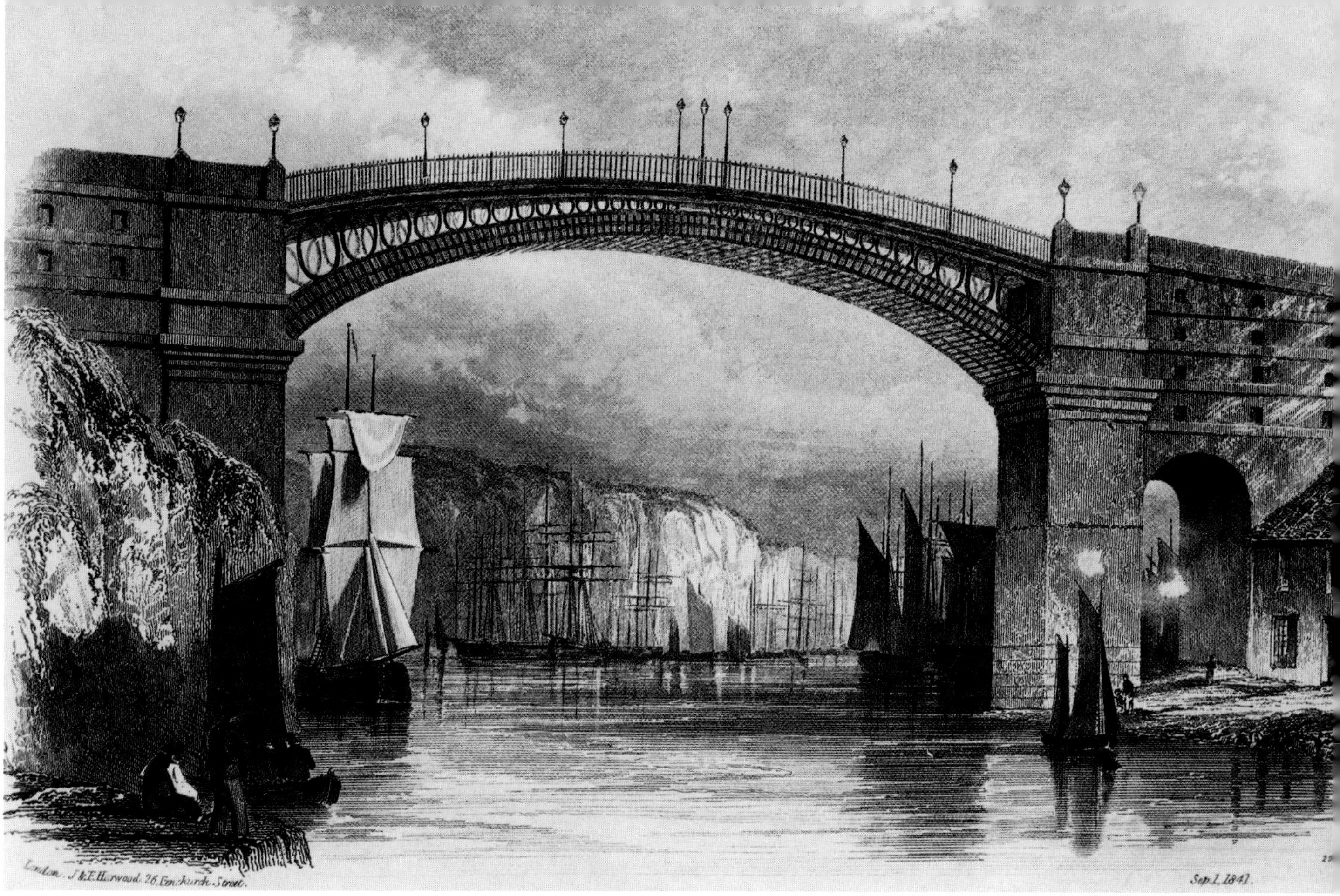

Sunderland Bridge by J. & E. Harwood, 26 Fenchurch Street, London. 1st September 1841.
Cat No: WPG018 Ref: T5415

Sunderland Bridge over the River Wear.
Cat No: WPG019 Ref: X1141

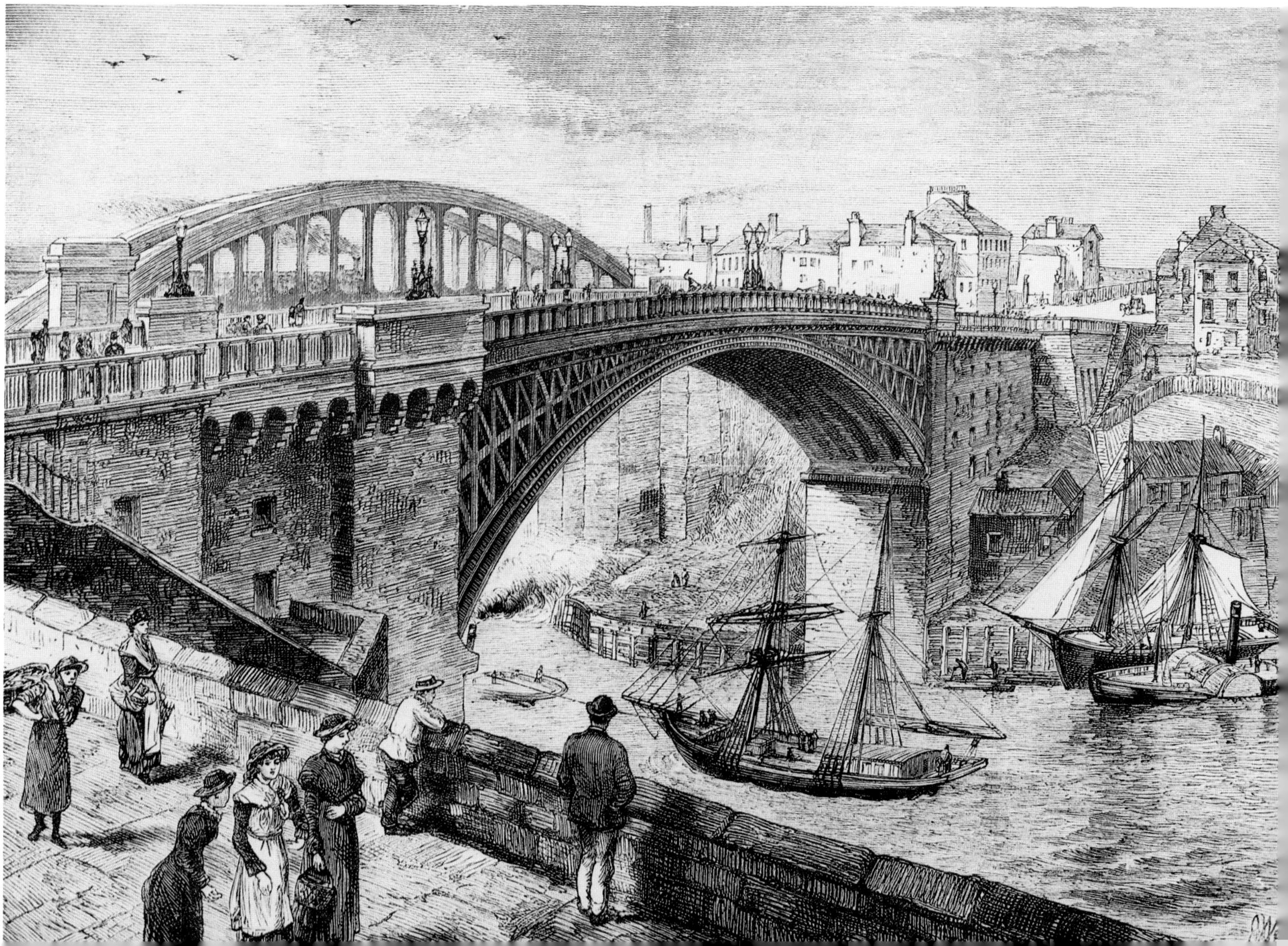

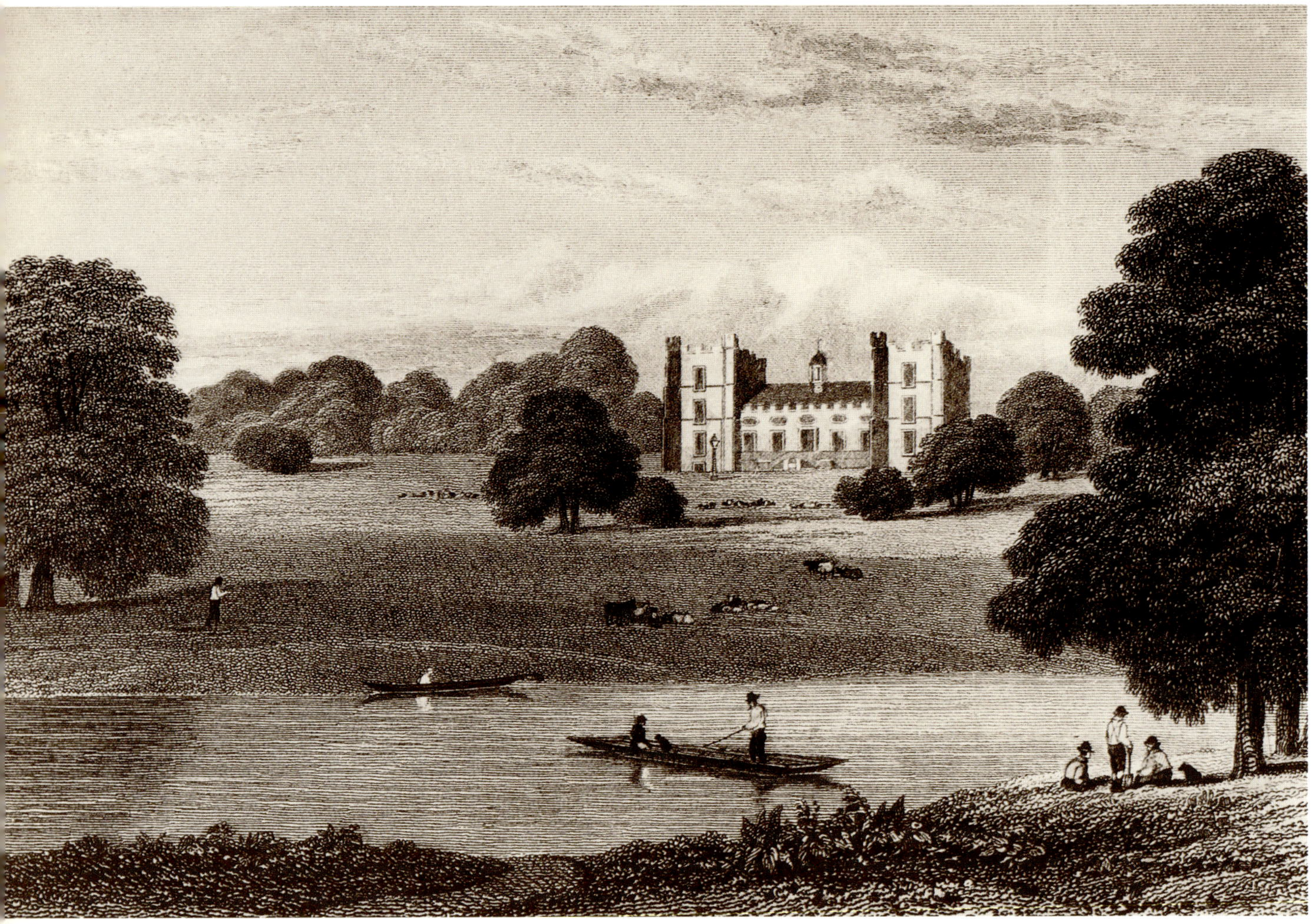

Lumley Castle near Chester-le-Street, Durham.
Cat No: WPG020 Ref: M5552

Castle Eden Hall, County of Durham - the seat of Rowland Burden Esq. by T. Jeavons.
Cat No: A123 Ref: R4960

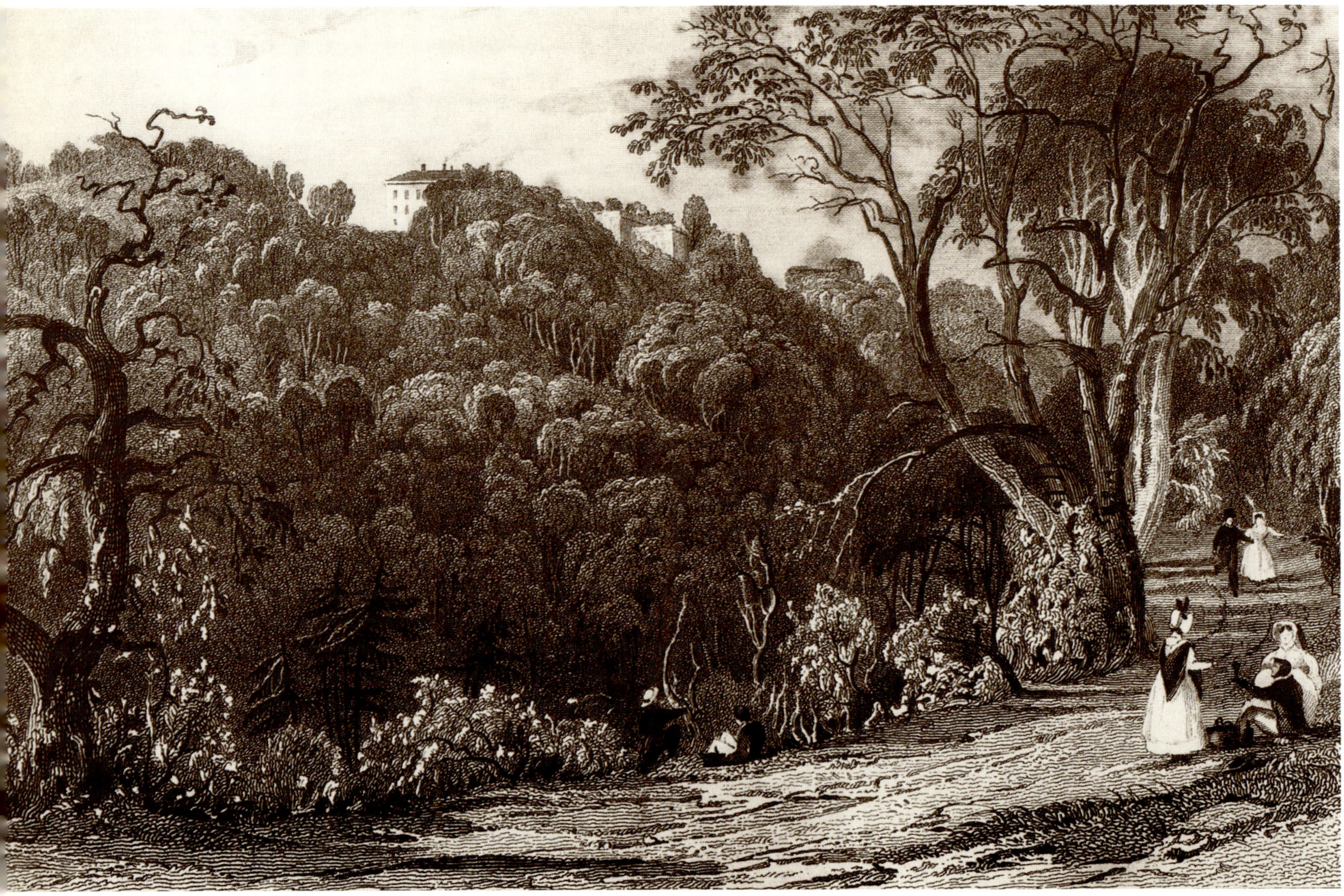

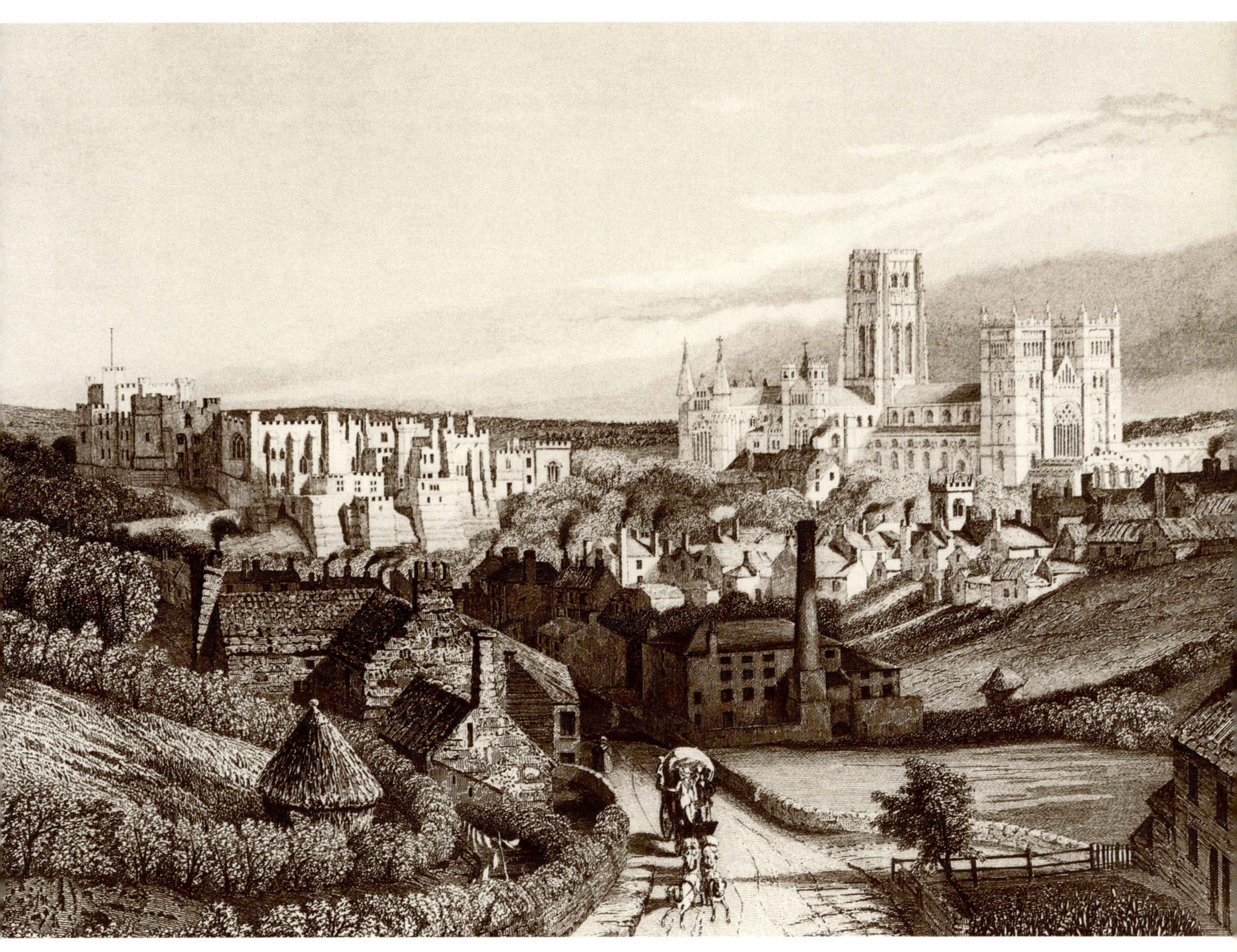

The Castle and Cathedral, Durham City from the Newcastle Road.
Cat No: WPG021 Ref: P4966

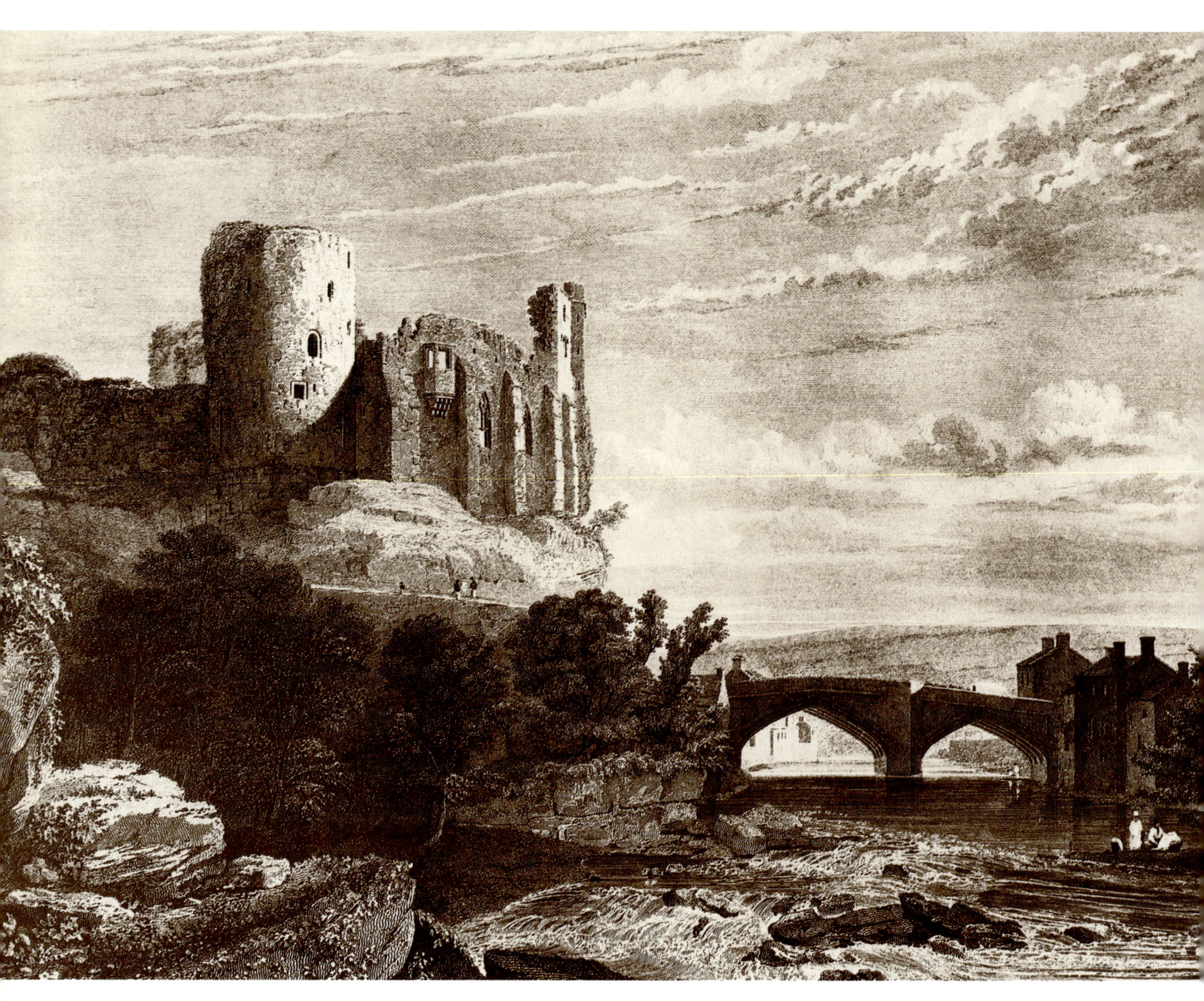

Barnard Castle and Bridge, County Durham.
Cat No: WPG022 Ref: X3879

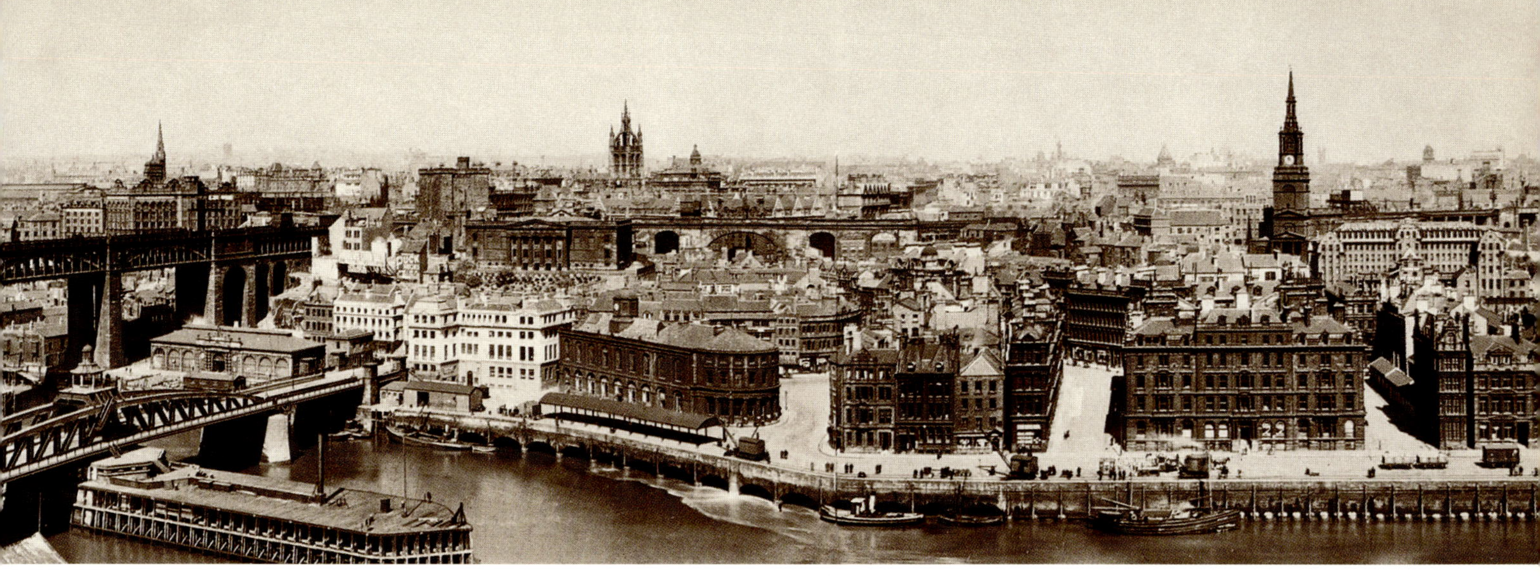

Newcastle upon Tyne in full
view before the Tyne Bridge.
Cat No: A126 Ref: H9176

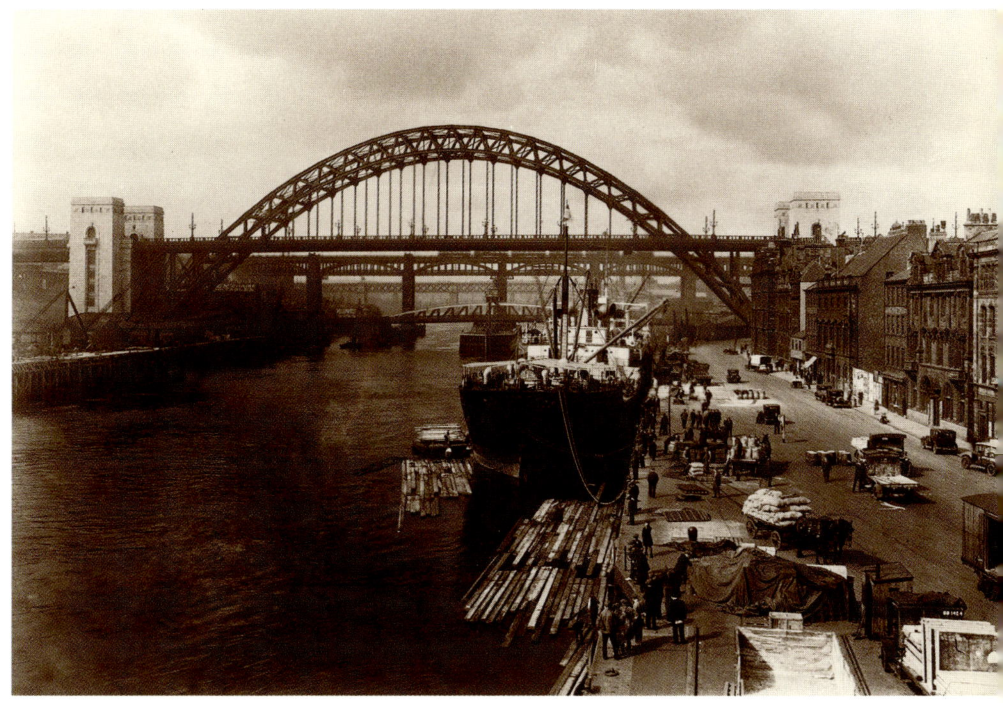

Loading the ships. The height of
trading activity with the loading of
cargo at the Newcastle Quayside.
Cat No: A127 Ref: H9177

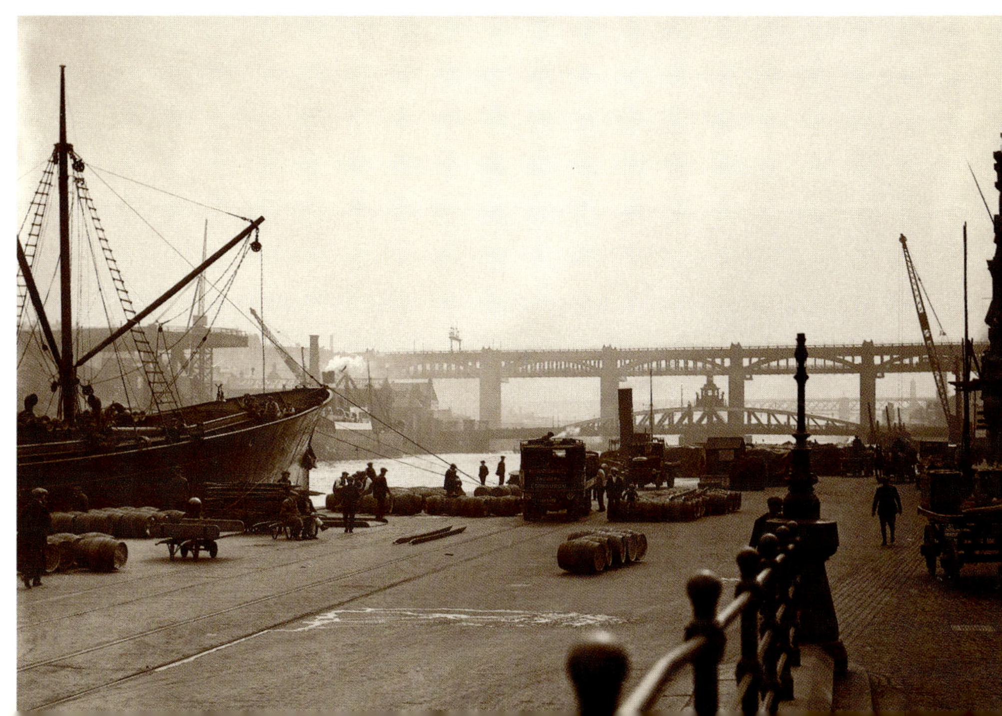

Loading the barrels as the Quayside
trades successfully while building of the
new Tyne Bridge Commences, circa 1925.
Cat No: WPG023 Ref: H7525

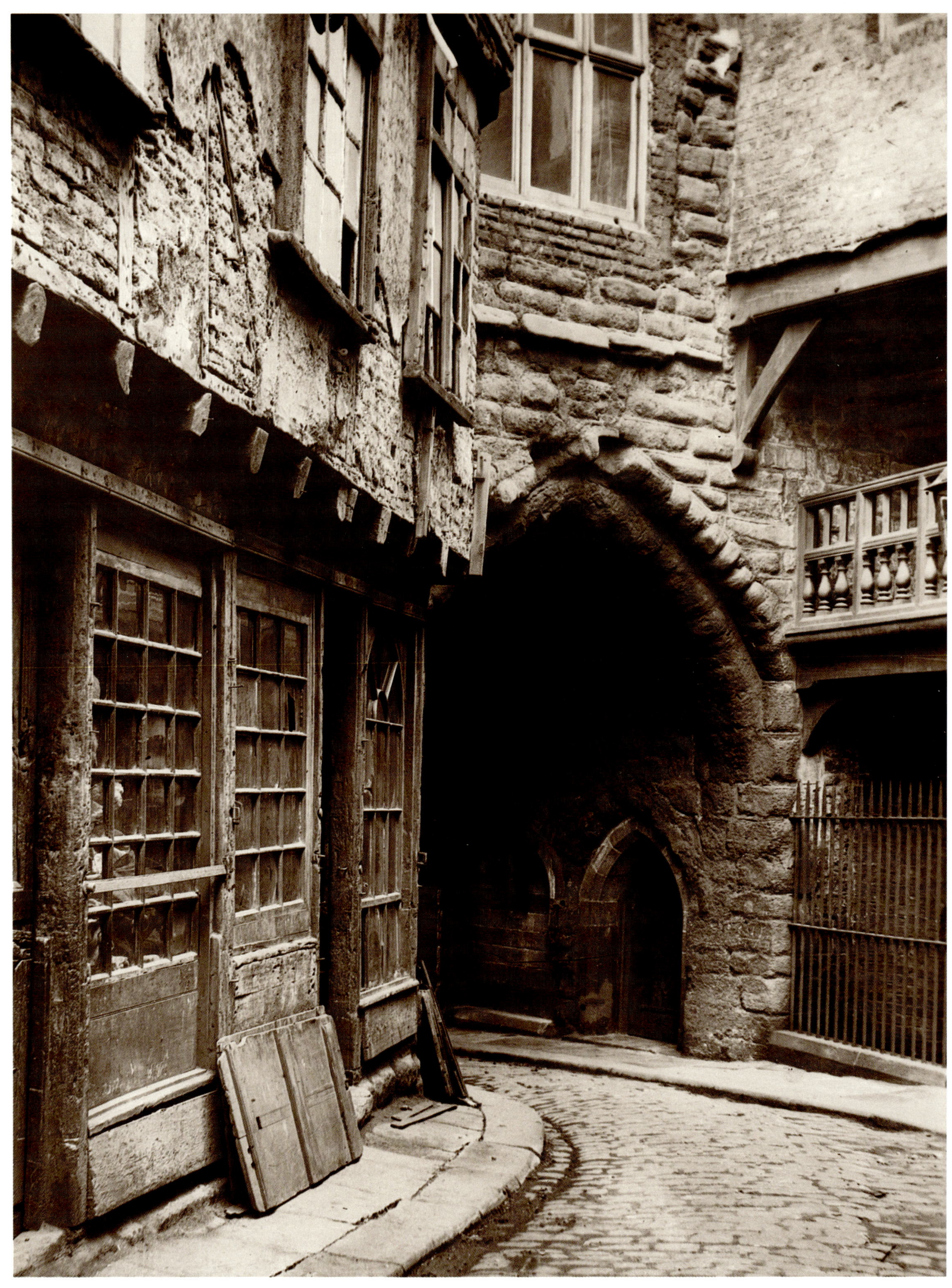

Black Gate, Newcastle upon Tyne.
Cat No: WPG024 Ref: C2436

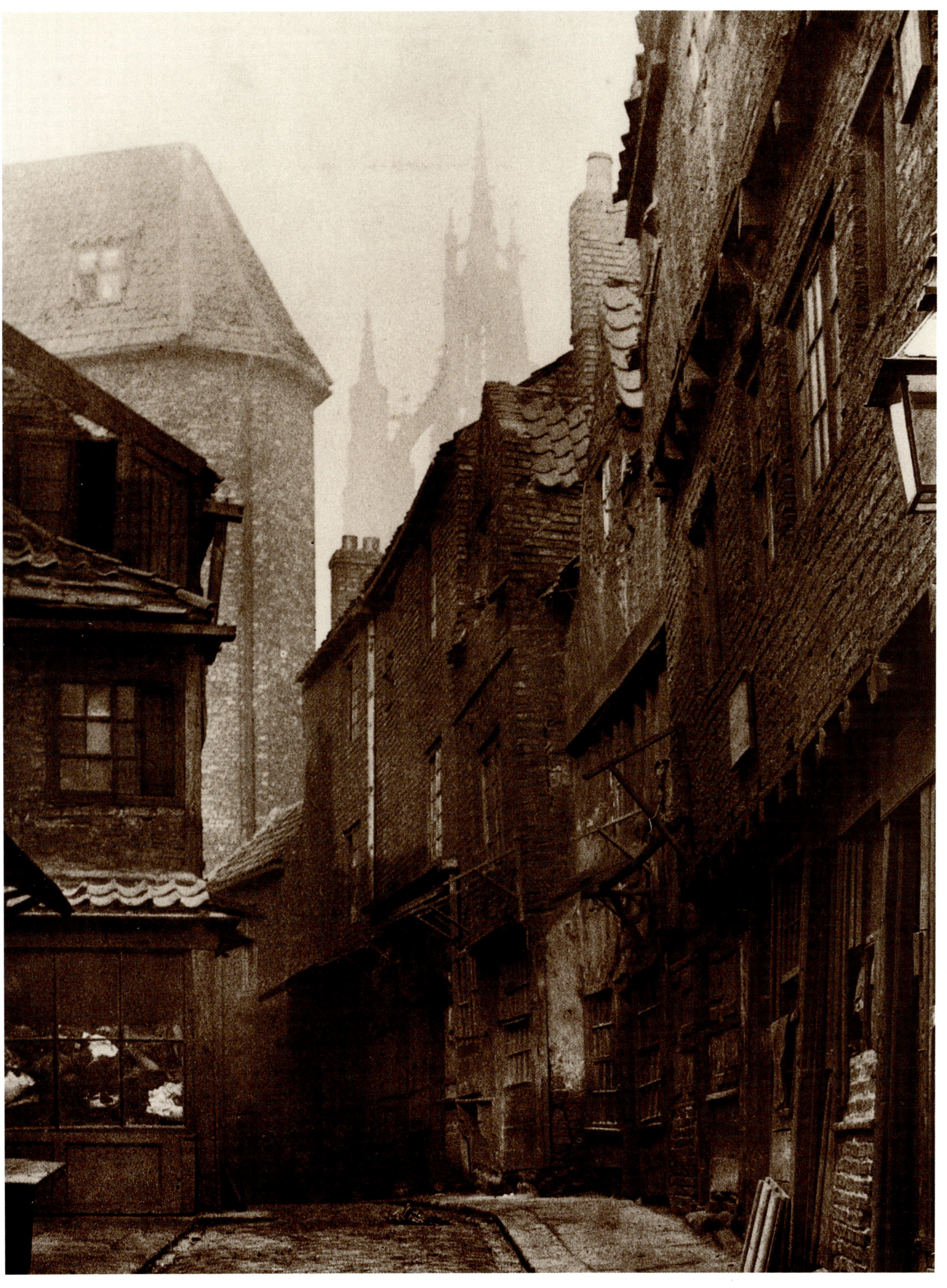

Near Dog Leap Stairs, Newcastle upon Tyne, in the shadows of St. Nicholas Cathedral.
Cat No: WPG025 Ref: H9155

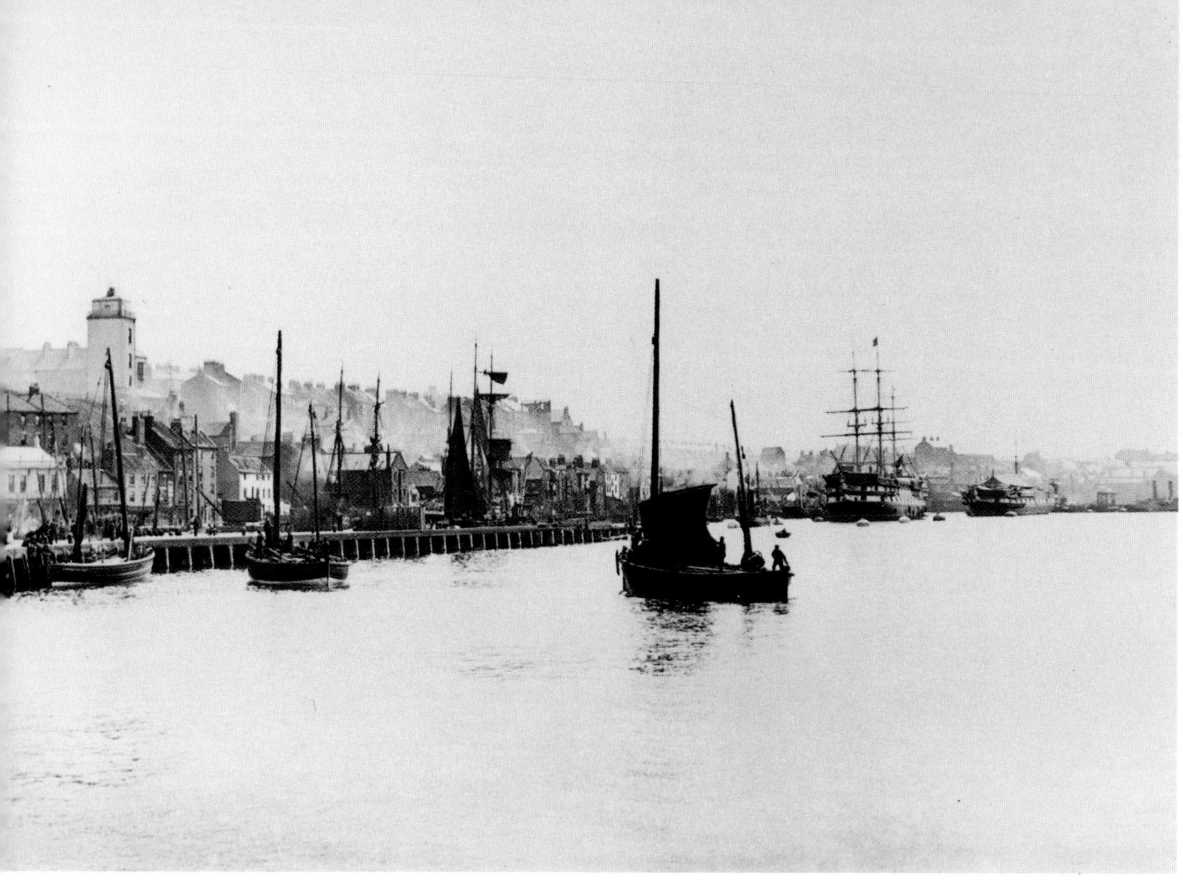

Coming into dock.
The Quayside awaits its cargo and sailors, North Shields.
Cat No: A128 Ref: H7371

Steam ships of all sizes, leaving the Tyne.
Cat No: A129 Ref: C631

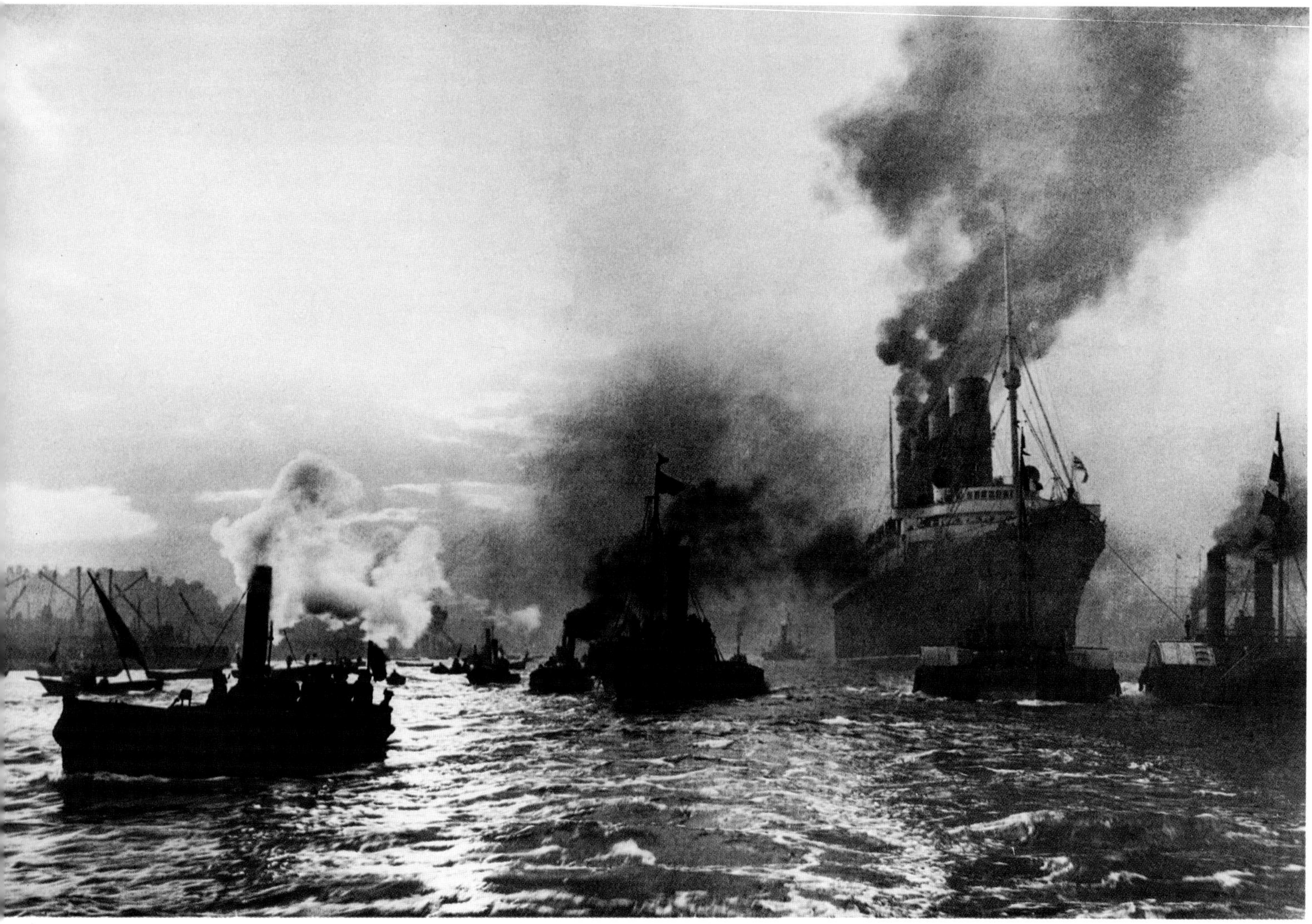

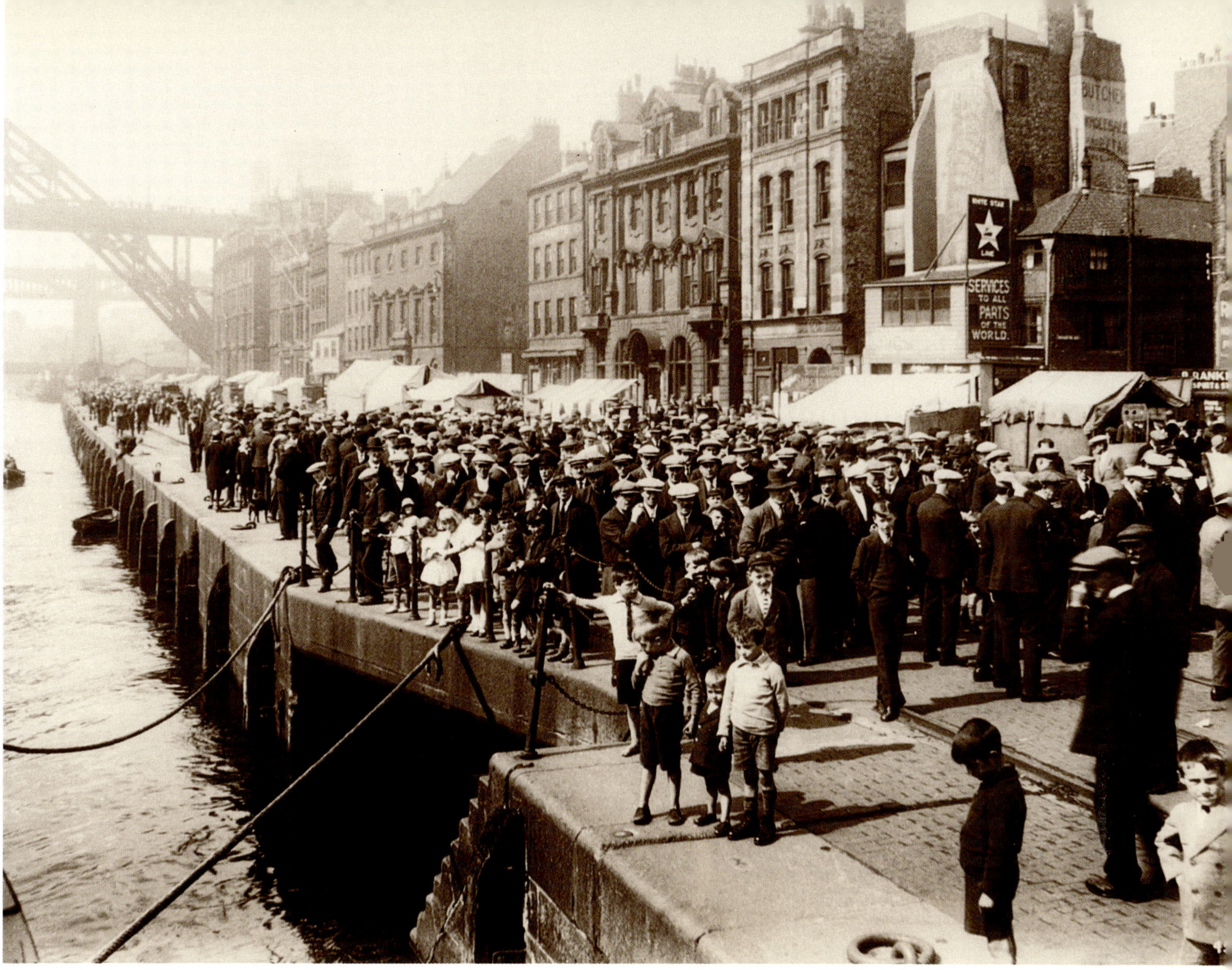

Market day at the Quayside, Newcastle upon Tyne.
The men, the children, but where are the women?
Cat No: A131 Ref: 458B

A fleet of paddle steamers
at North Shields Quayside.
Cat No: A130 Ref: X1540

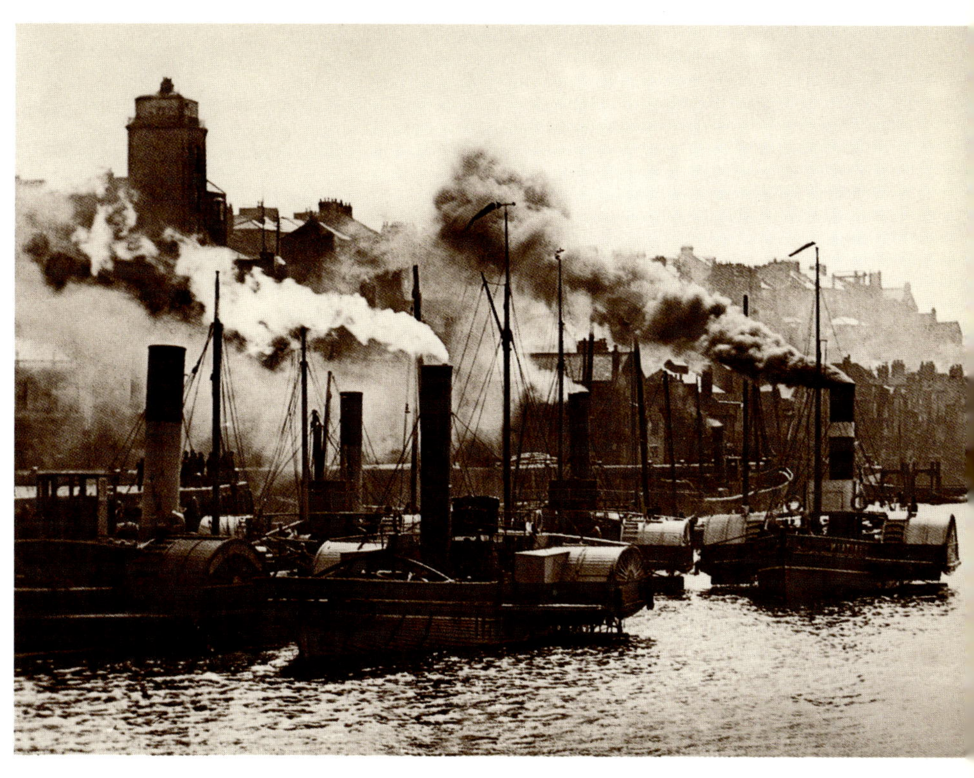

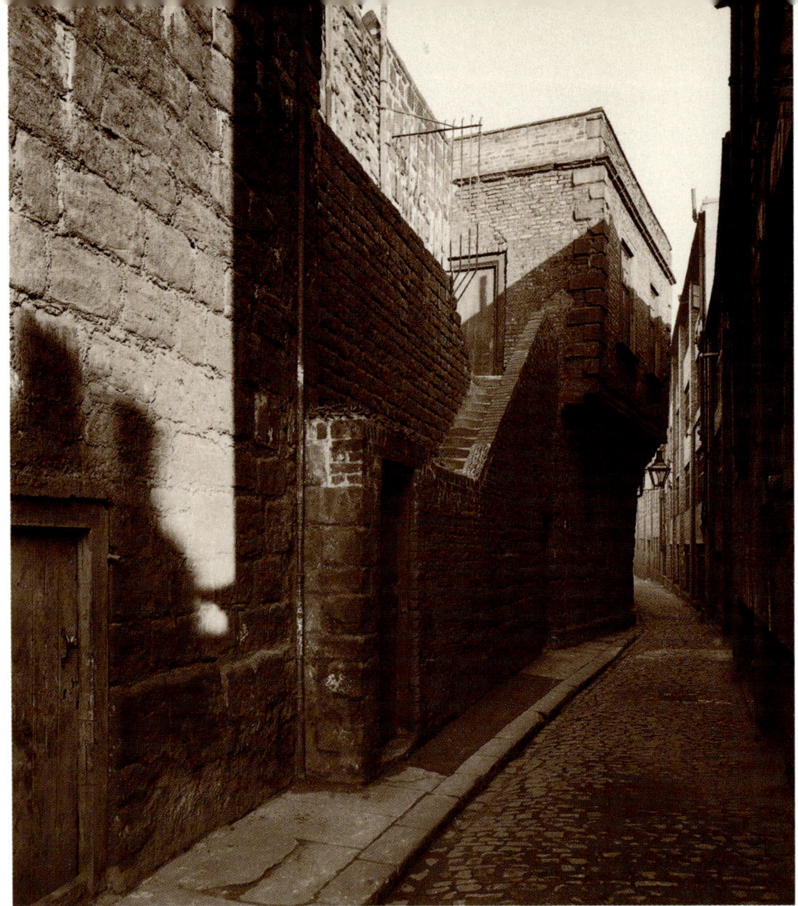

Morden Tower, Stowell Street,
Newcastle upon Tyne.
Cat No: A135 Ref: WP6100

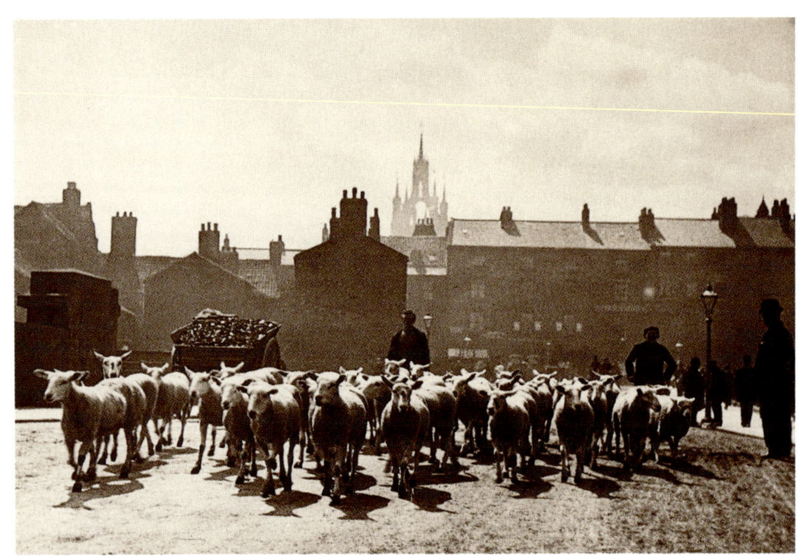

Coming home from market. Sheep herd leaving the City of Newcastle.
Cat No: A136 Ref: X1542

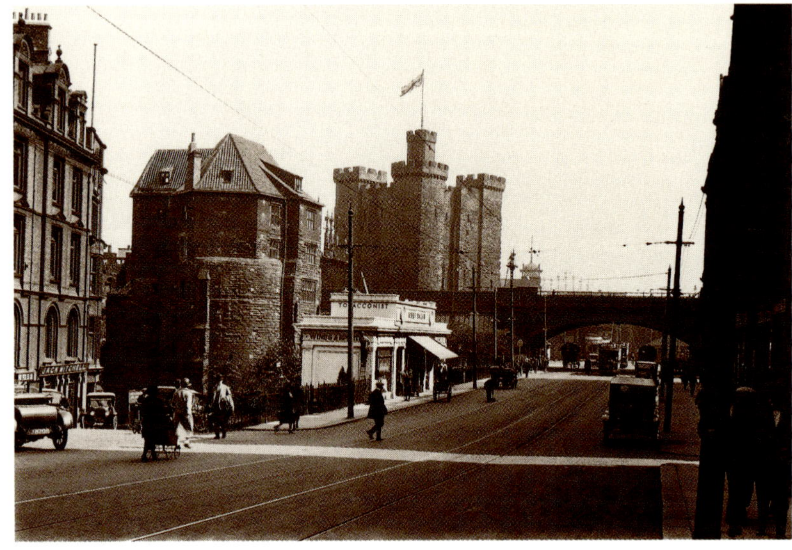

St. Nicholas Street, Newcastle upon Tyne with the Railway Bridge and Castle in the background.
Cat No: A137 Ref: 316B

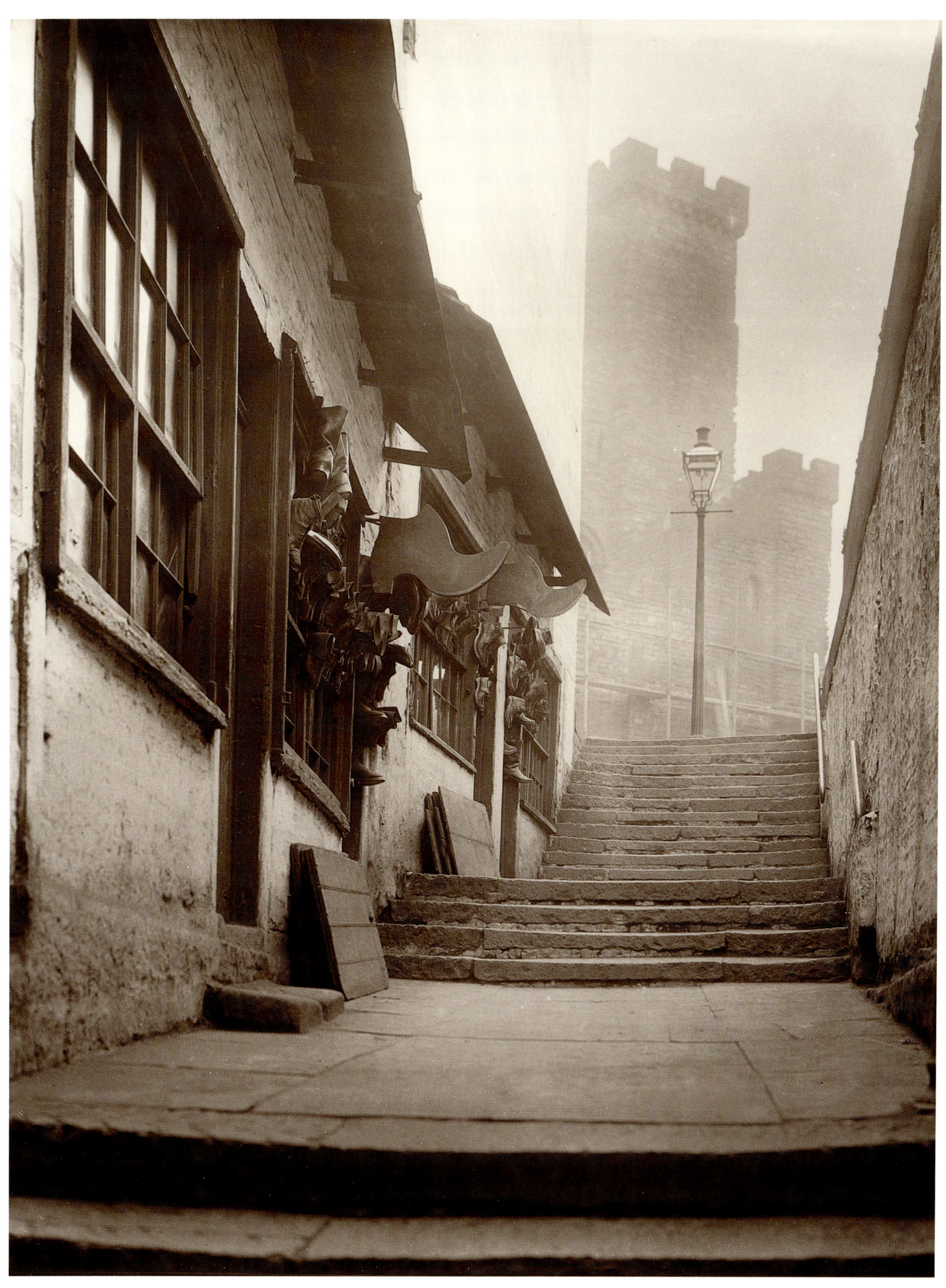

The cloggers' shops on the Castle Stairs. A corner of the old Keep of the new castle is glimpsed across the Garth at the head of the stairs.
Cat No: WPG026 Ref: 128B

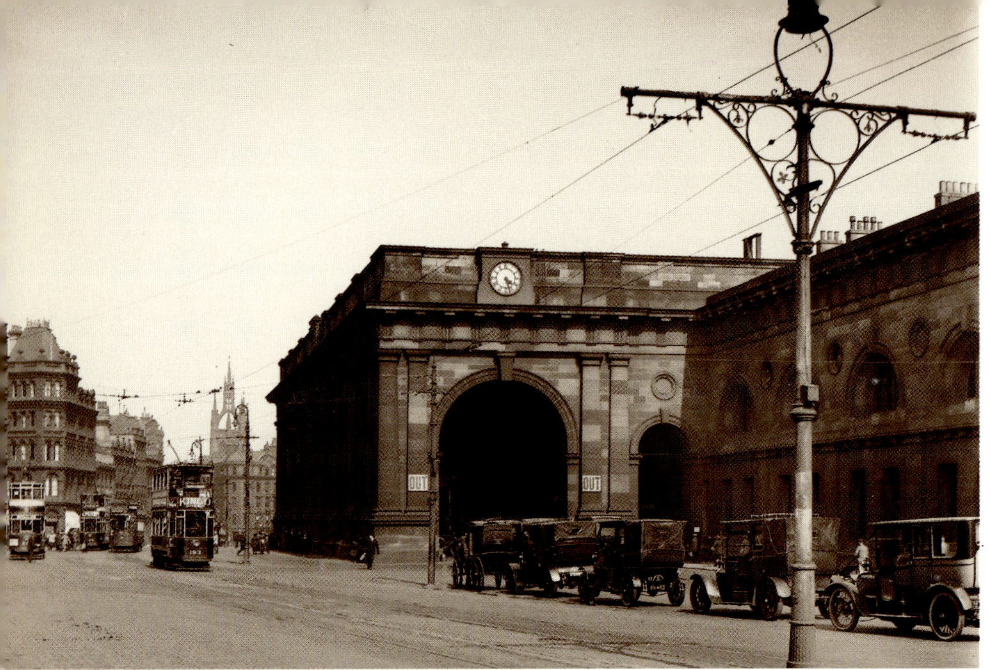

Trams and taxis to the station,
Neville Street, Newcastle upon Tyne.
Cat No: A138 Ref: H9178

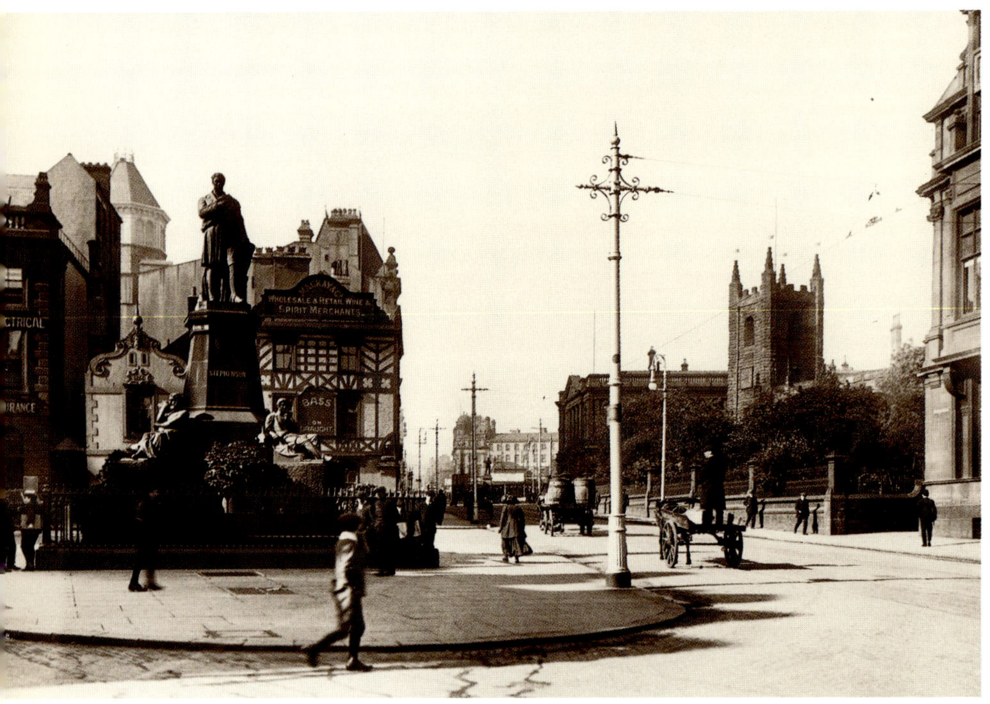

Westgate Road, Newcastle upon Tyne,
with horse drawn vehicles carrying
barrels of beer to Mackay & Co.,
Wholesale and Retail Wines and Spirits
Merchants selling 'Bass on Draught'.
Cat No: A139 Ref: S3598

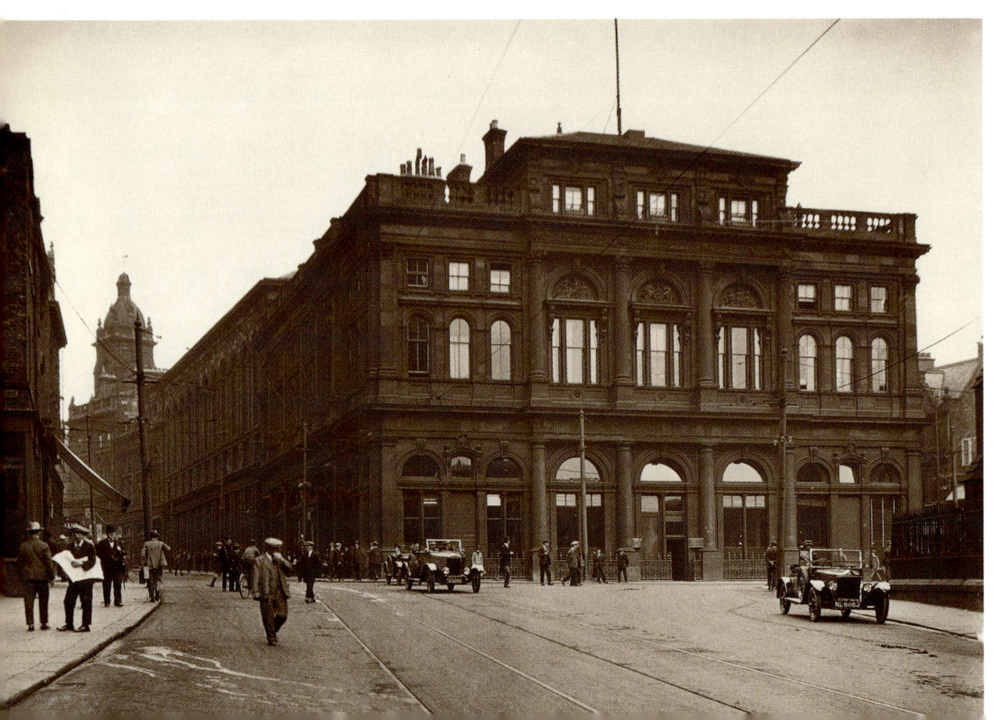

The Town Hall, Newcastle upon Tyne,
Which was situated on the corner of the
Groat Market and Mosely Street.
Cat No: A140 Ref: 325B

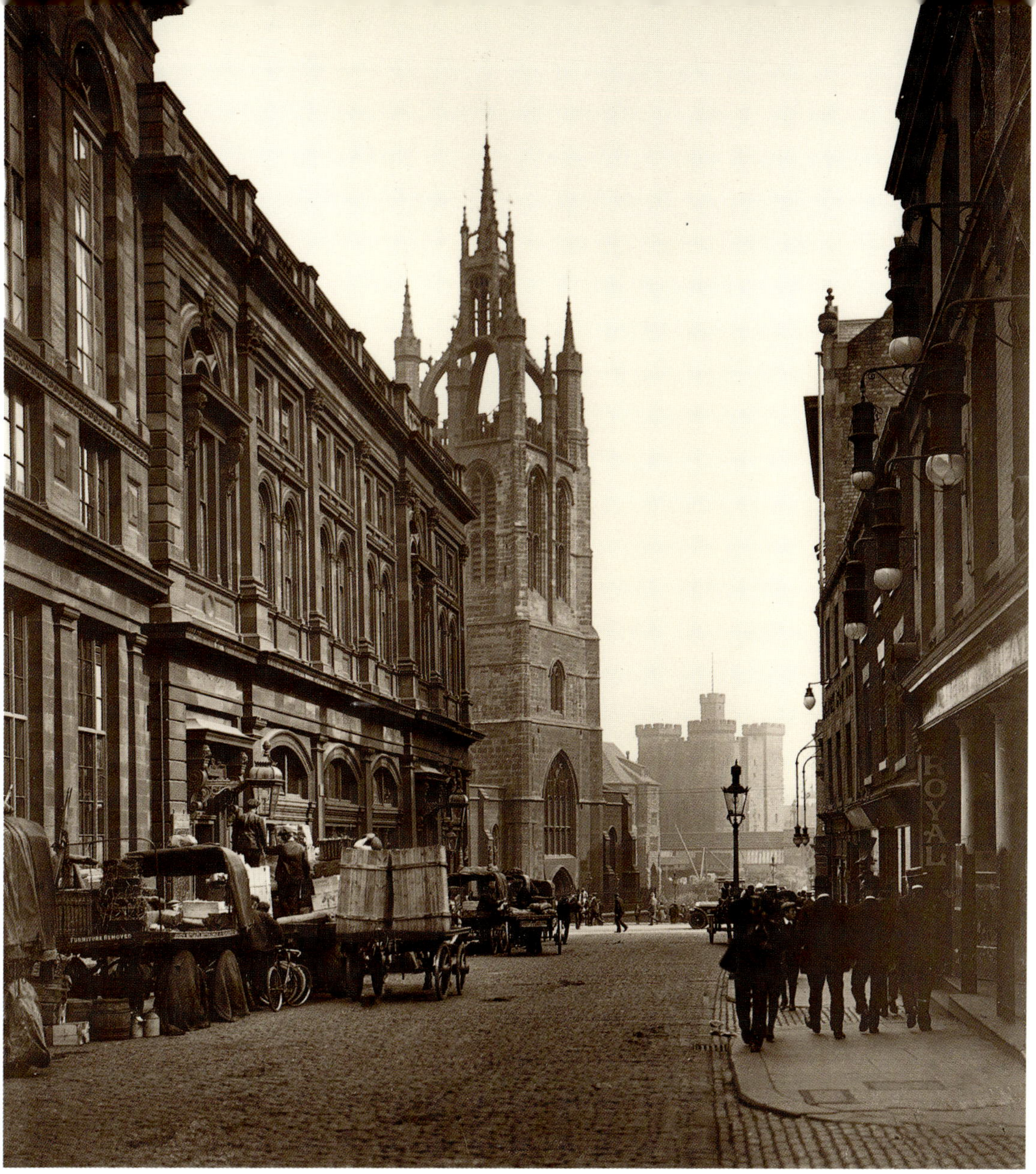

Groat Market and Town Hall at the height of transport activity.
Cat No: WPG027 Ref: H7729/12 E1265

Theatre Royal, Grey Street, Newcastle upon Tyne
with Grey's Monument in the distance, circa 1924.
Cat No: A141 Ref: 1293

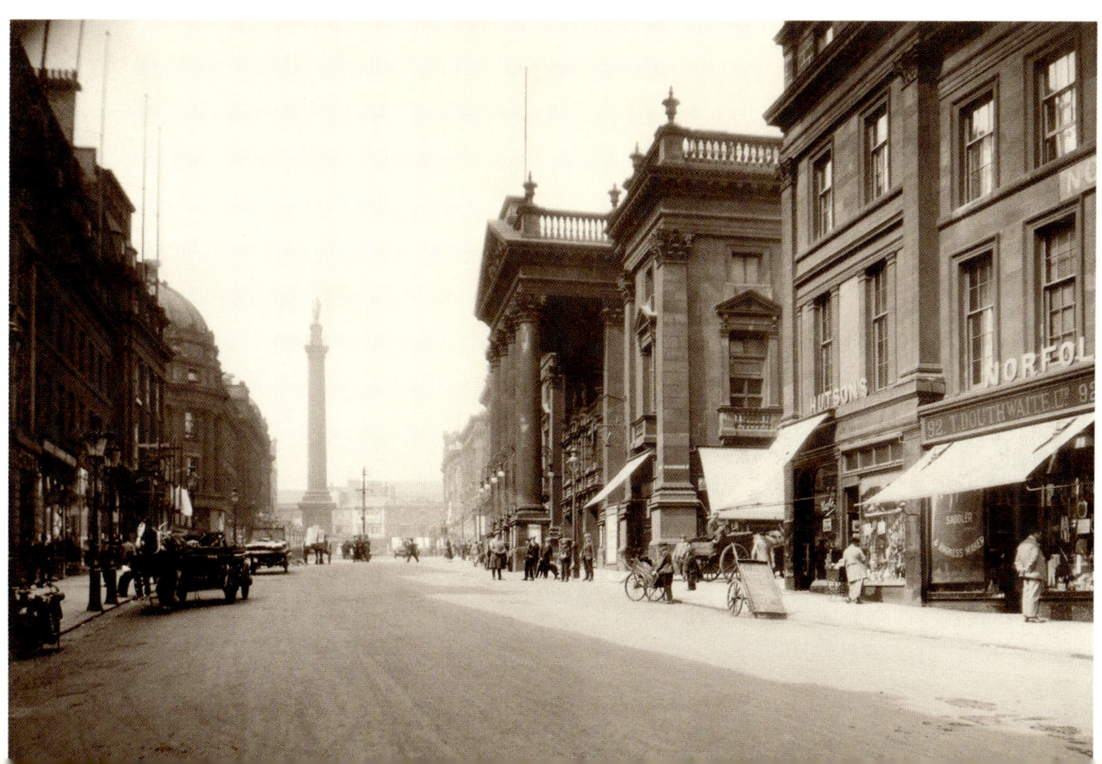

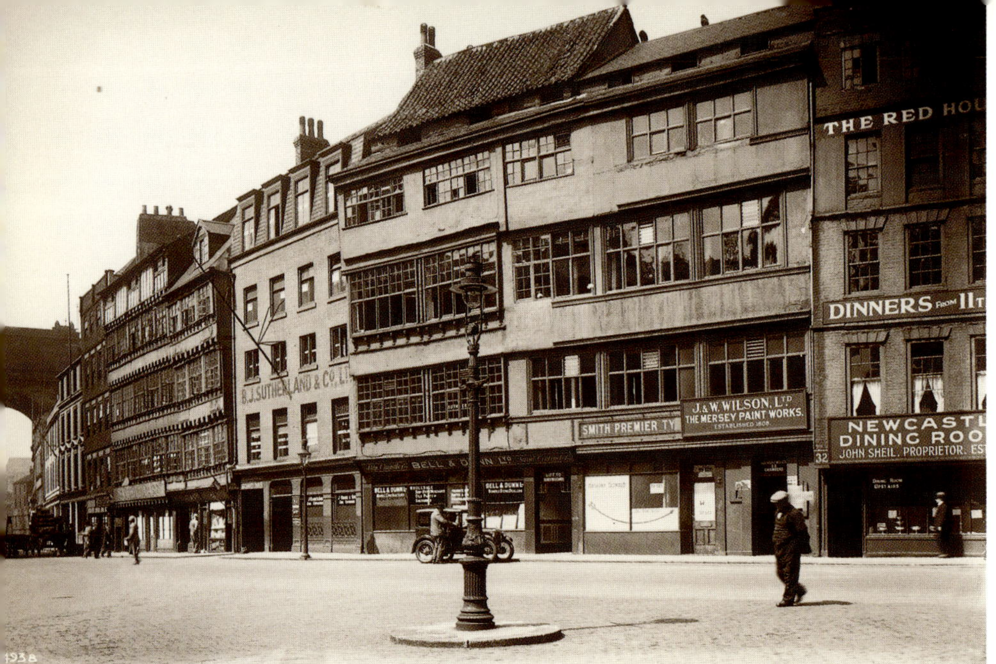

The Newcastle Dining Rooms, Sand Hill, Quayside, Newcastle upon Tyne with Bessie Surtees House to the left of B. J. Sutherland & Co. Ltd.
Cat No: A142 Ref: 493B/E4763

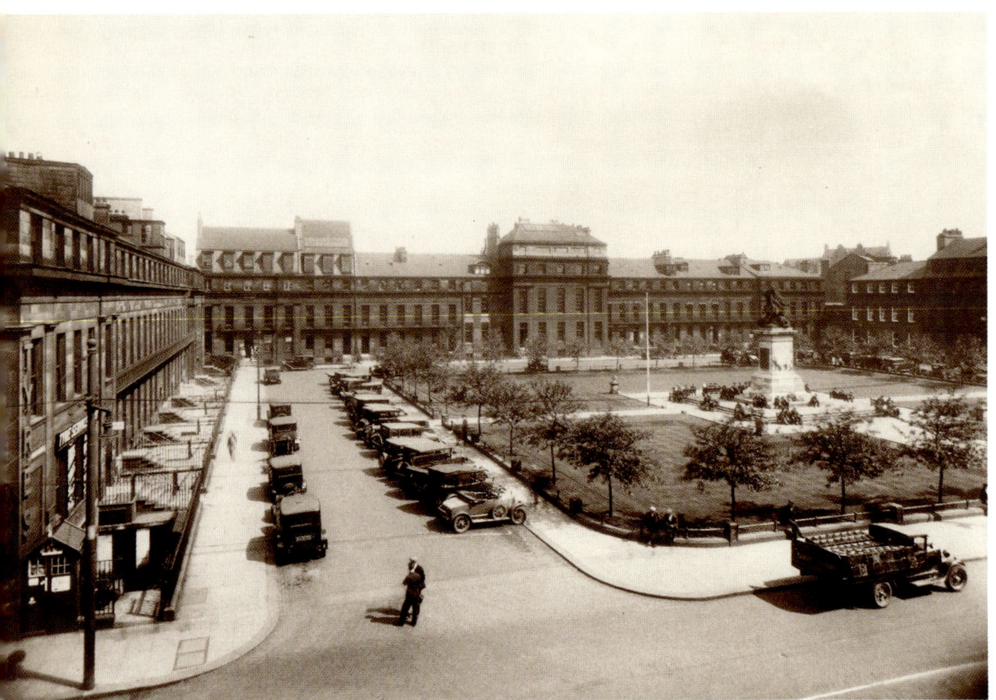

Eldon Square, Newcastle upon Tyne.
Cat No: A144 Ref: 442B

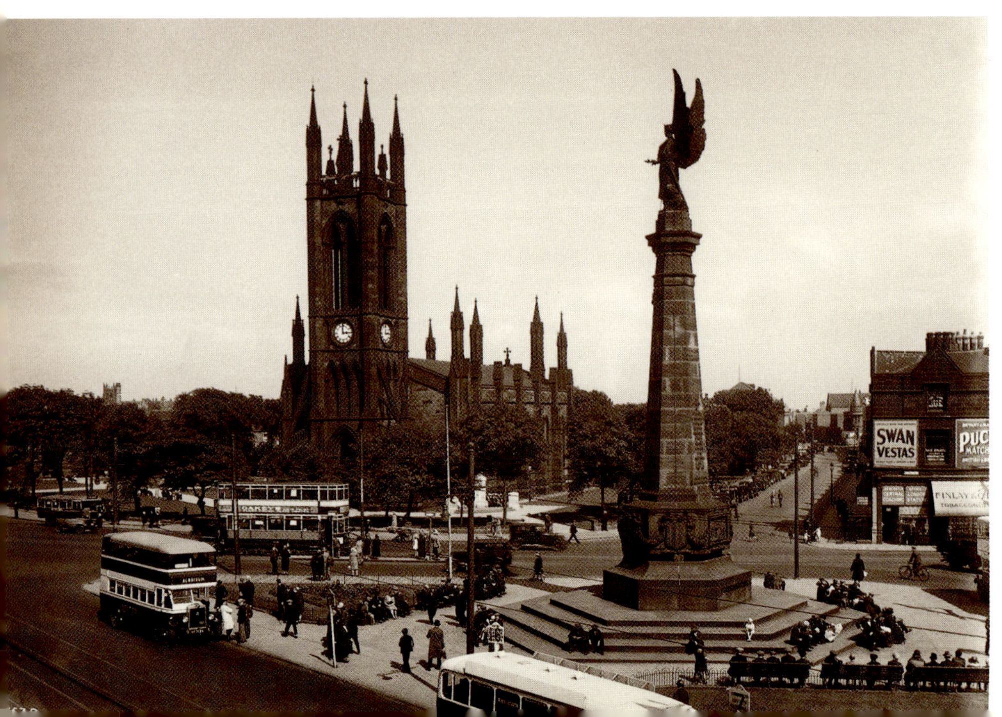

Catch the bus to Newbiggin at the Haymarket, Newcastle upon Tyne.
Cat No: A145 Ref: 457B

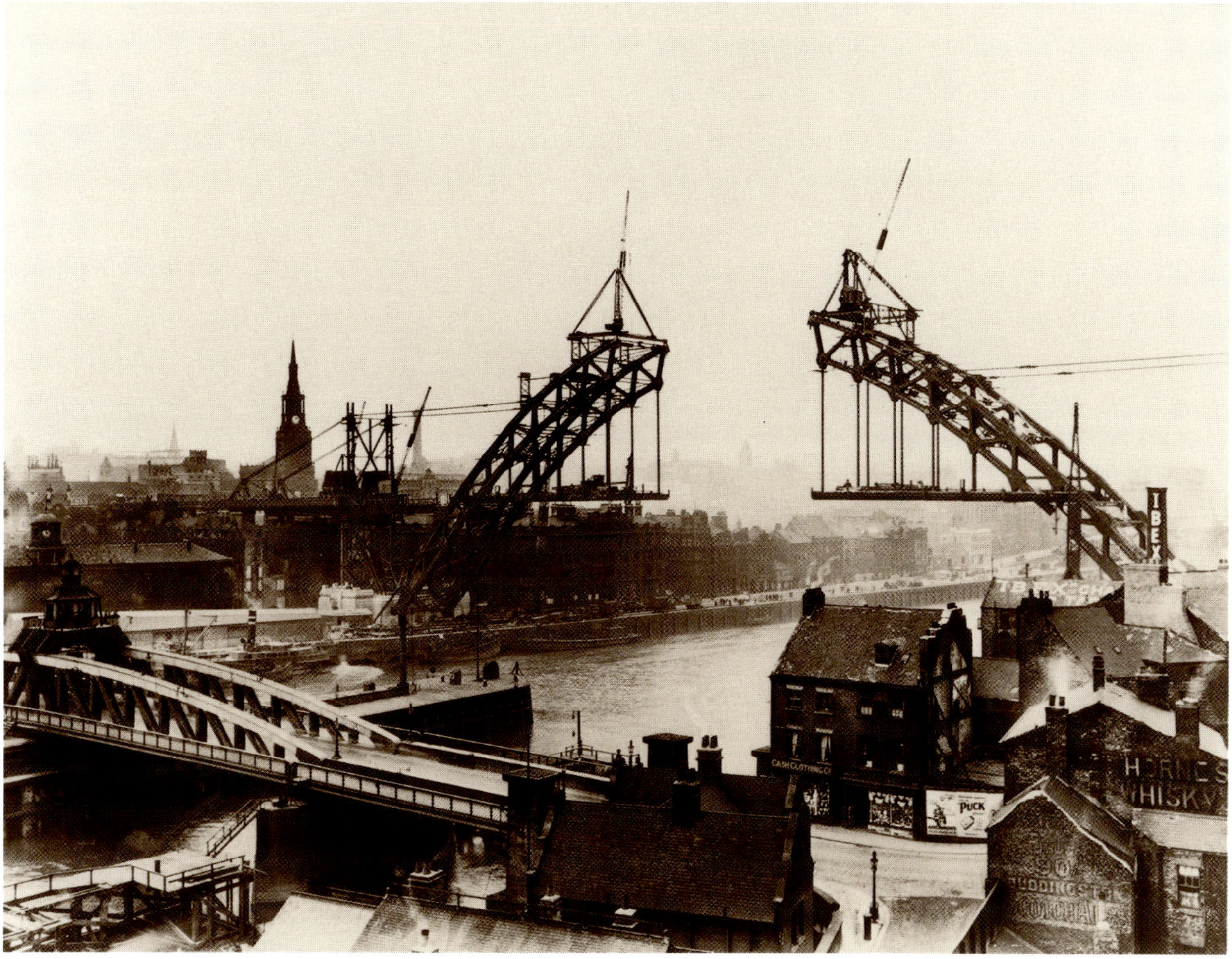

A bridge of two halfs. Construction of the Tyne Bridge from Gateshead, circa 1926.
Cat No: A146 Ref: H9158

Completing the Gateshead end of the Tyne Bridge, circa 1927.
Cat No: A147 Ref: H7523

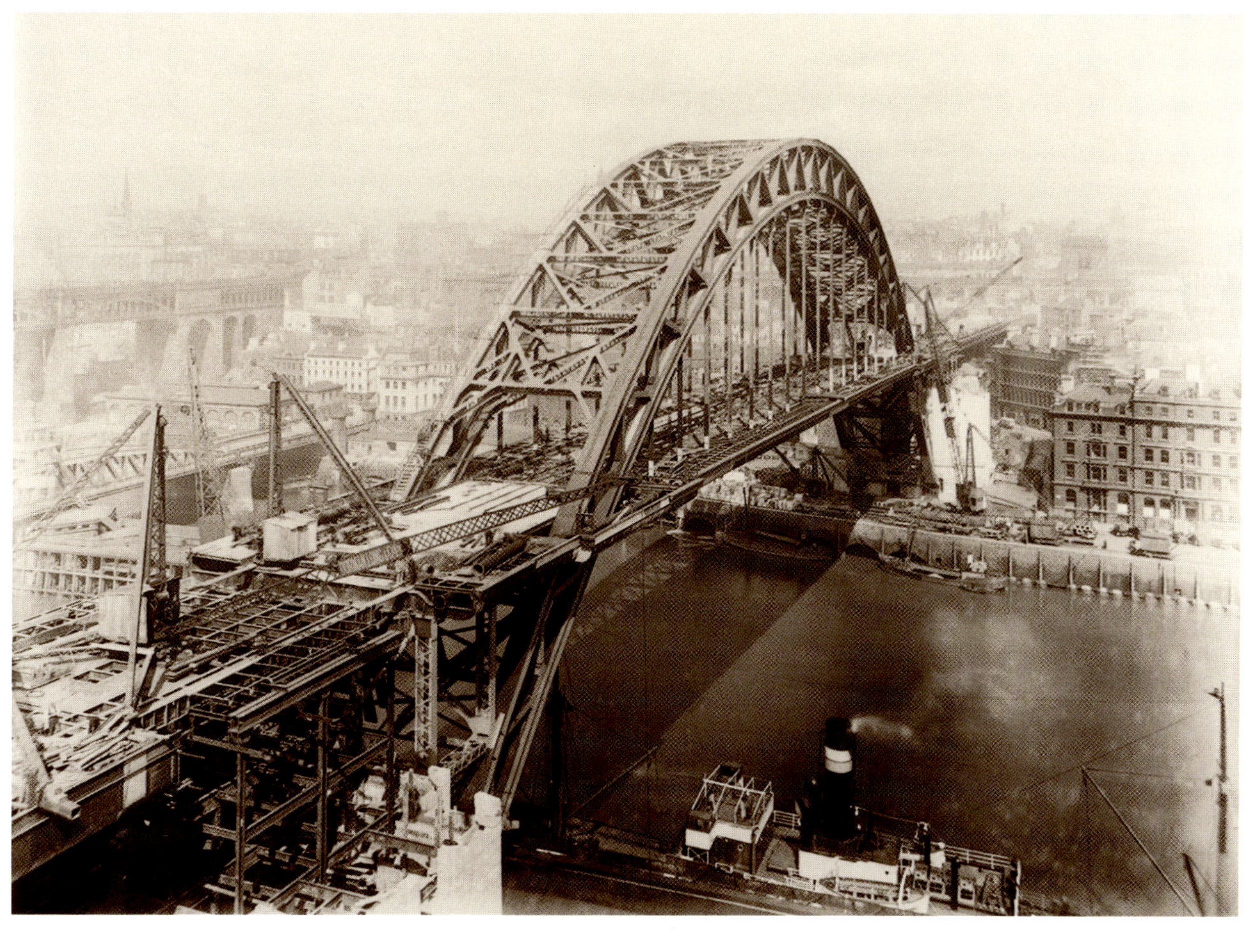

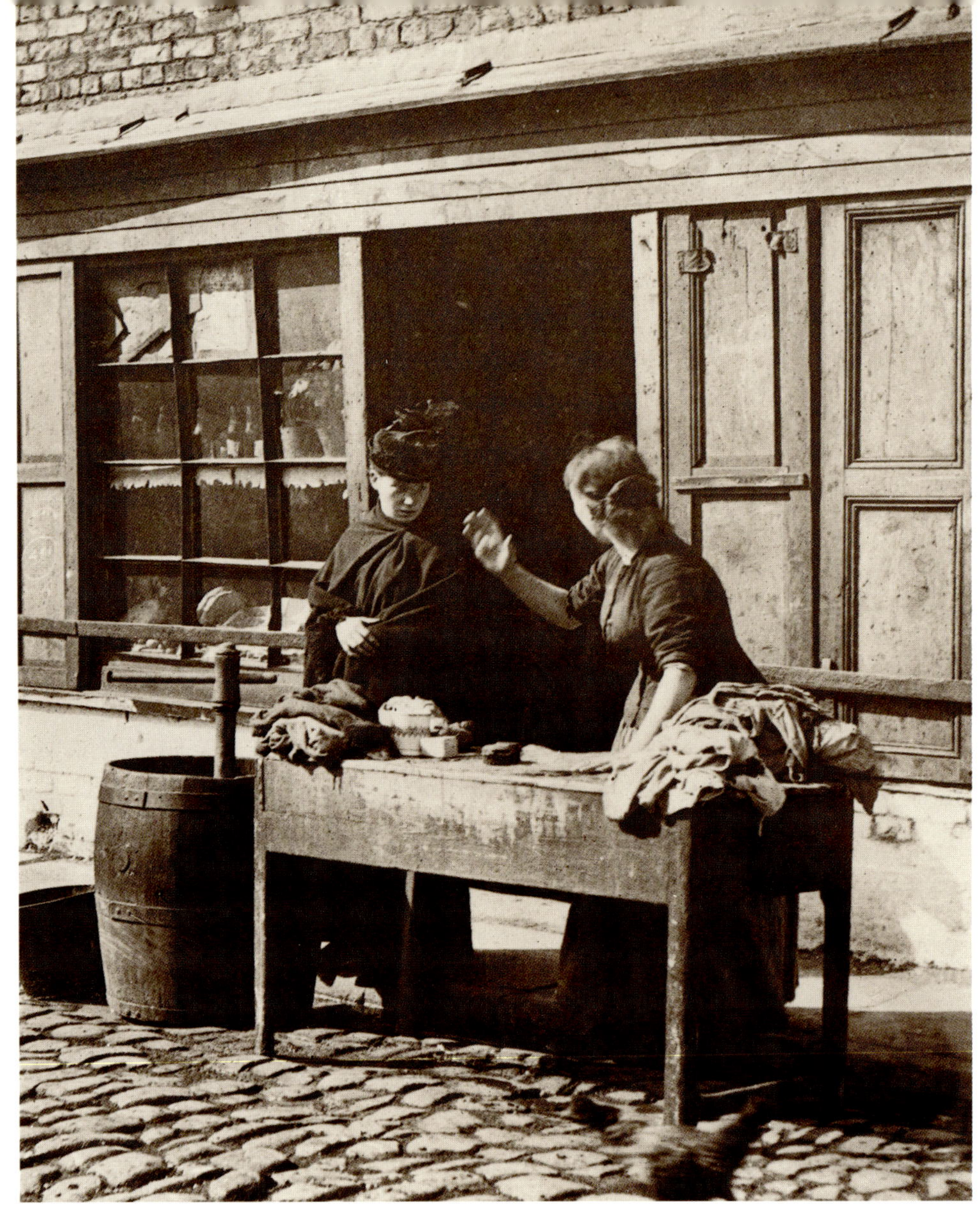

The laundry women at work - dealing with a customer.
Cat No: WPG028 Ref: X1570

A break for lunch - waiting for a sale.
Cat No: WPG029 Ref: X1547

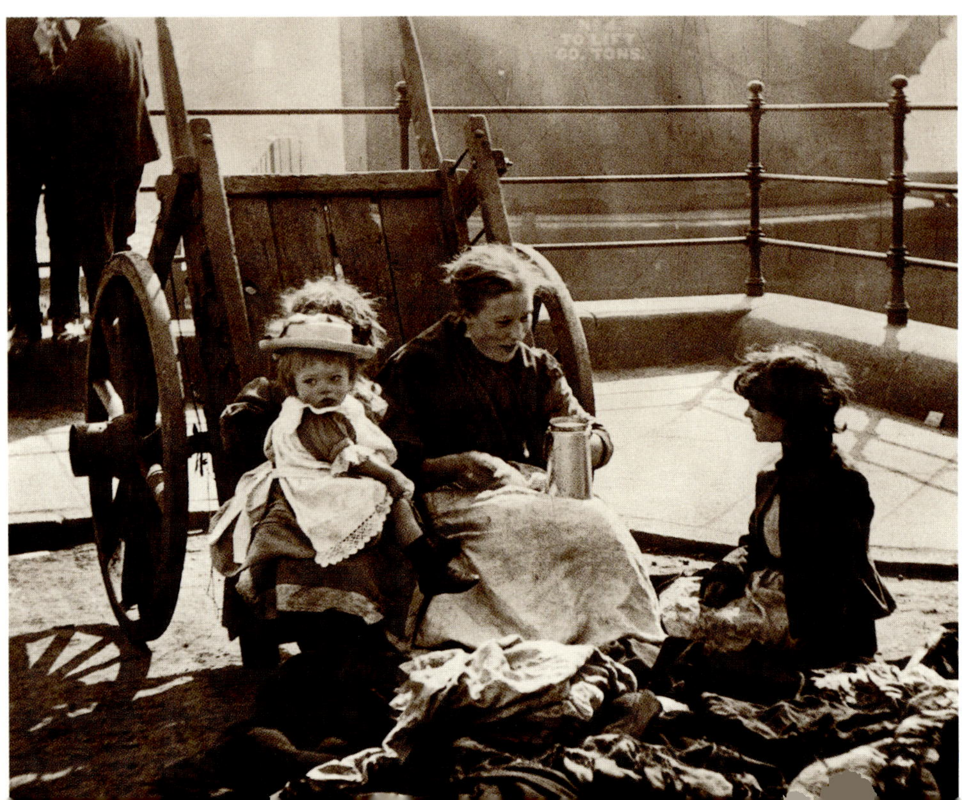

My boat is bigger than yours! But mine
is here and it sails with the wind.
Cat No: WPG030 Ref: H7637/15

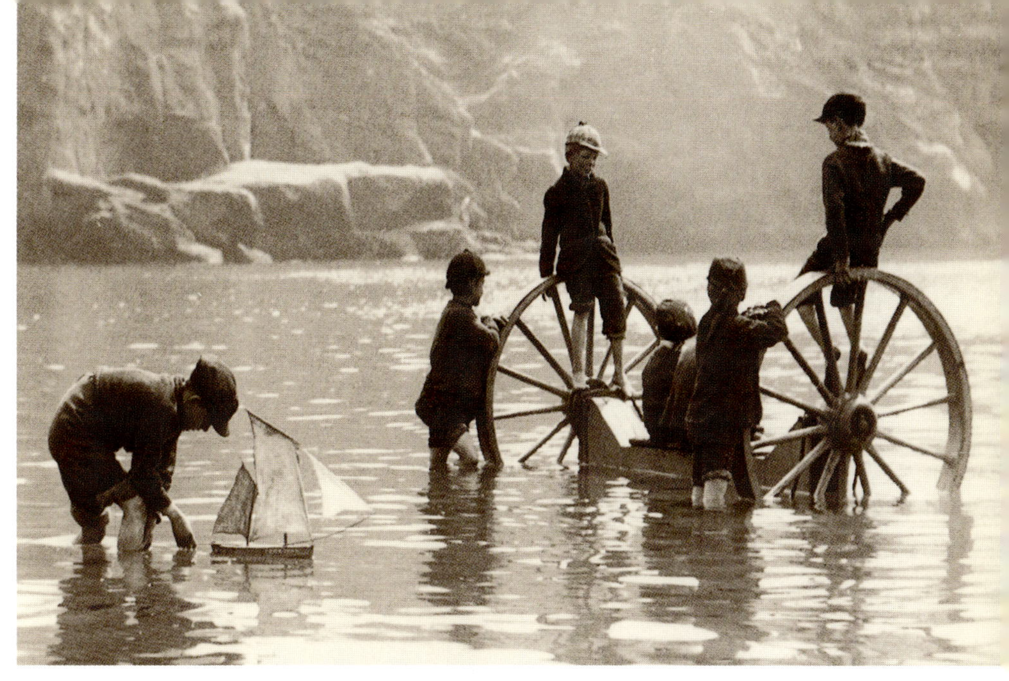

An early stroll with my baby and perambulator.
Cat No: WPG031 Ref: H7636/12 CH171

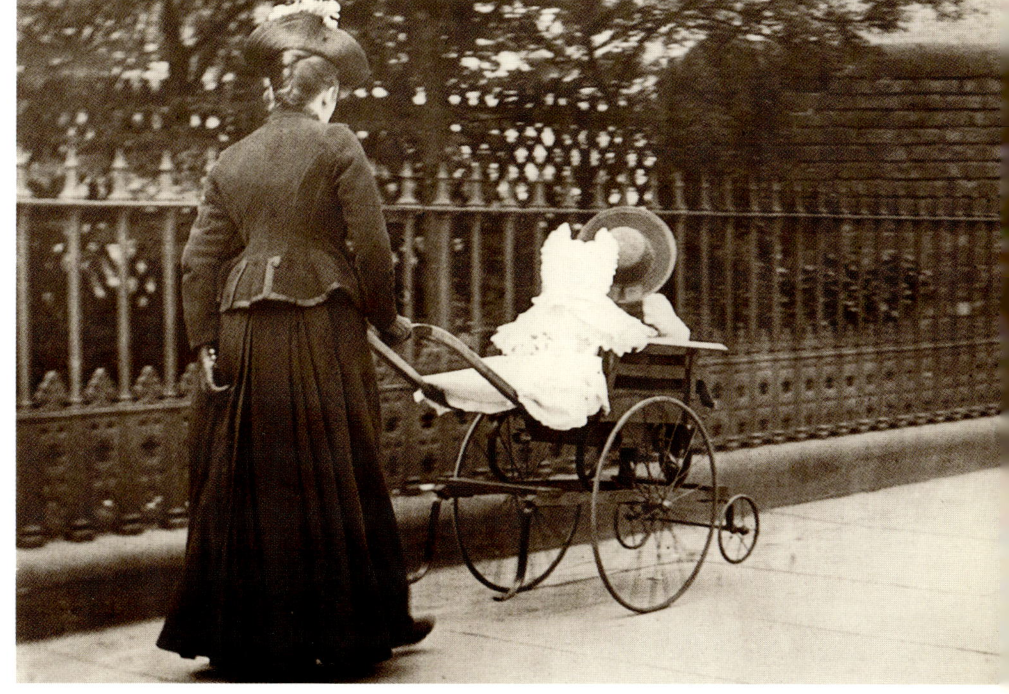

A country scene, a crumbling bridge, a
sincere plea…what will the answer be?
Cat No: WPG032 Ref: H7637/4

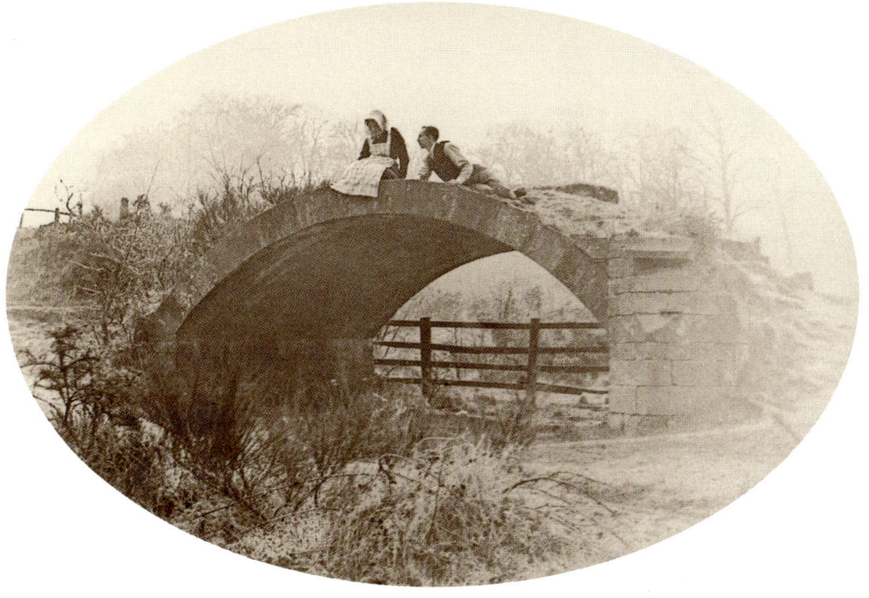

Choosing fish at the Quay.
Cat No: WPG033 Ref: C4417

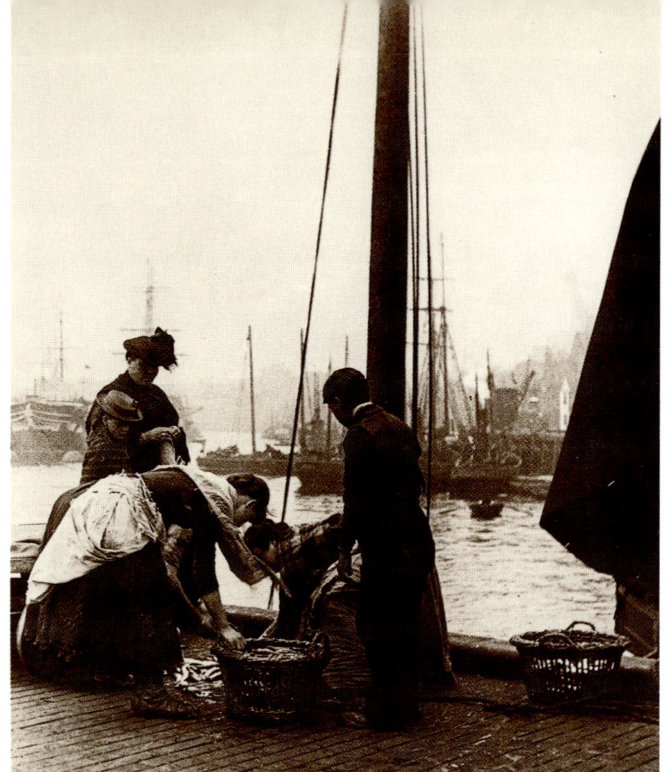

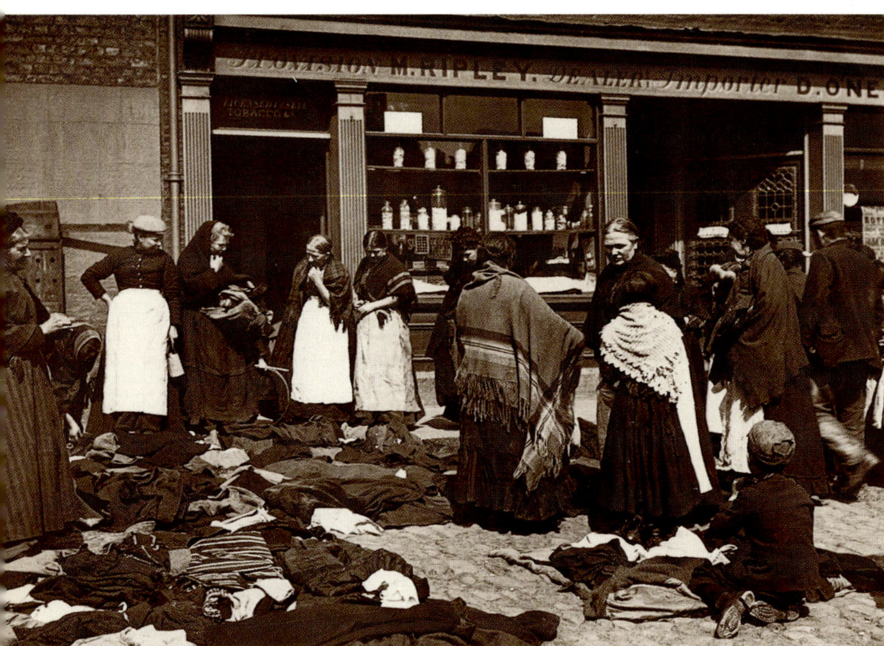

Picking clothes outside
M. Ripley, provisions dealers.
Cat No: WPG034 Ref: 9

Shoes for sale at the Quayside,
Newcastle upon Tyne.
Cat No: WPG035 Ref: 17

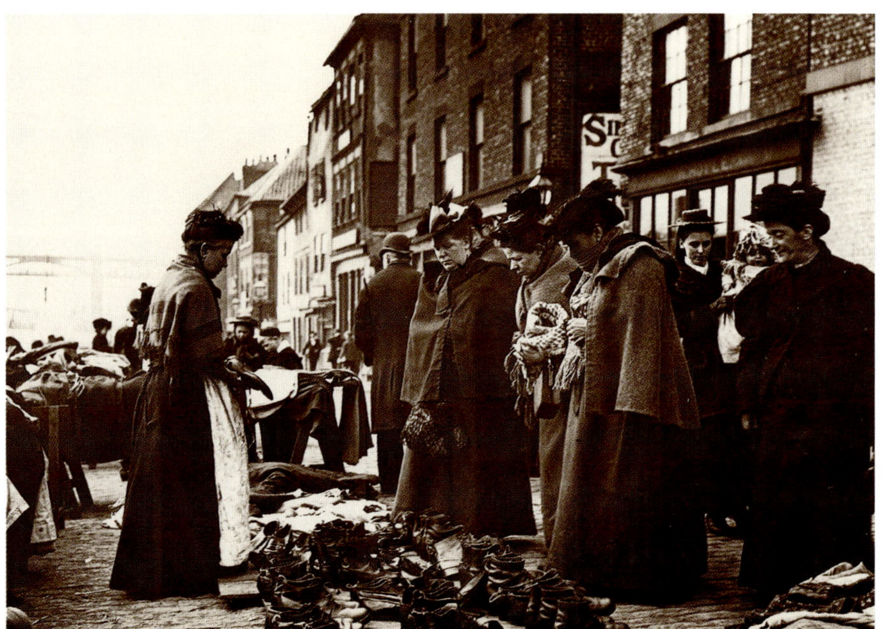

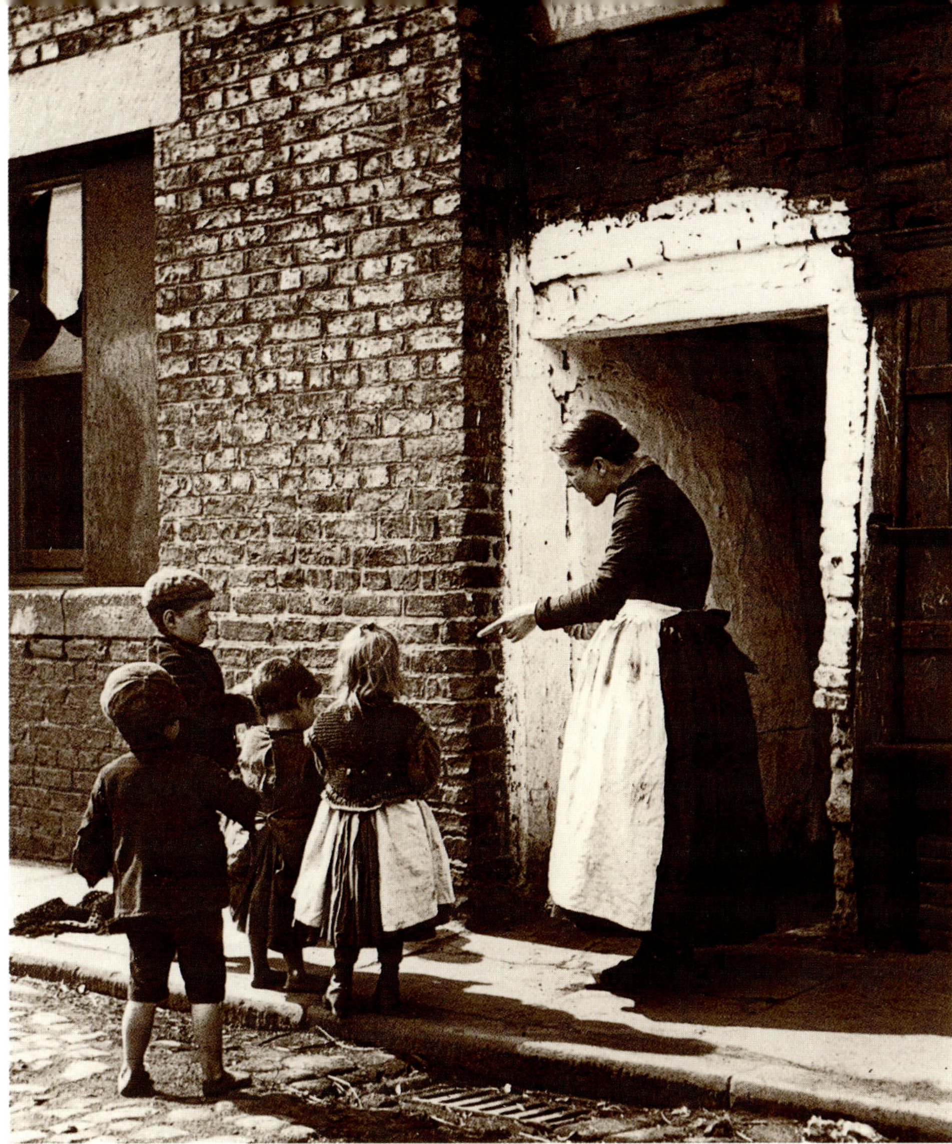

"Wait till your father gets home!", Wranghams Lane.
Cat No: WPG036 Ref: C4416

"Please play with me!" - a small girl stands with her skipping rope while others play. A unique photograph reproduced from an old collection of glass photographic plates.
Cat No: WPG 037 Ref: H7637/5

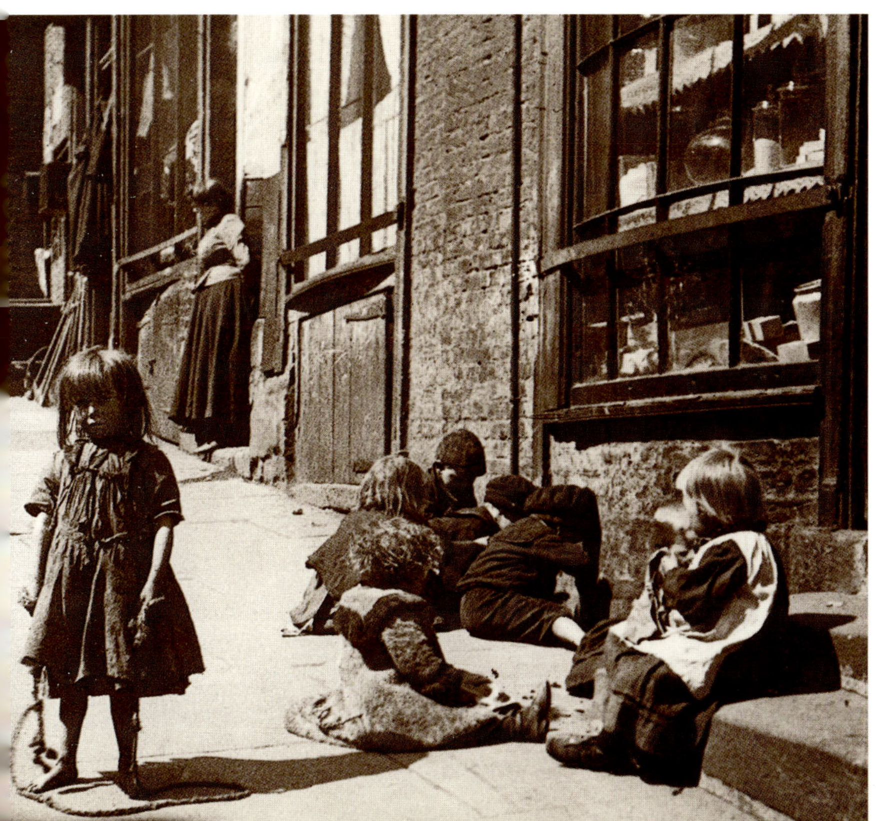

Going to the shops - an old glass plate negative.
Cat No: WPG038 Ref No:X1543

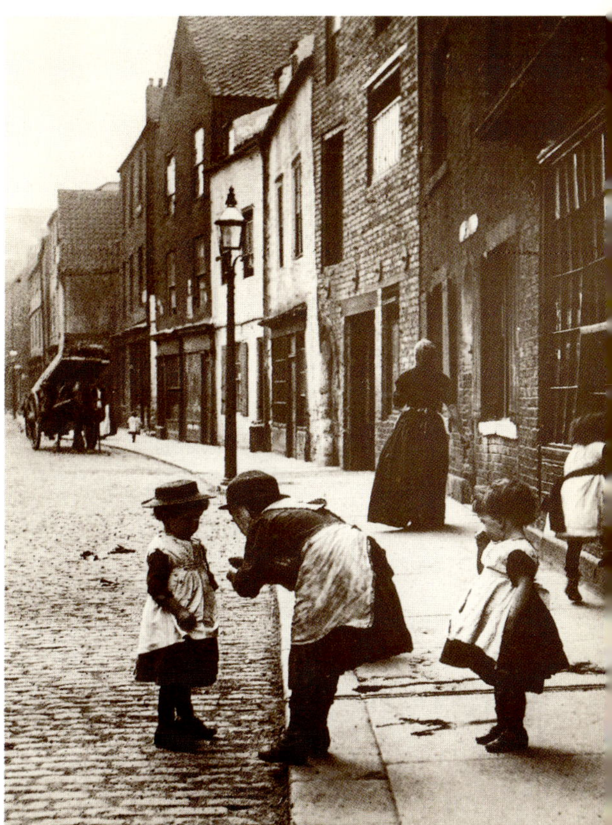

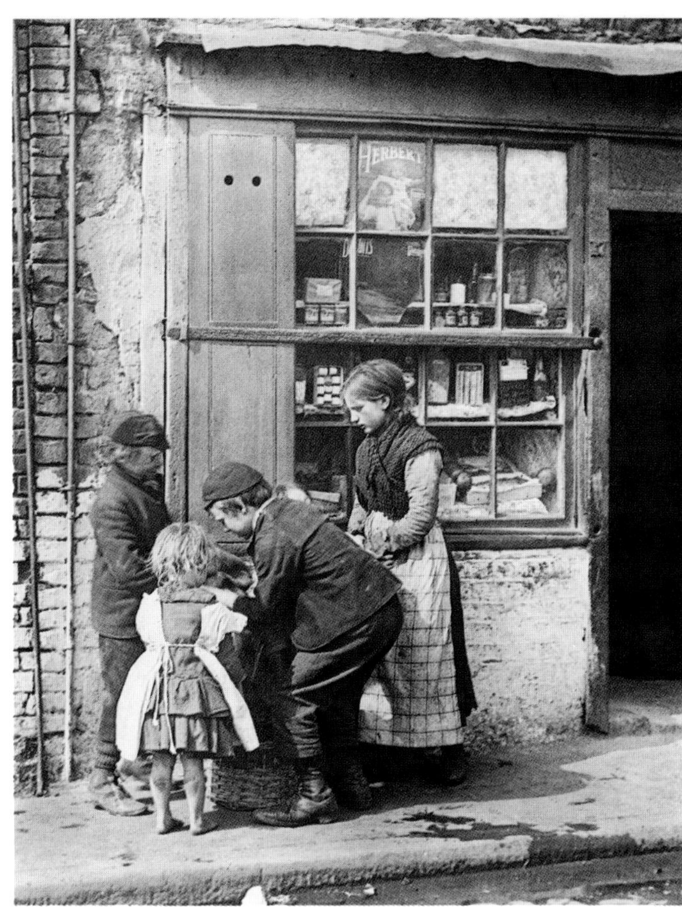

"Let me help you!" Early photography, reproduced from an original glass plate.
Cat No: WPG039 Ref: X1545

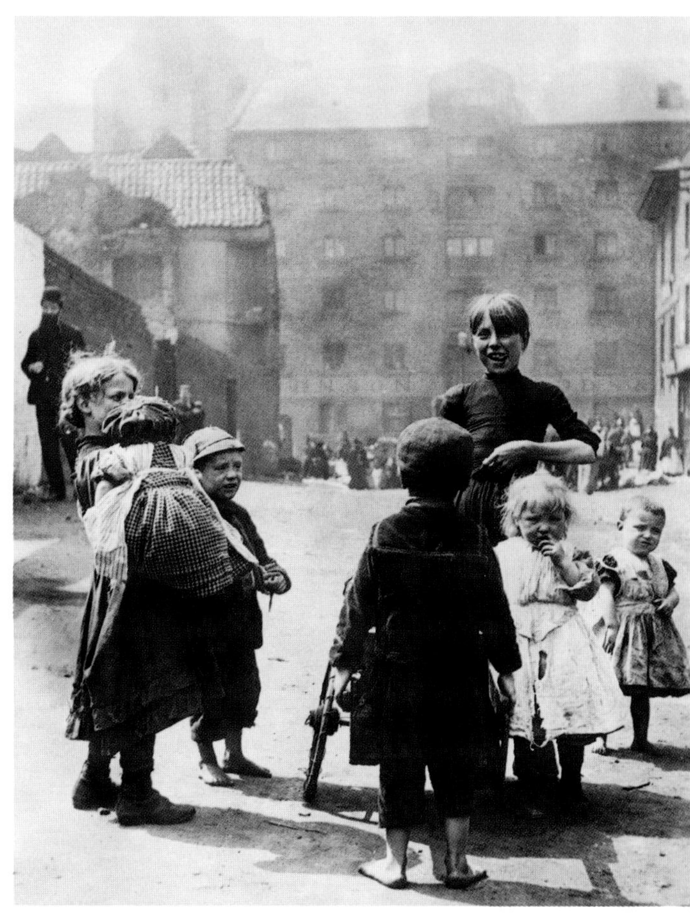

"What's in your barrow?" Children of the city.
Cat No: WPG040 Ref: X1573

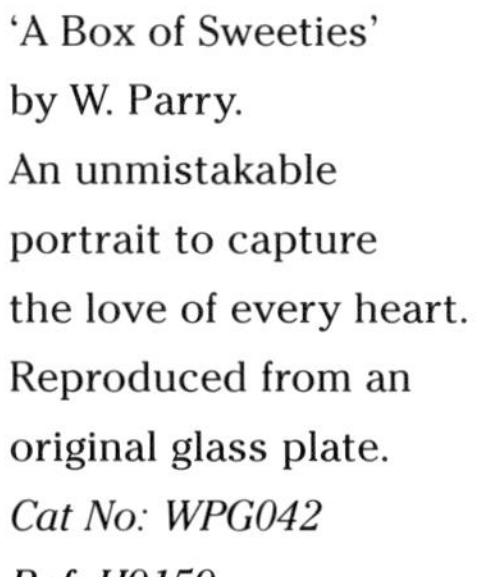

'A Box of Sweeties' by W. Parry.
An unmistakable portrait to capture the love of every heart.
Reproduced from an original glass plate.
Cat No: WPG042
Ref: H9159

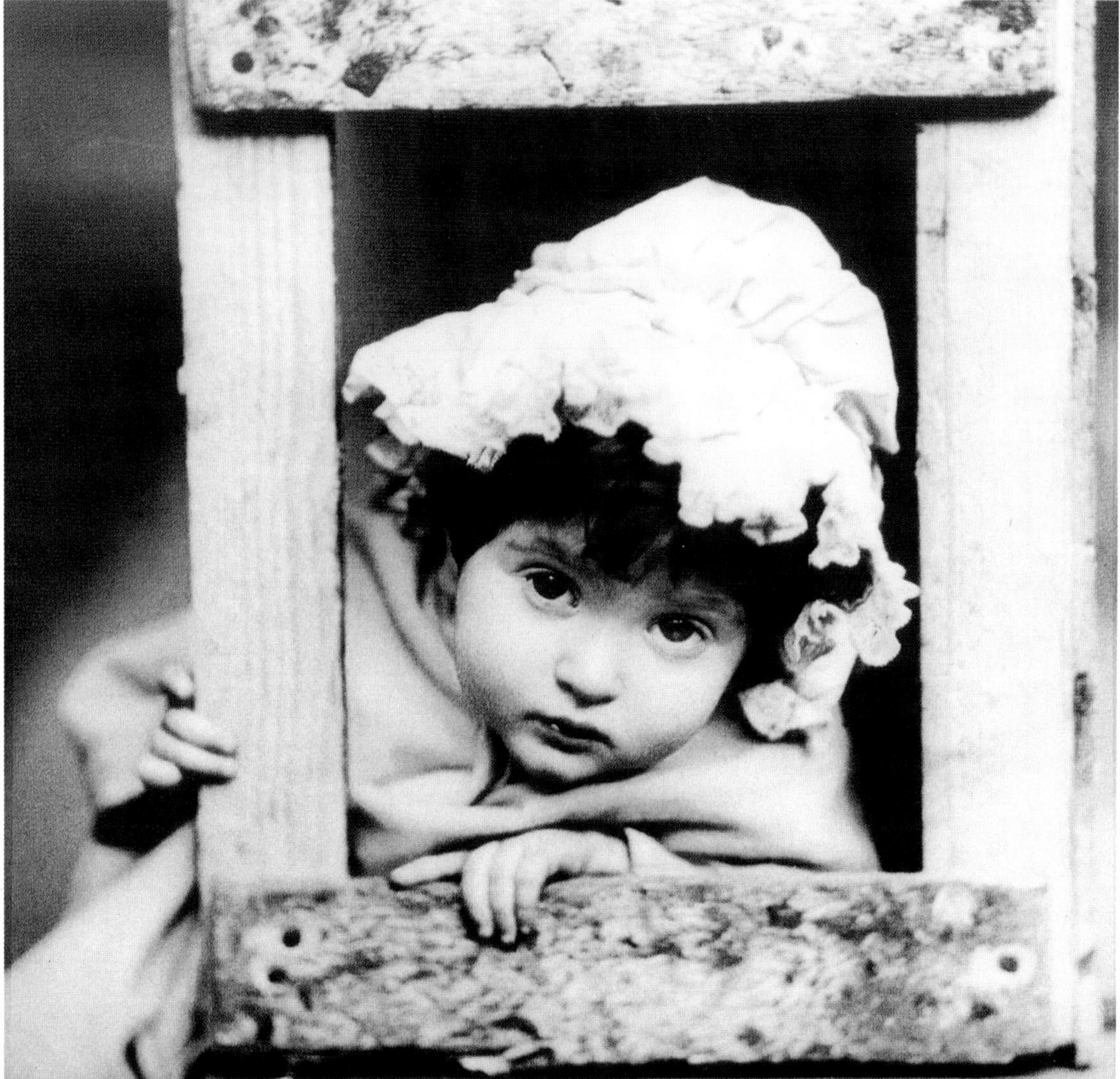

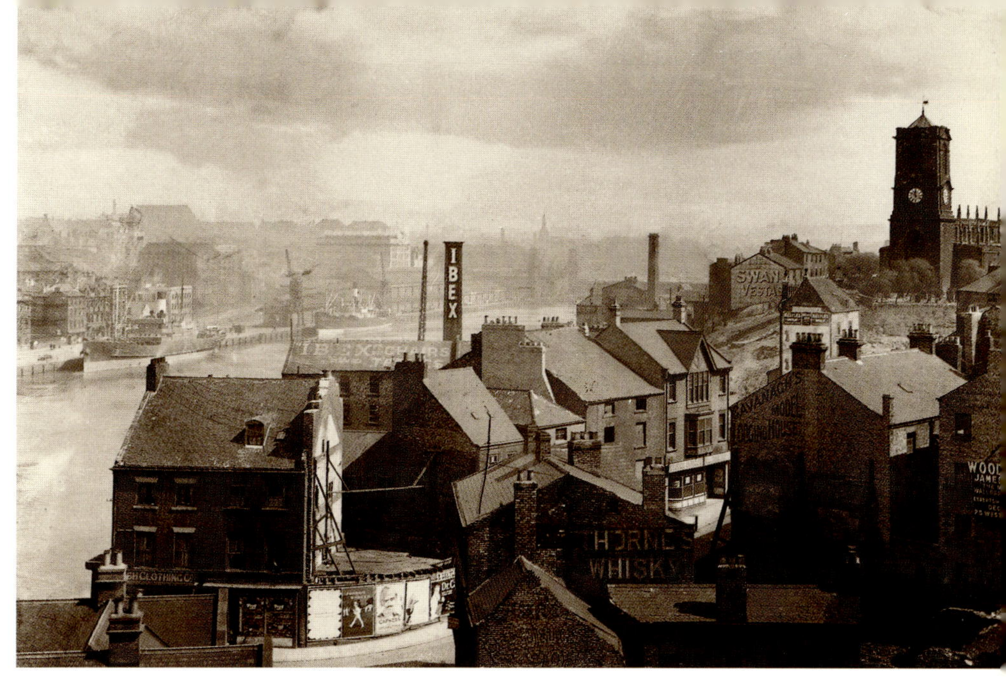

South Side of the Tyne, including
St. Mary's church, Gateshead.
Cat. No. A149 Ref. No. D1408

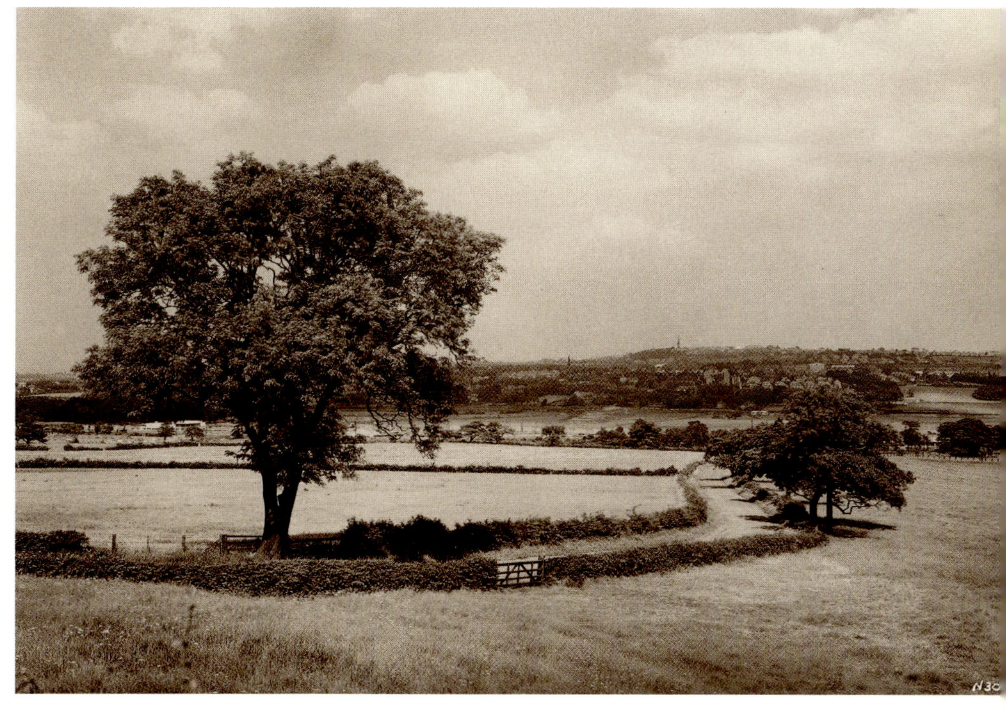

Team Valley, Gateshead.
Cat. No. A150 Ref. No. N3003

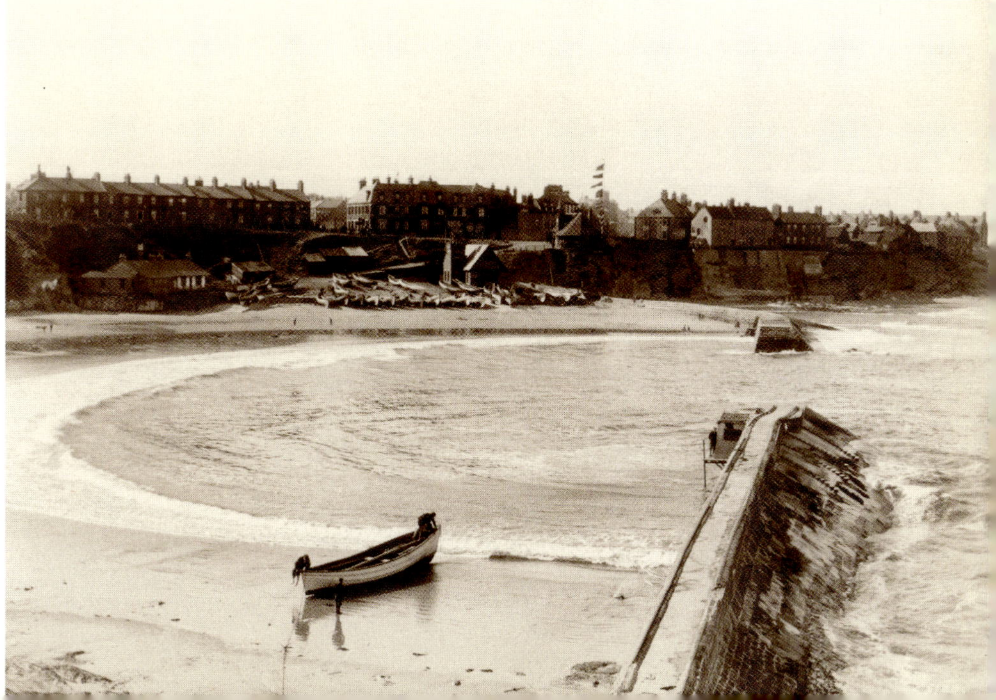

Whitley Bay.
Cat No. A151 Ref. No. H9226

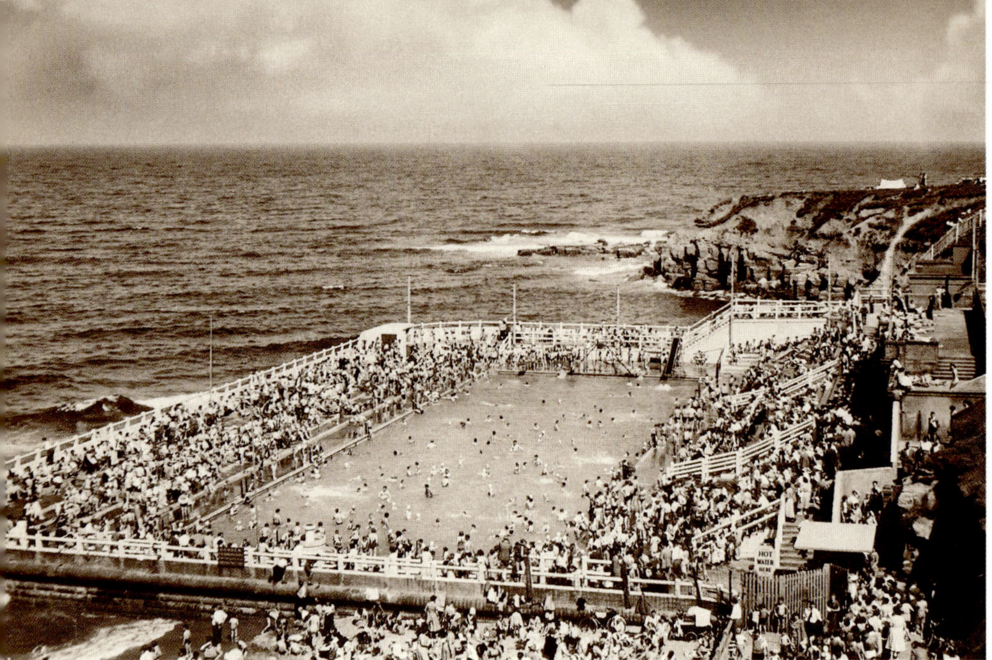

Tynemouth outdoor swimming and bathing pool.
Cat No: A153 Ref: B1280

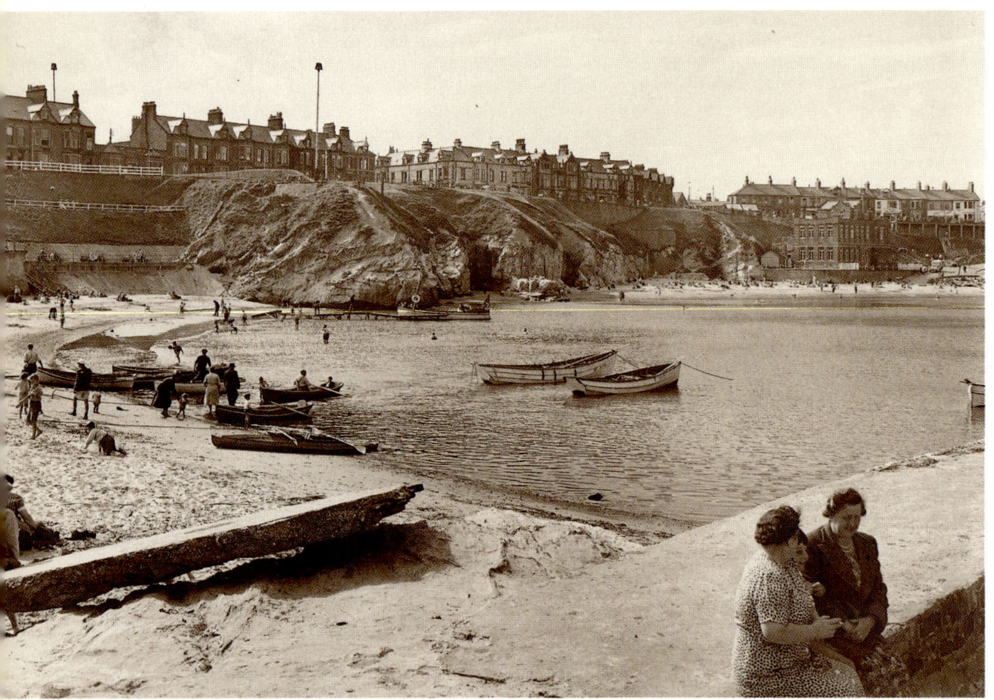

Cullercoats Bay from South Breakwater.
Cat No: A154 Ref: H2998

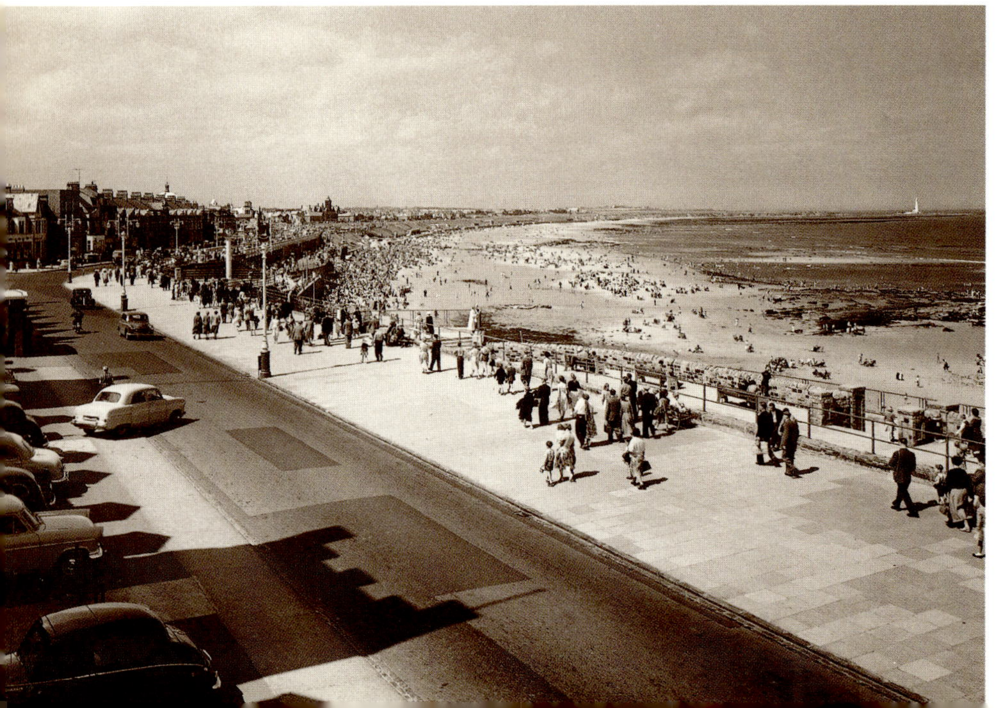

The promenade and coast of Whitley Bay, Northumbrian Coast, with St. Mary's Lighthouse visible in the distance, August 1957.
Cat No: A155 Ref: G286

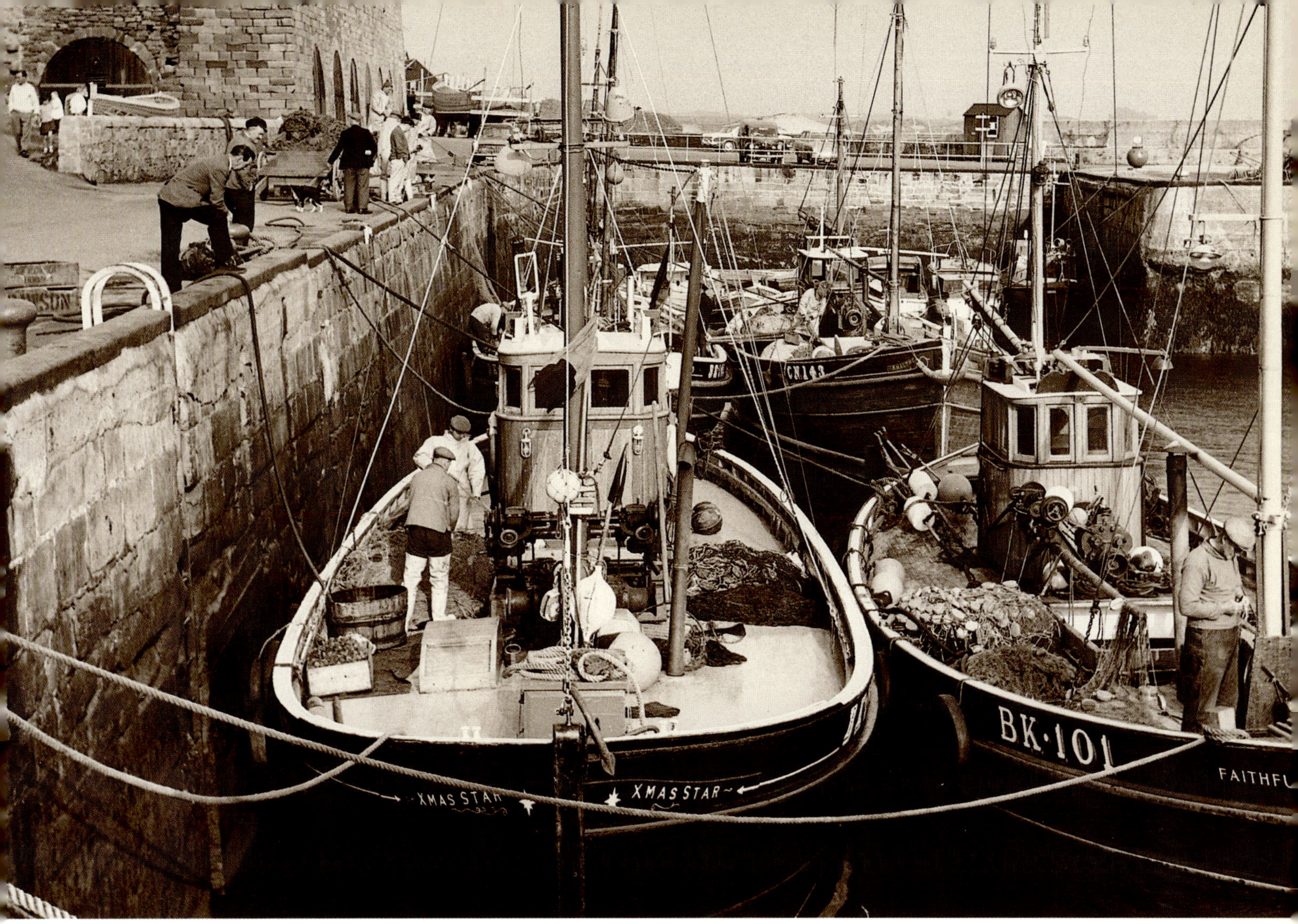

'Xmas Star' and 'Faithful' in the harbour at Seahouses.
Cat No: A156 Ref: R3549

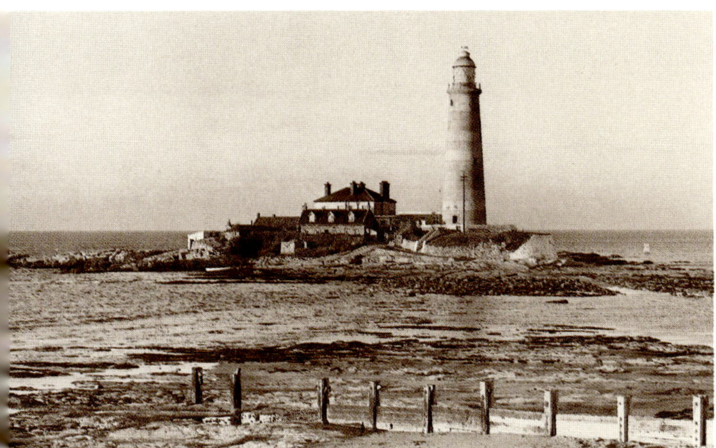

St. Mary's Lighthouse, Whitley Bay, Northumberland, 1952.
Cat No: A157 Ref: B1701

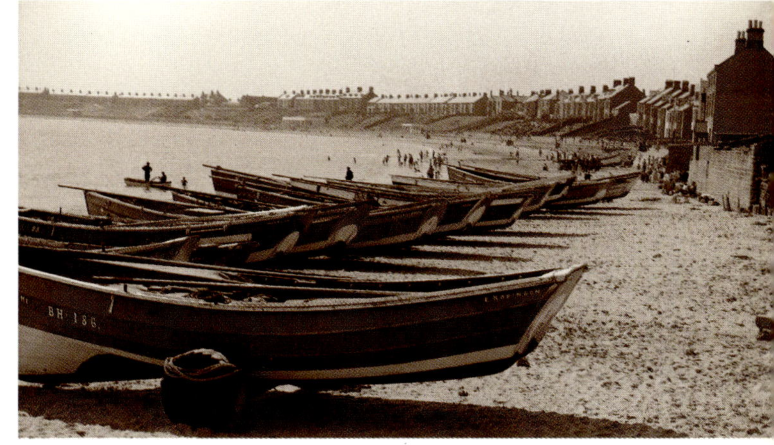

Boats at rest on the beach at
Newbiggin-by-the-Sea, Northumberland.
Cat No: A158 Ref: J2937

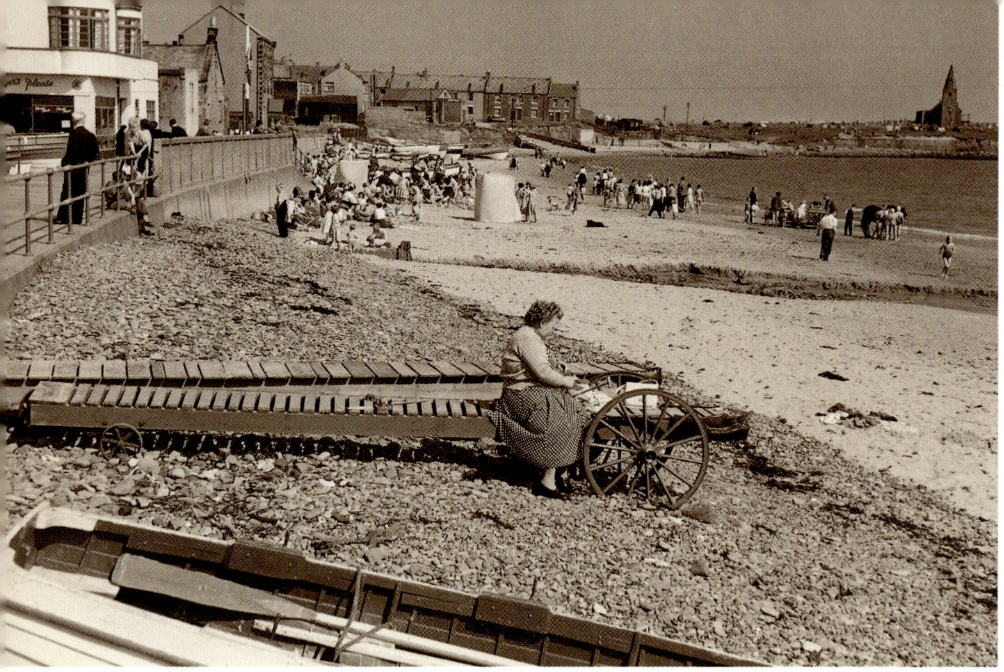

A day at the beach, Newbiggin-by-the-Sea, Northumberland, 1958. *Cat No: A159 Ref: J2940*

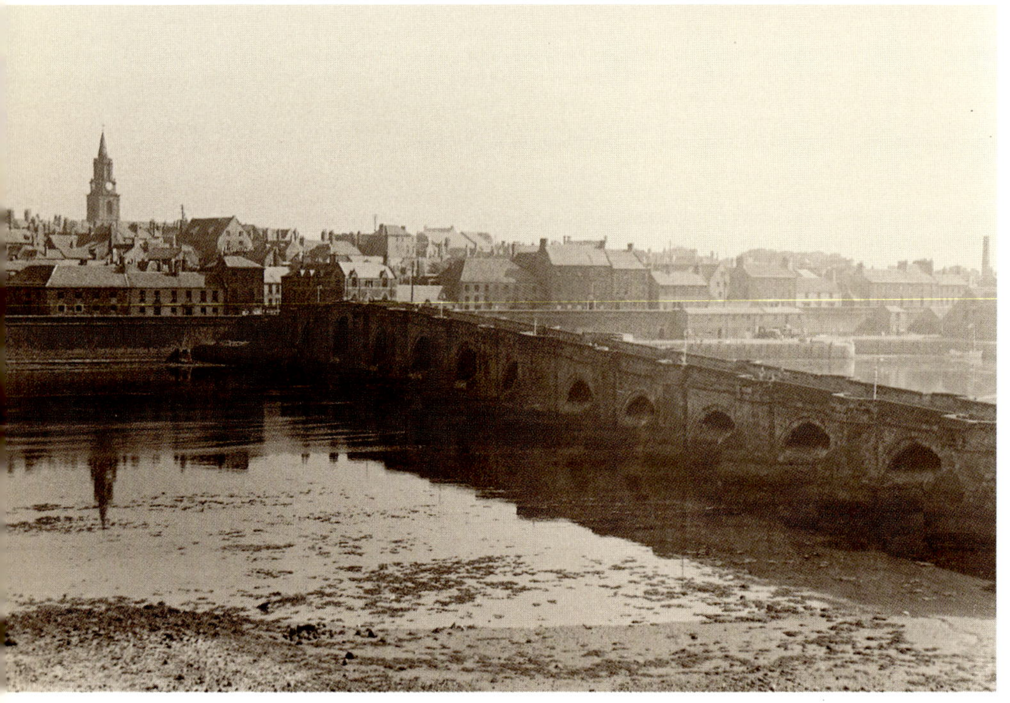

The old bridge at Berwick-upon-Tweed. *Cat No: A161 Ref: 2/9/D17*

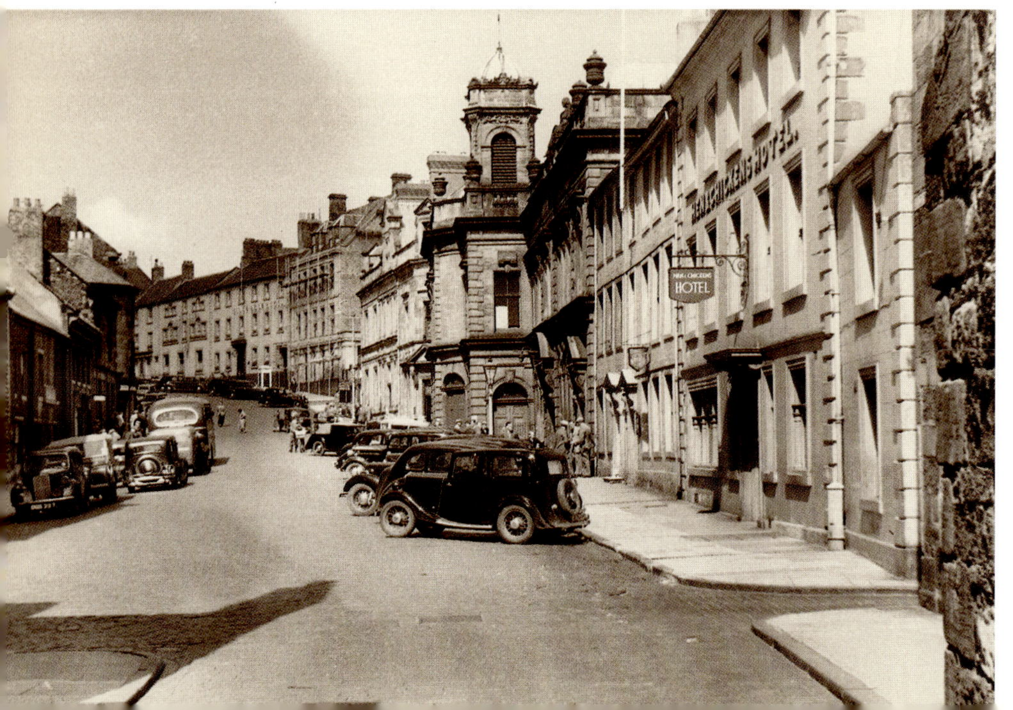

Main Street, Berwick-upon-Tweed, with the Hen & Chickens Hotel open for business. *Cat No: A162 Ref: H9151*

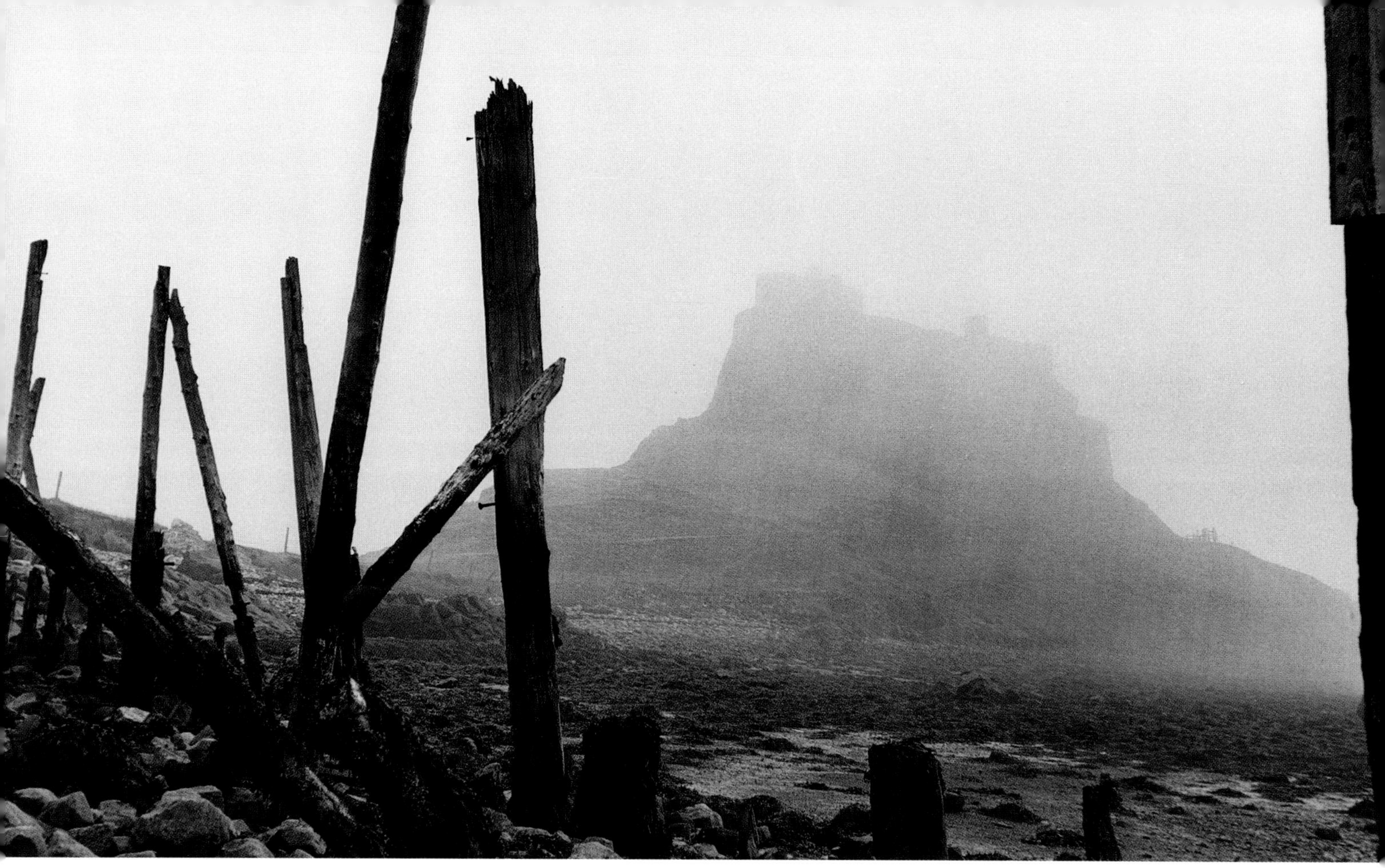

Lindisfarne, Holy Island, in the mist.
Cat No: WPG 043 Ref: K4425

The end of a day's fishing
at Lindisfarne, Holy Island.
Cat No: WPG044 Ref: D5045

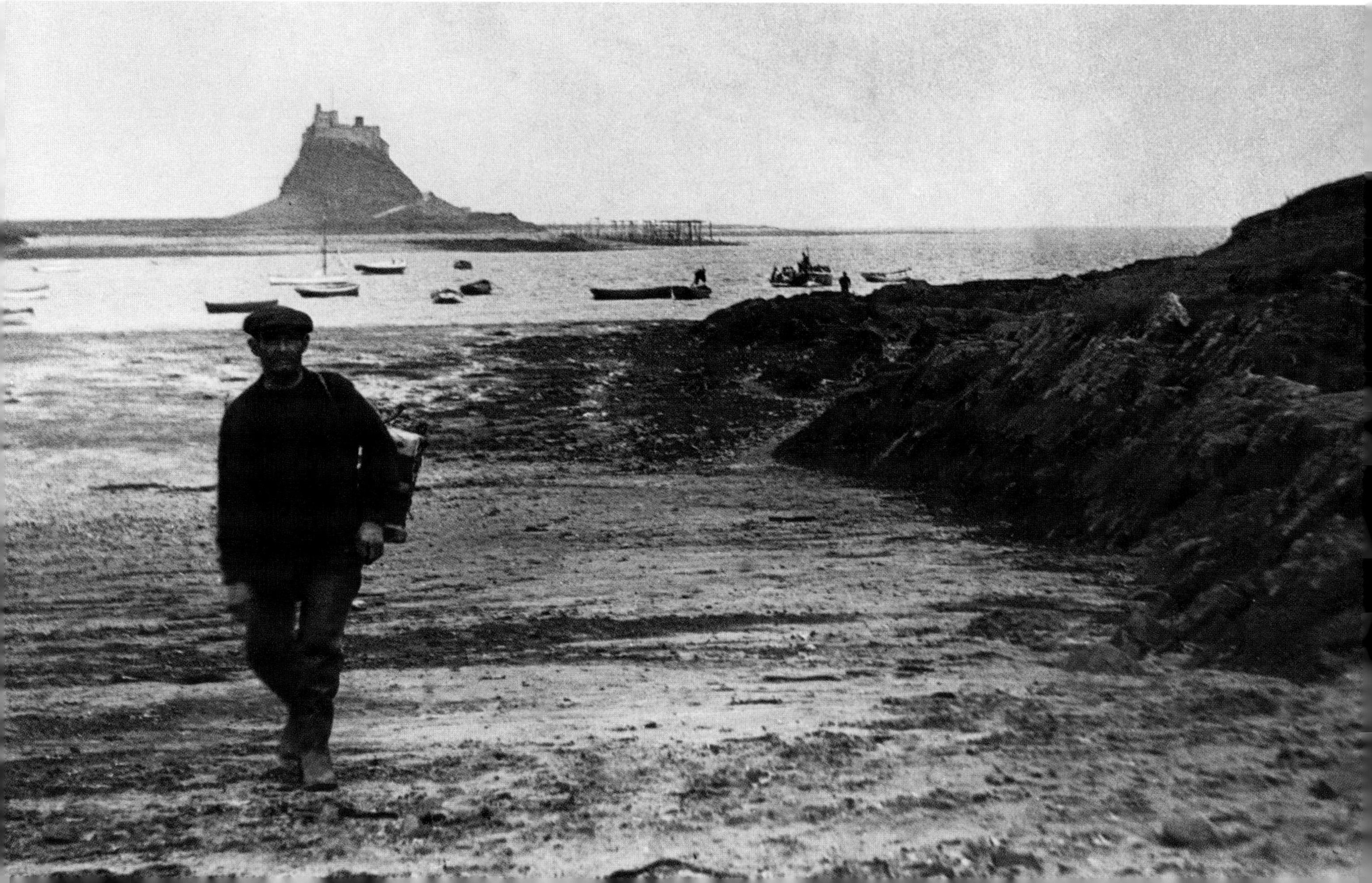

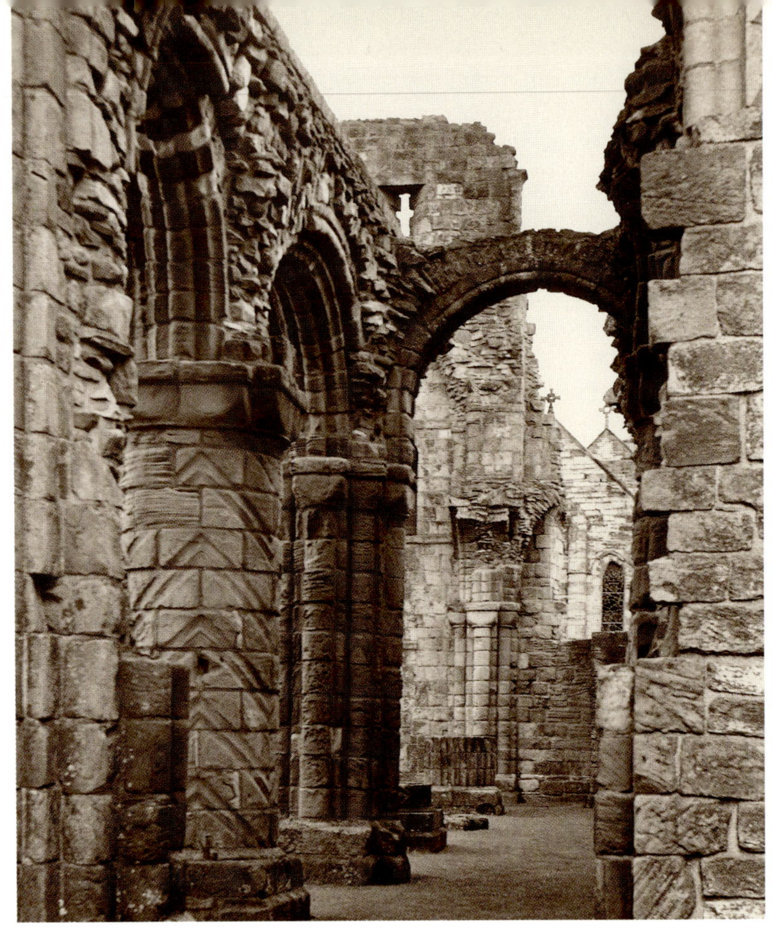

Part of the ruins of the Priory on the Holy Island of Lindisfarne.
Cat No: A163 Ref: G2836

Launching the lifeboat at Lindisfarne, Holy Island on the Northumbrian Coast.
Cat No: A164 Ref: G2825

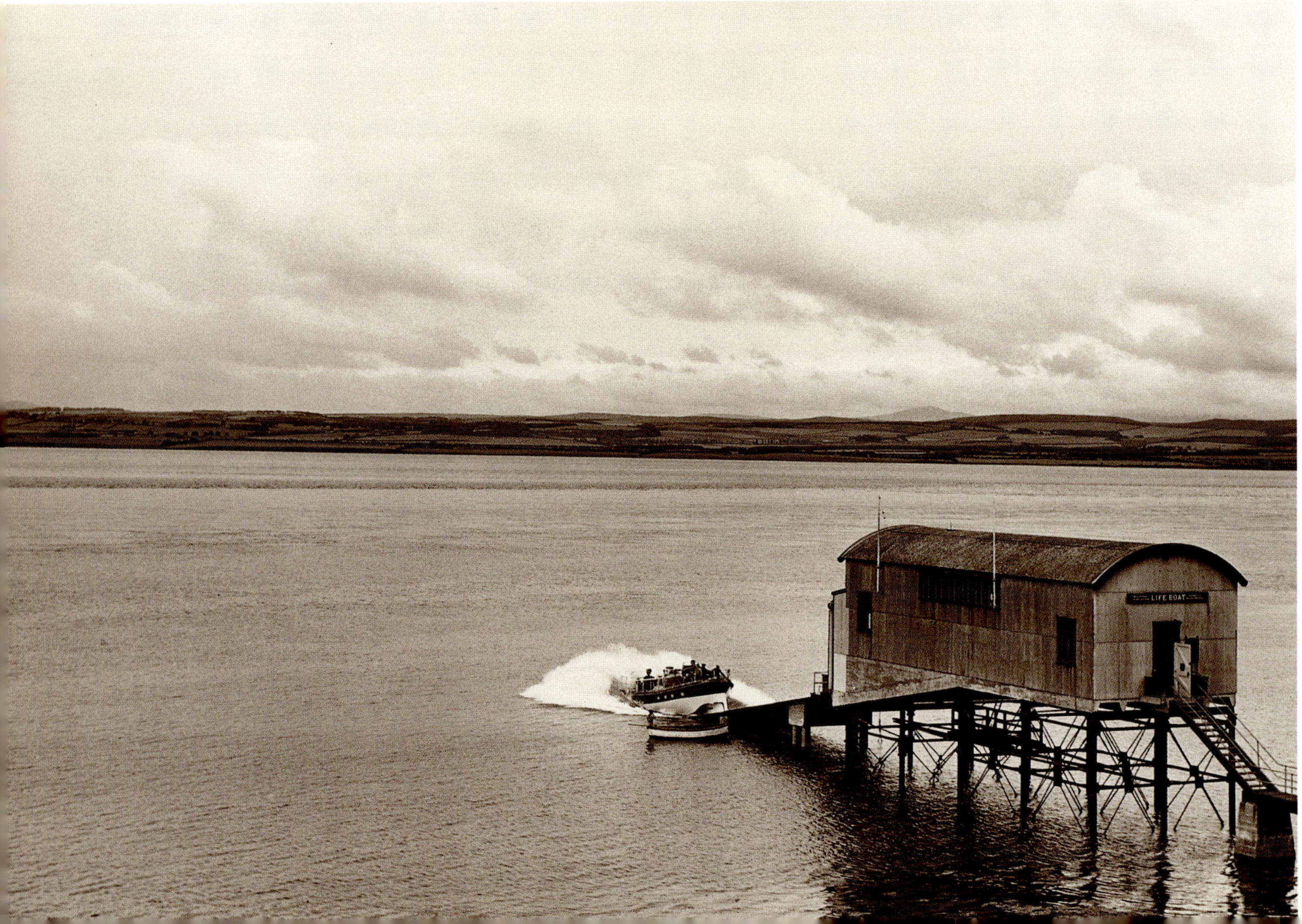

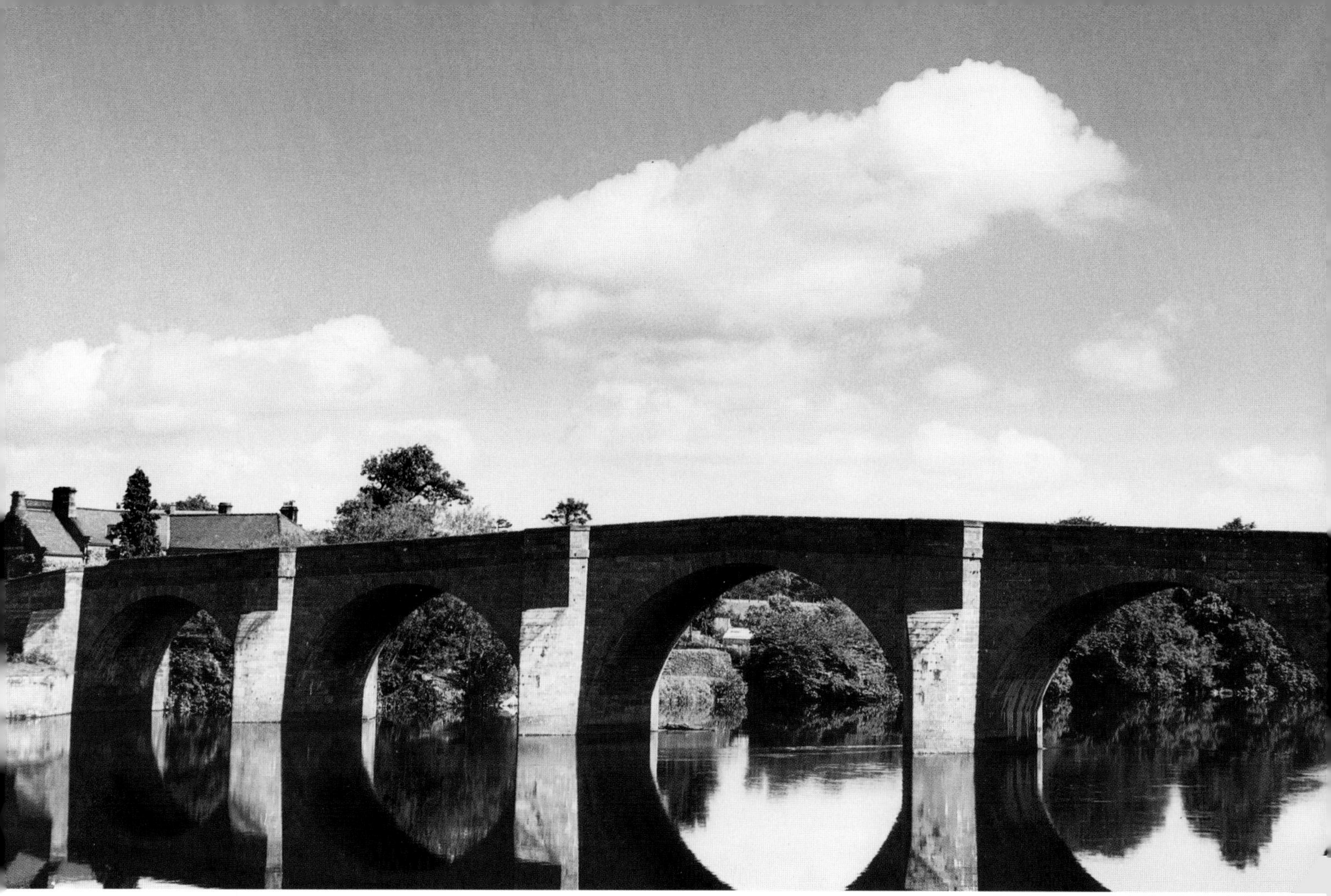

The bridge over the North Tyne at Chollerford.
The well known George Inn is visible to the left of the bridge.
Cat No: A167 Ref: D2727

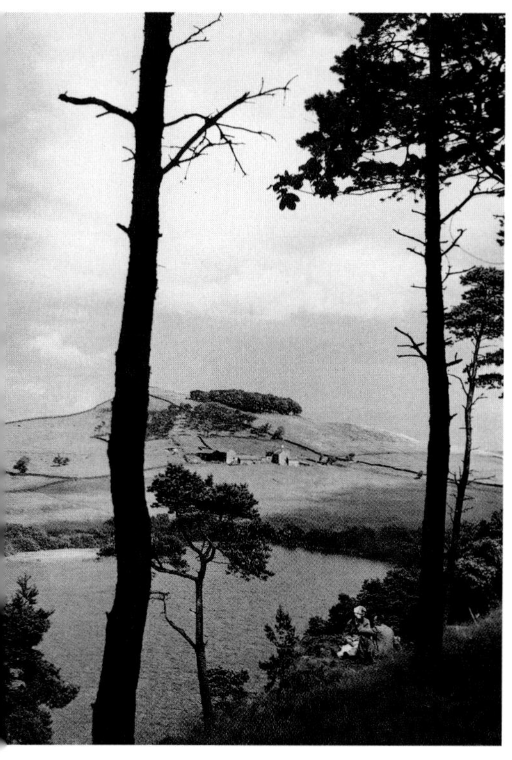

Crag Lough and the Roman Wall.
Cat No: A165 Ref: 2728(B)

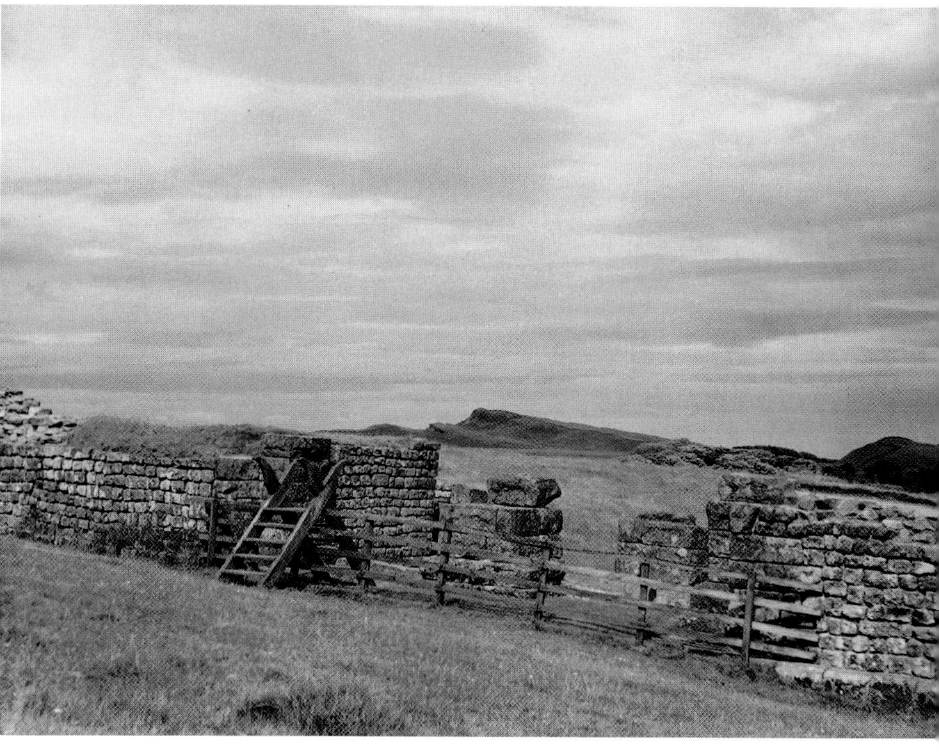

Chester's North West Gate, the Roman Wall, Northumberland.
Cat No: A166 Ref: P3528

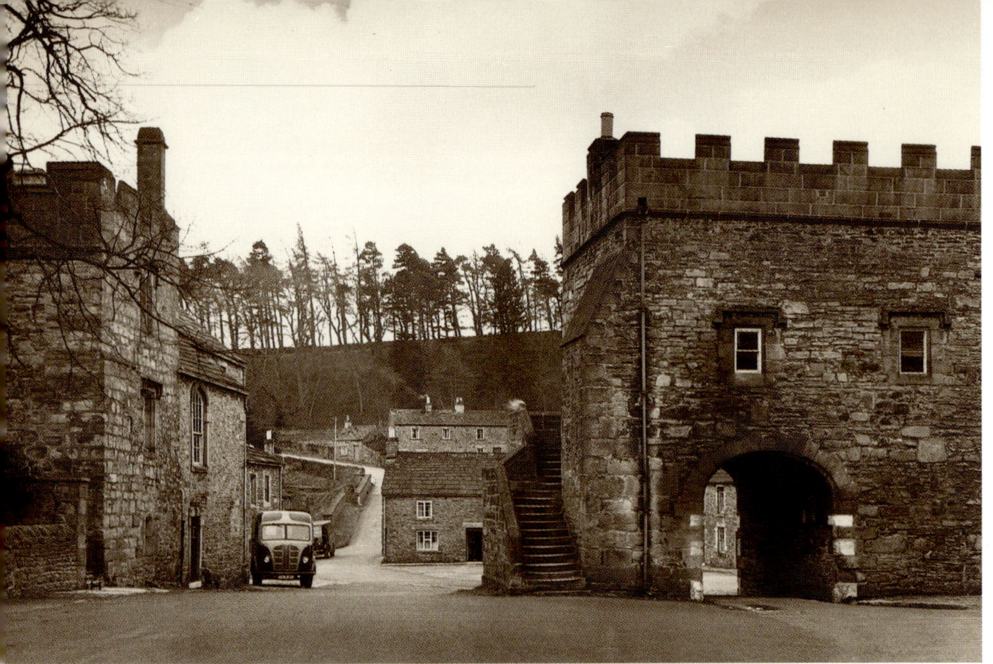

The village of Blanchland is one of the most attractive in Northumberland. It owes much of its character to its stone walls and roofs and to the square form which it inherits from the premonstratension abbey, the remains of which may be seen in the church and inn.
Cat No: A168 Ref: 2494

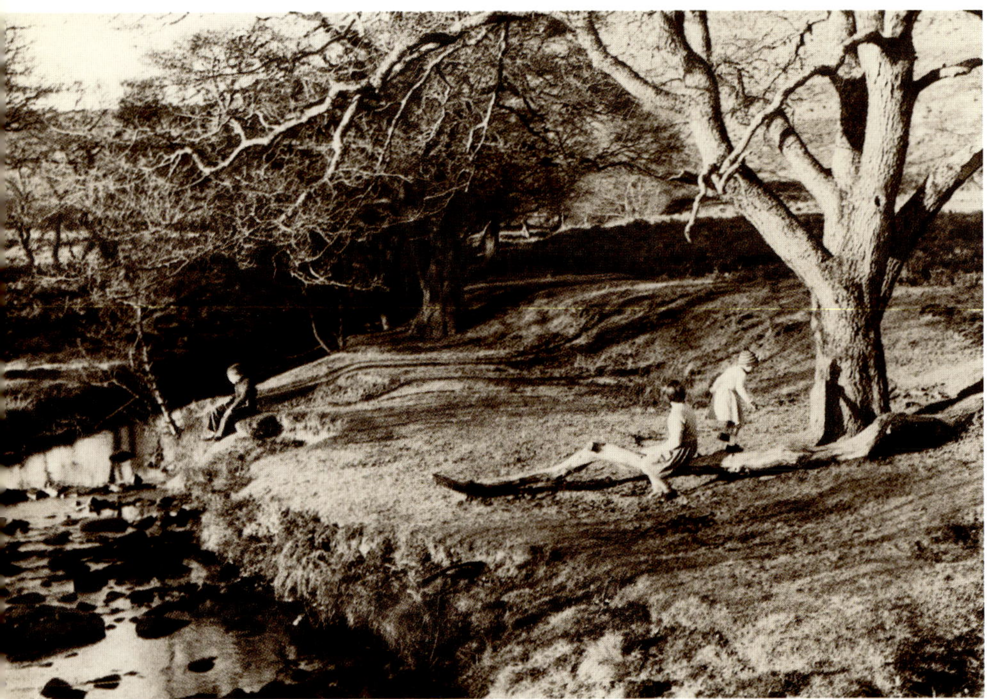

Children at play by the Keenshaw Burn in Bilsmoor Valley, Upper Coquetdale.
Cat No: A169 Ref: C2175

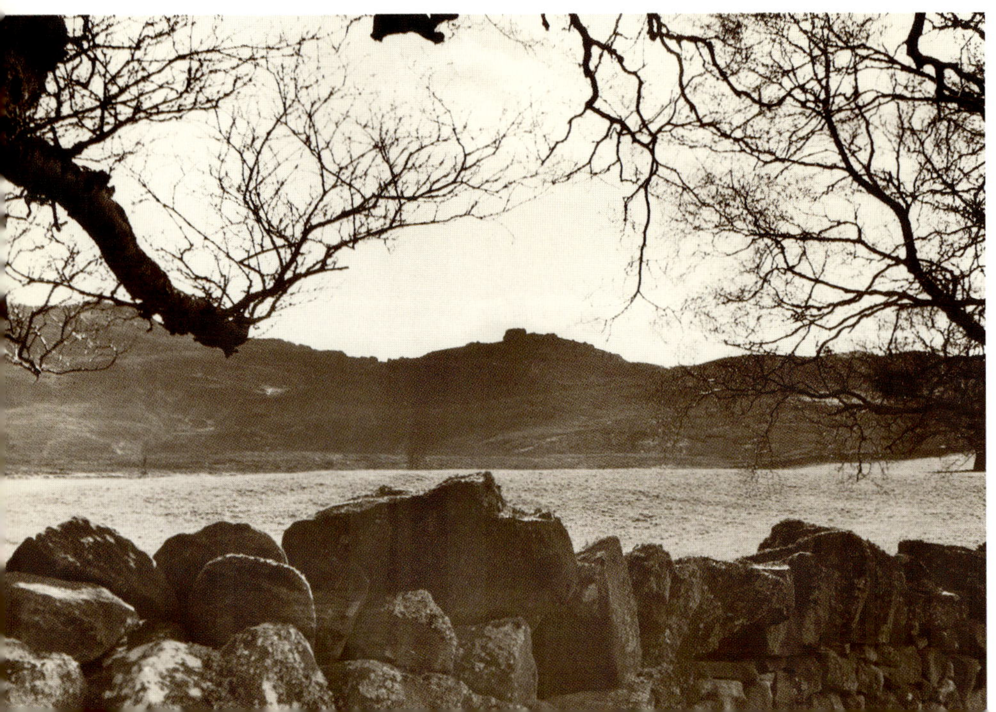

The Harbottle Hills, Northumberland seen from the road near the manse. The Drake Stone can be seen standing against the sky in the centre of the photograph. Owing to its broken surface and varied vegetation, the fells are known to change colour daily and hourly throughout the year.
Cat No: A170 Ref: R4026

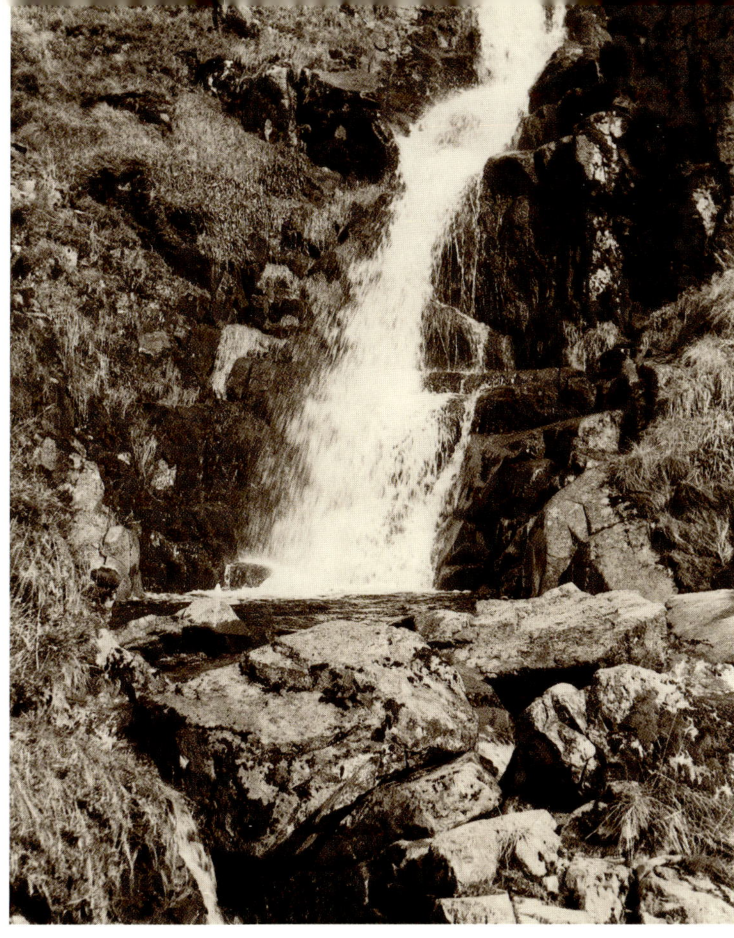

One of the fine series of waterfalls in the Hen Hole on the Cheviot.
Cat No: A171 Ref: H9148

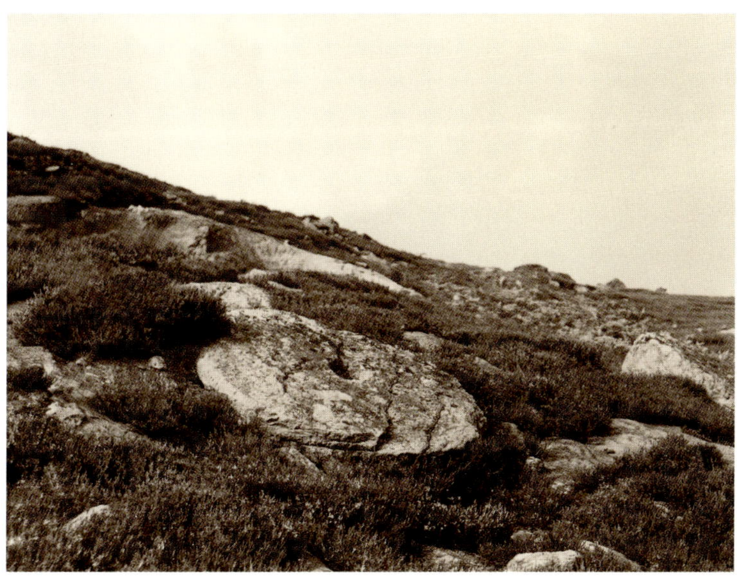

The old industry of cutting millstones on the Harbottle Hills, Coquetdale, Northumberland is evident from abandoned stones such as this.
Cat No: A172 Ref: H9149

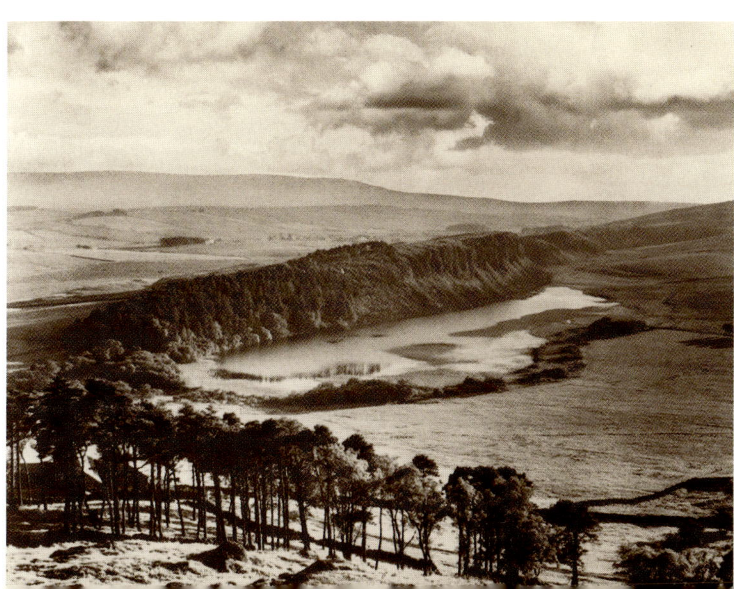

Crag Lough, Northumberland, seen from above Hotbank. The Roman Wall runs along the crown of the crag which overhangs the lough.
Cat No: A173 Ref: W7879

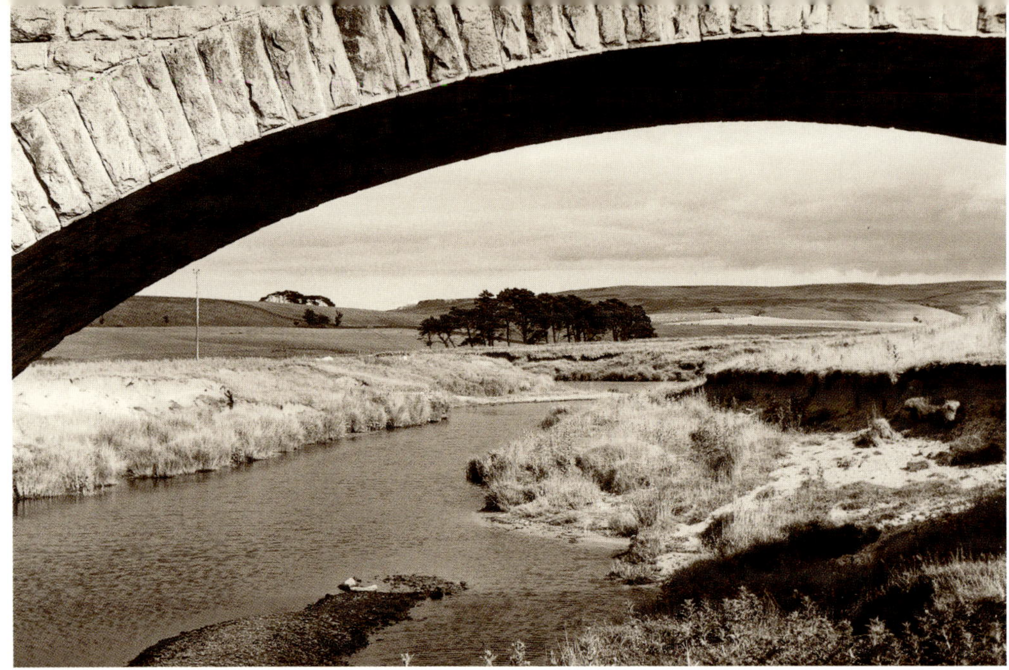

River Rede at Otterburn.
Cat No: A174 Ref: P3945

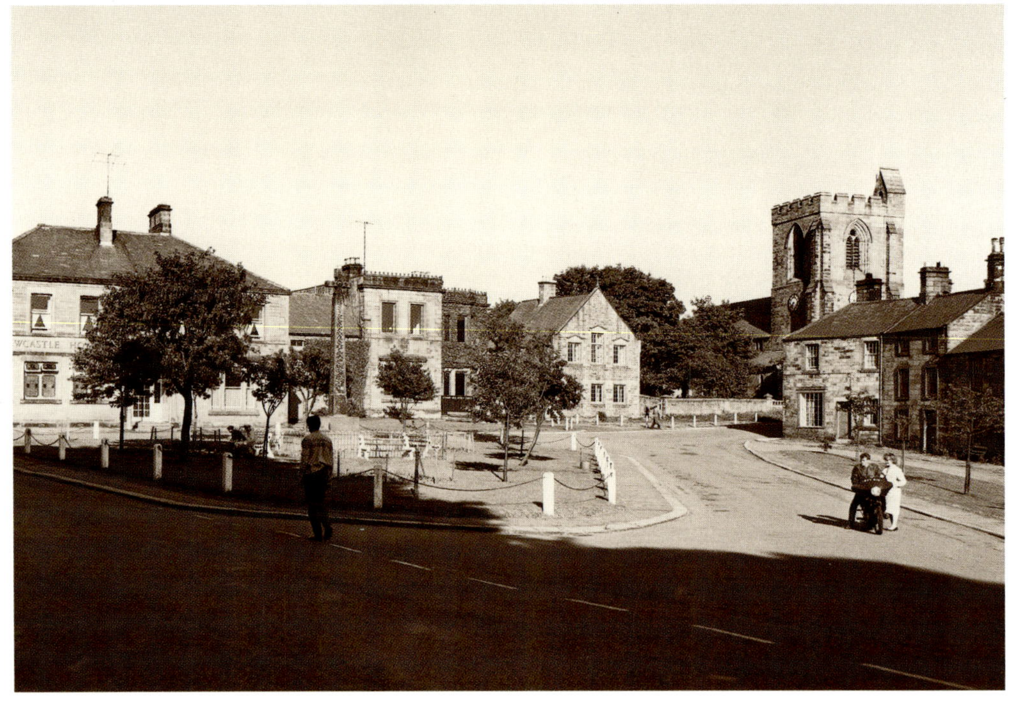

The centre of Rothbury, Coquetdale. The tower of the parish church can be seen on the right.
Cat No: A175 Ref: P3752

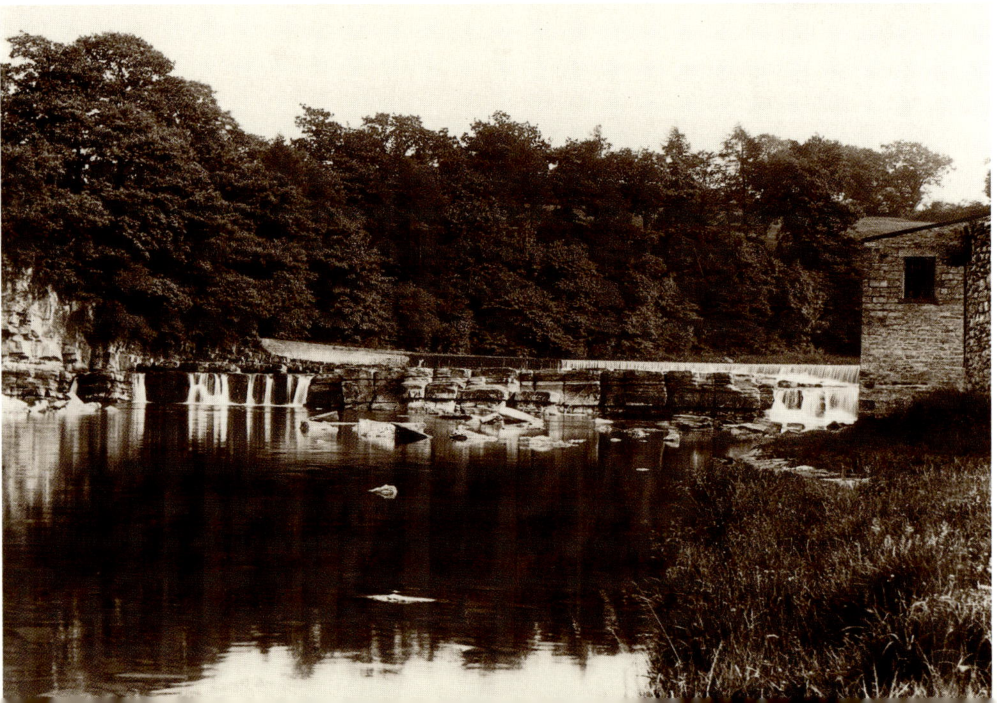

Thrum Mill, on the River Coquet, near Rothbury, Northumberland.
Cat No: A176 Ref: H9146

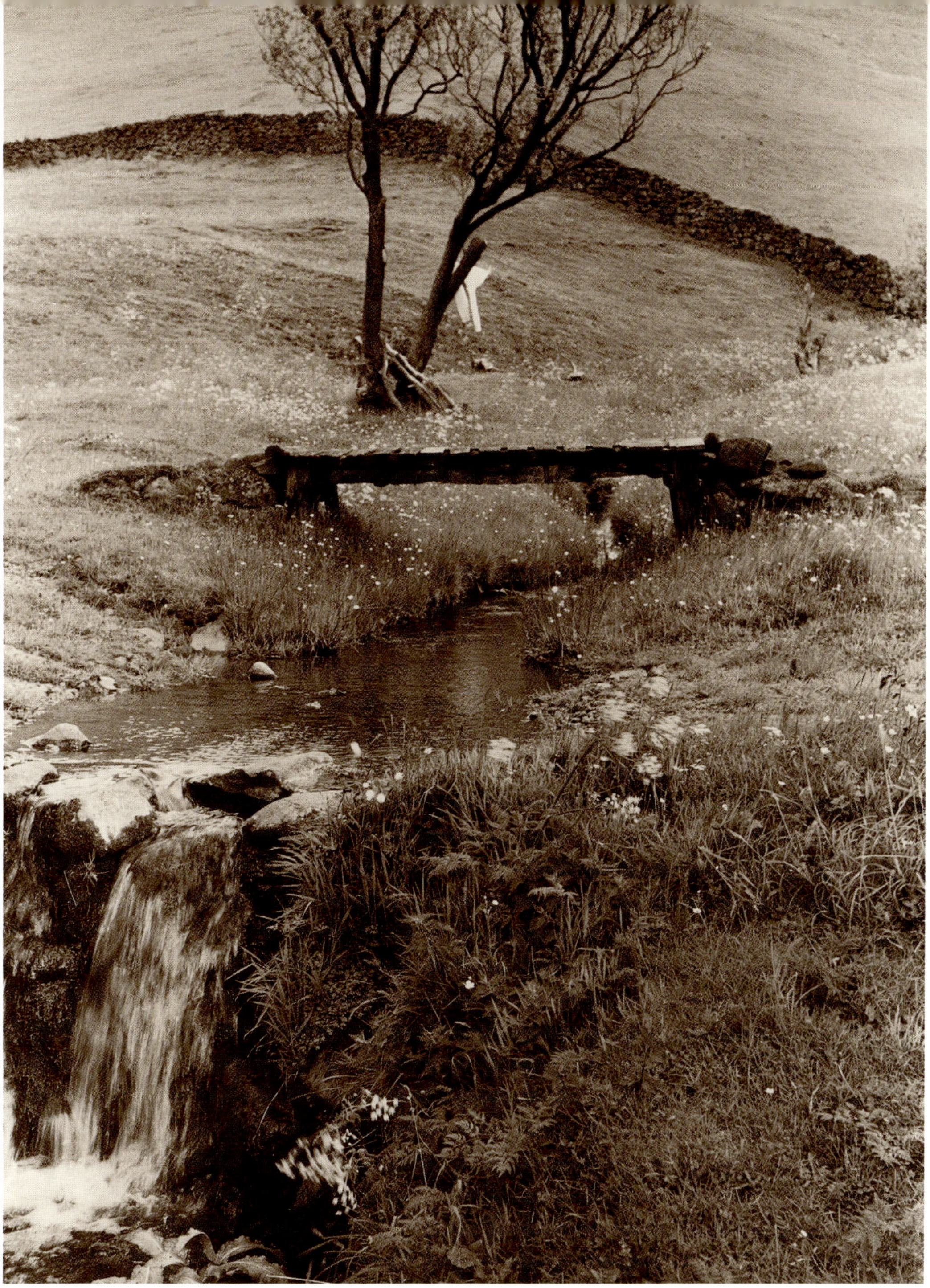

Ford and footbridge across the Battalsheil Burn near the farm of Battalsheil up the Usway Valley, Upper Coquetdale.
Cat No: A177 Ref: H9147

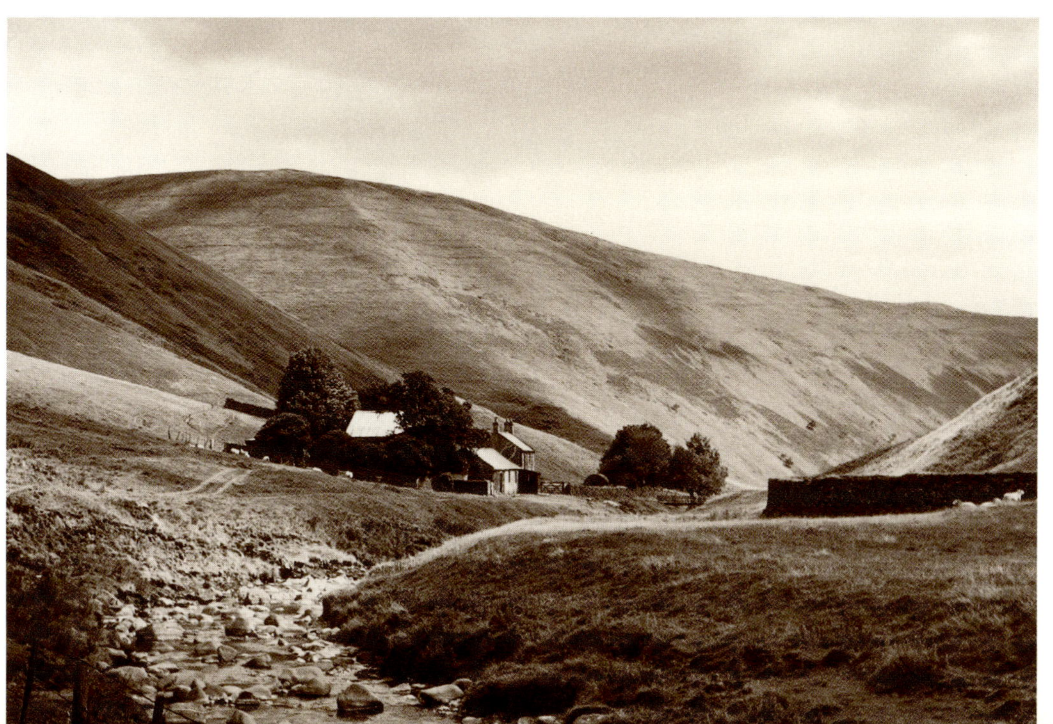

Battalsheil, a farm on the Usway Burn. There was no proper road nor any bus service to this isolated hill farm, nor could the housewife depend opon visiting tradesmens' vans. The winter stocks had to be laid in on a generous scale to meet the danger of snow storms.
Cat No: A178 Ref: P7005

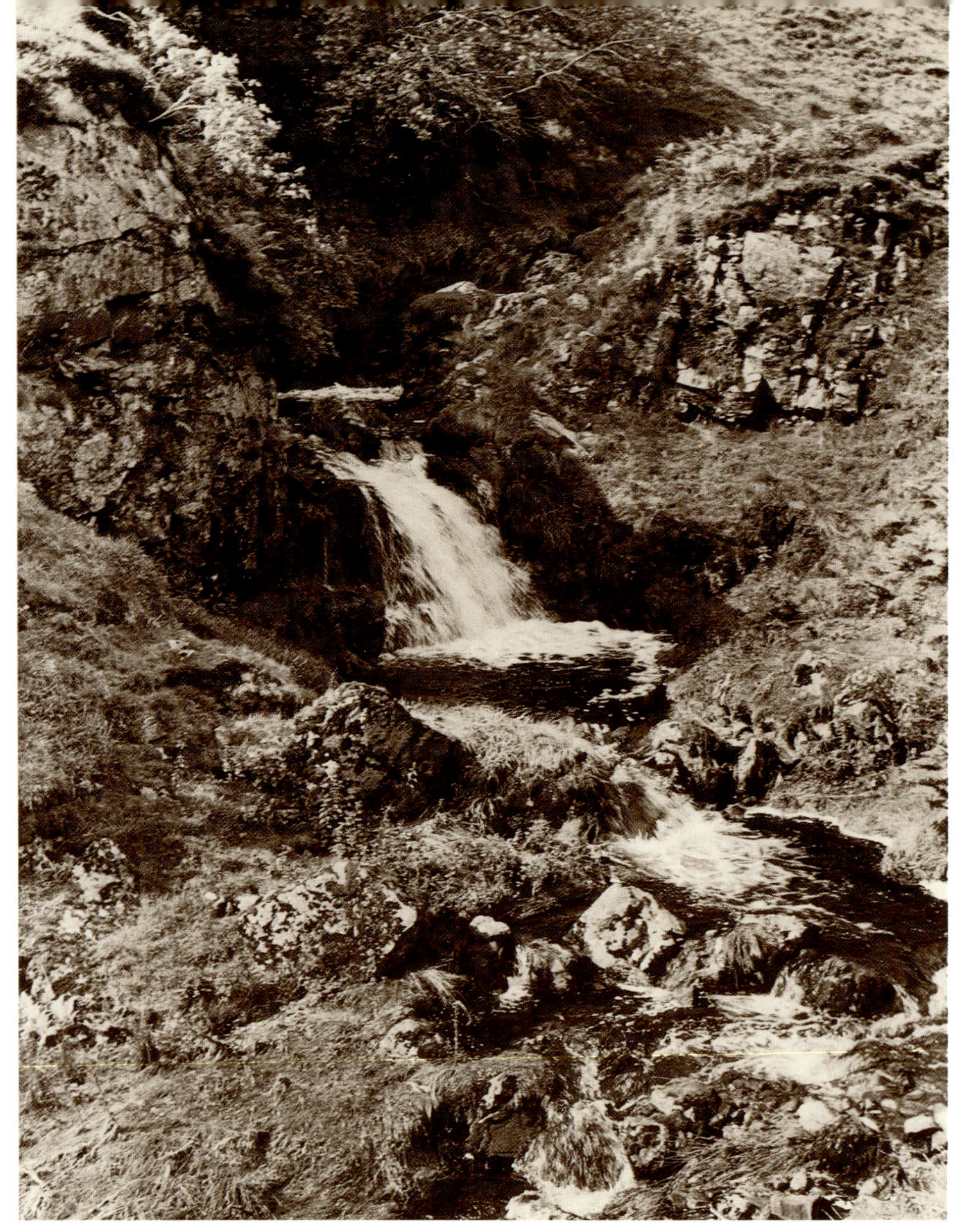

Lindhope Linn - a waterfall on a tributary of the Coquet.
Cat No: A180 Ref: H9144

View of Hedgehope and the Cheviot Hills across the valley of the Till from near Chillingham.
Cat No: A181 Ref: B1907

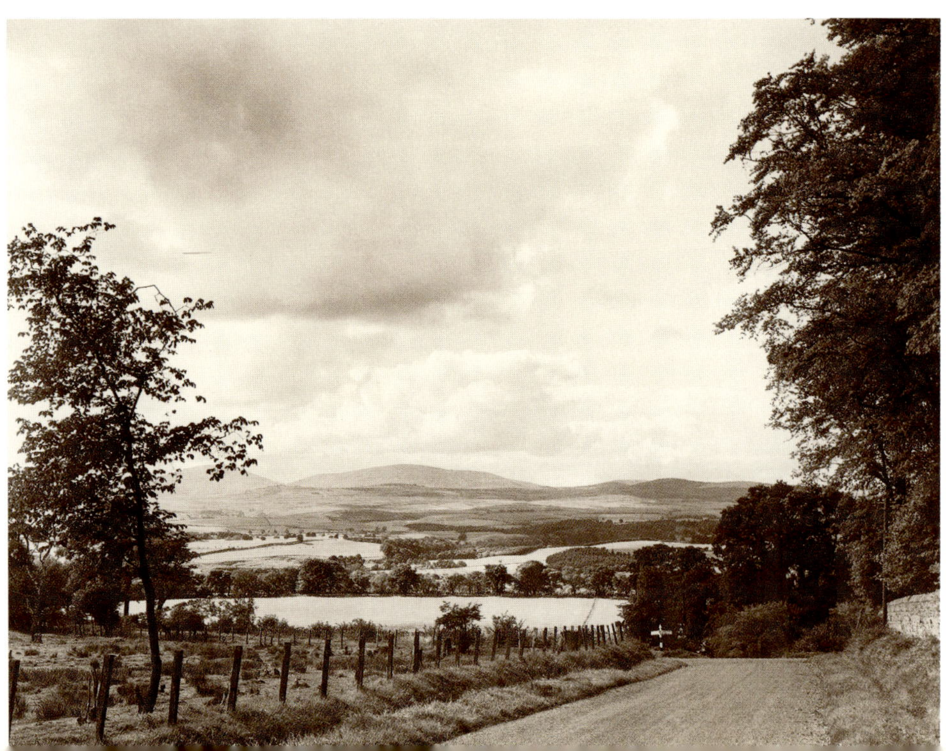

Farming in Northumberland - making a stack
Cat No: A183 Ref: 1637NI

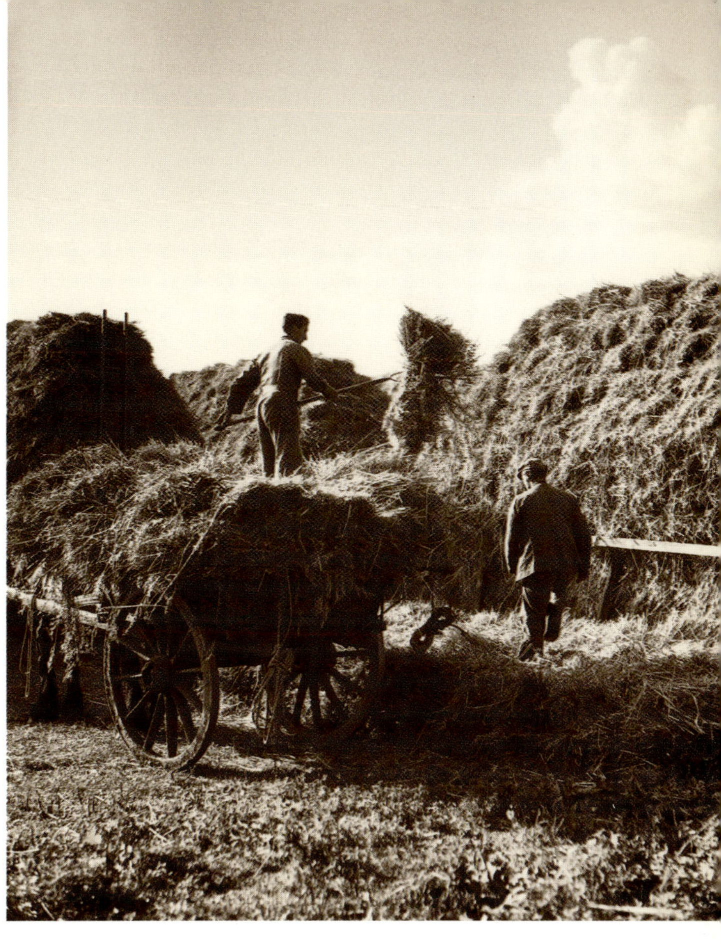

Farming in Northumberland - loading the horse-drawn trailer.
Cat No: A184 Ref: 1634NI

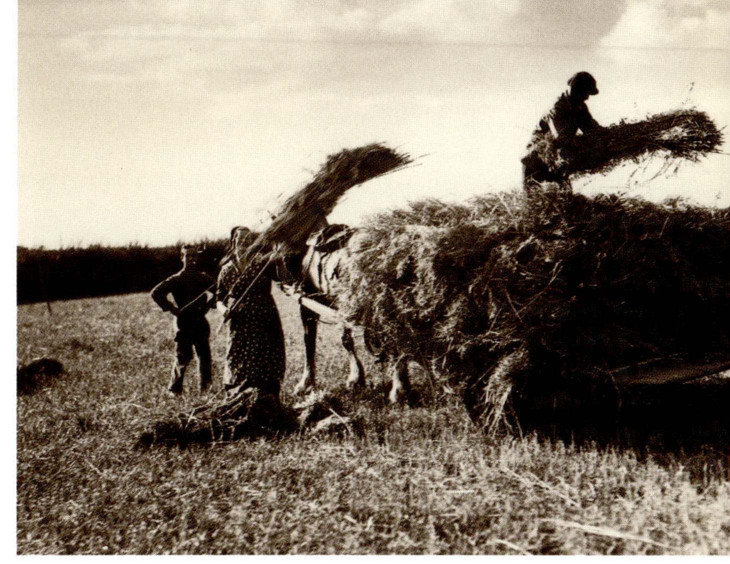

On the Wallington Estate which was covenanted to the National Trust by the Rt. Hon. Sir Charles Trevelyan Bart.
Cat No: A185 Ref: H9145

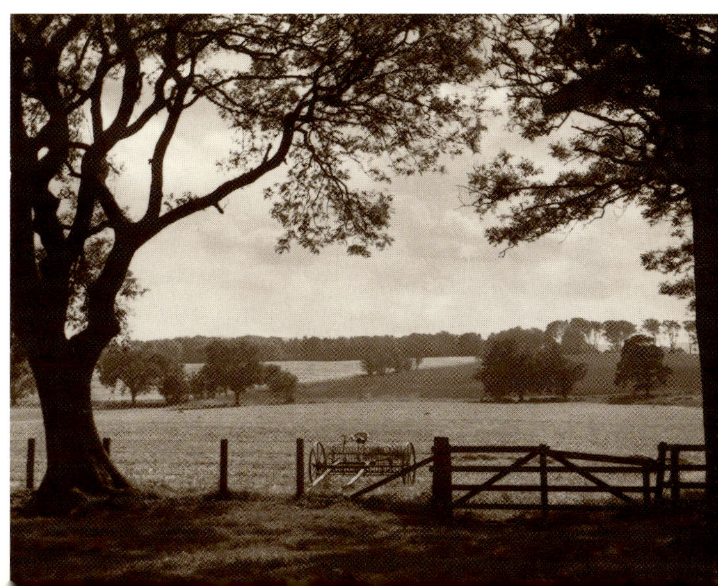

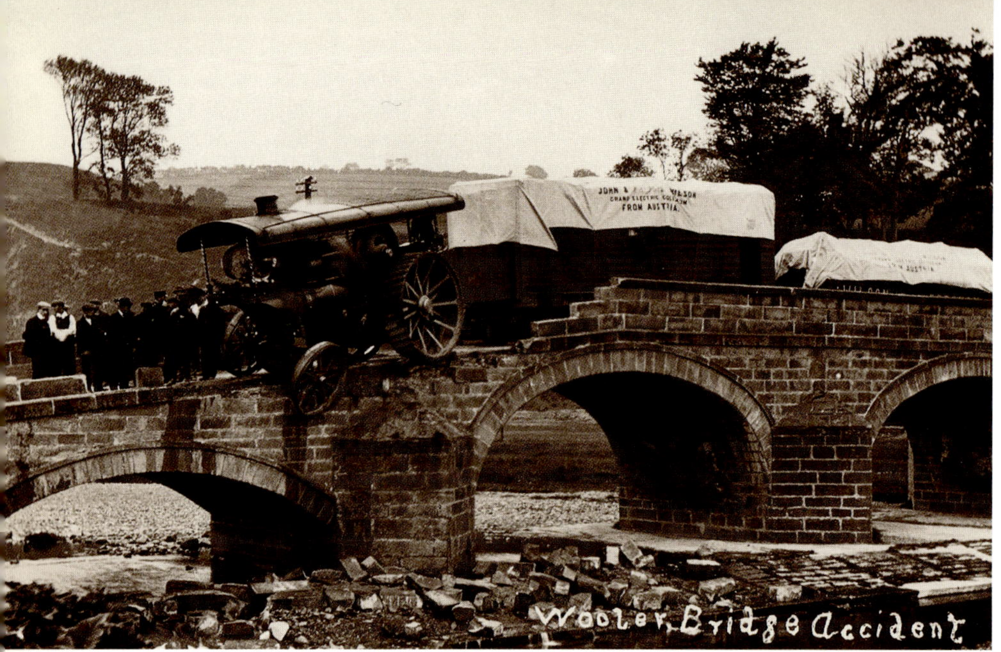

A slight accident with steam traction engine on the bridge at Wooler, Northumberland.
Cat No: A186 Ref: H9143

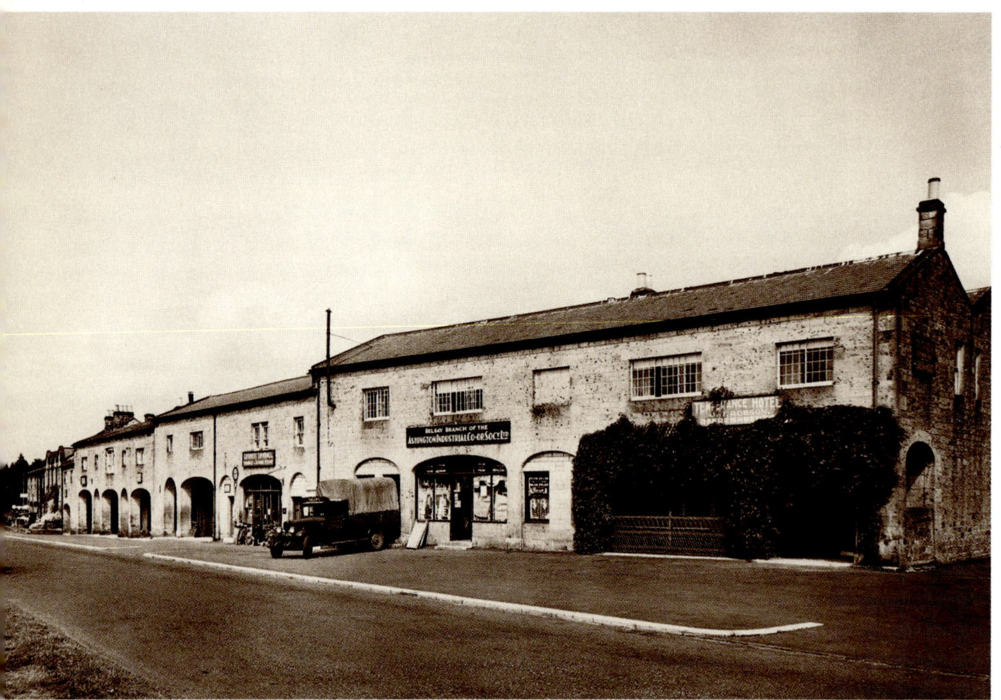

The Arcade, Belsay Village, Northumberland. Home of the Temperance Hotel and a branch of the Ashington Industrial Co-op Society Limited.
Cat No: A187 Ref: N3272

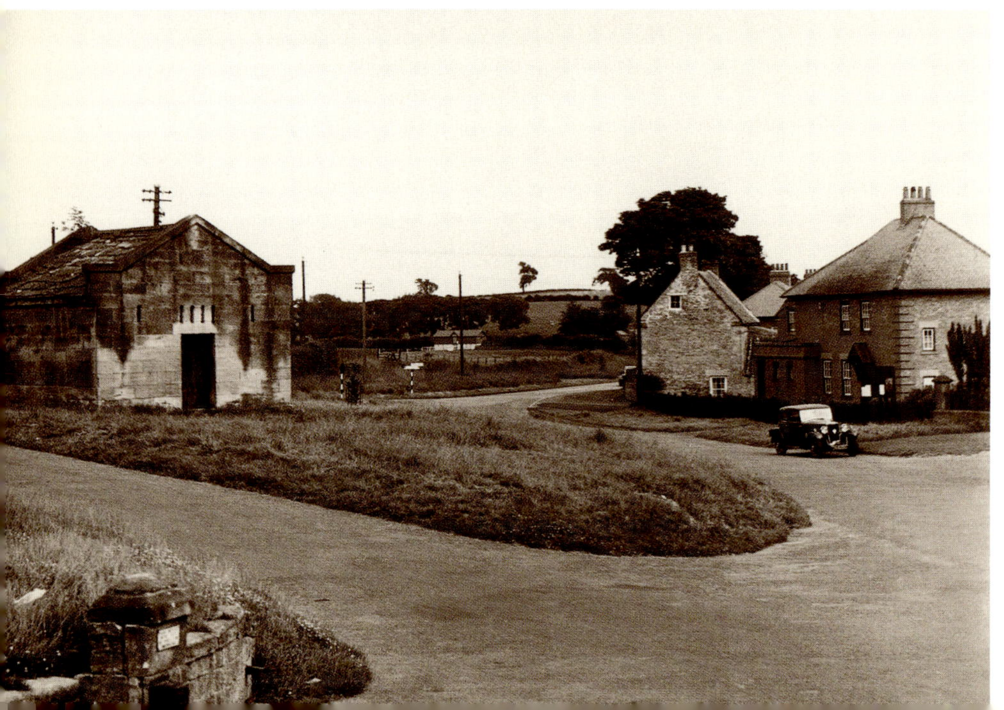

Pound and Water Pump, Stamfordham, Northumberland.
Cat No: A188 Ref: 1458NI

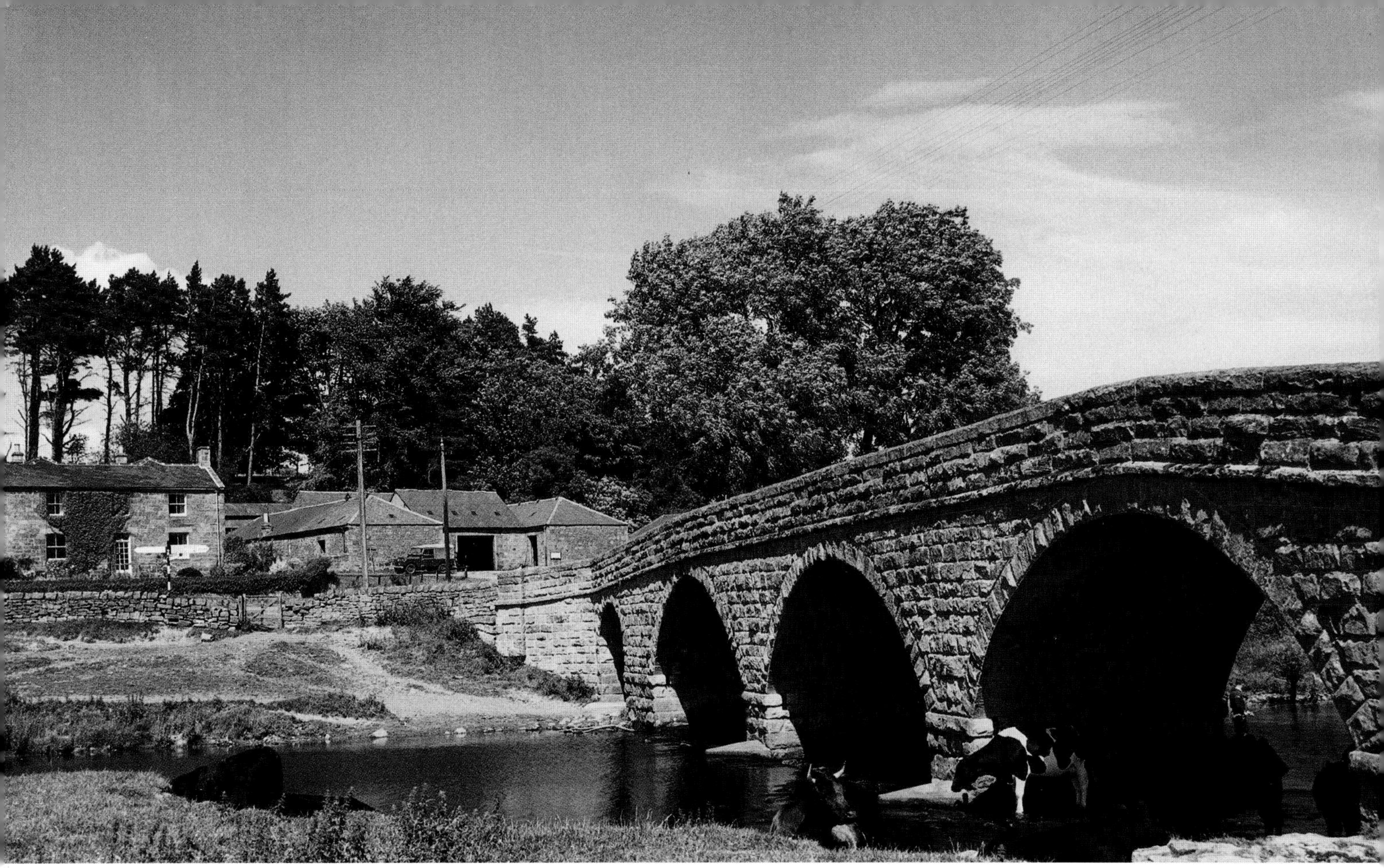

Pauperhaugh near Brinkburn Priory.
Cat No: A189 Ref: P3932

Bedlington Village, Northumberland was the centre of a prosperous coal mining area. Bedlingtonshire had long been administered by the Bishops of Durham and did not form part of the County of Northumberland.
Cat No: A190 Ref: J2932

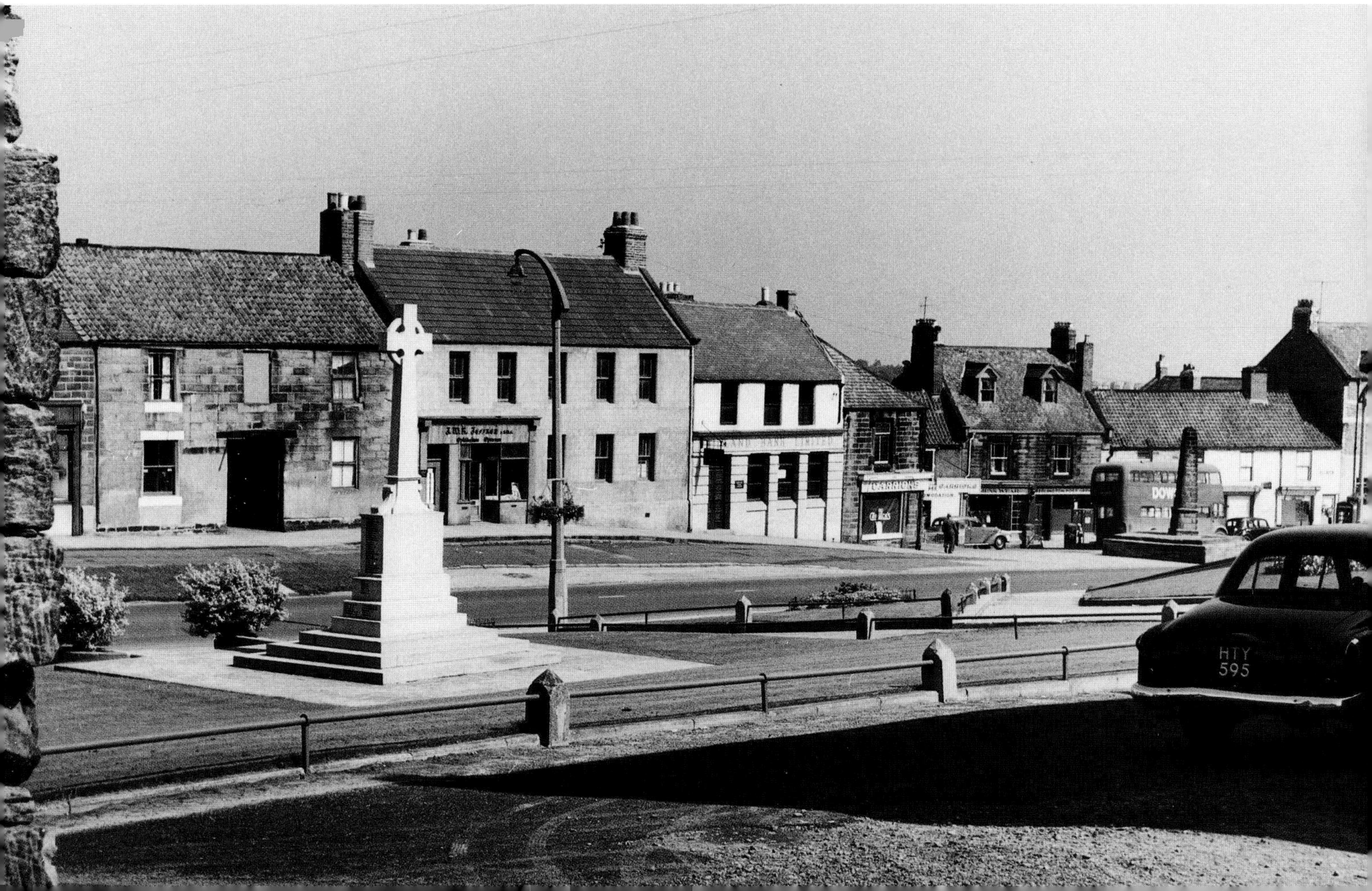

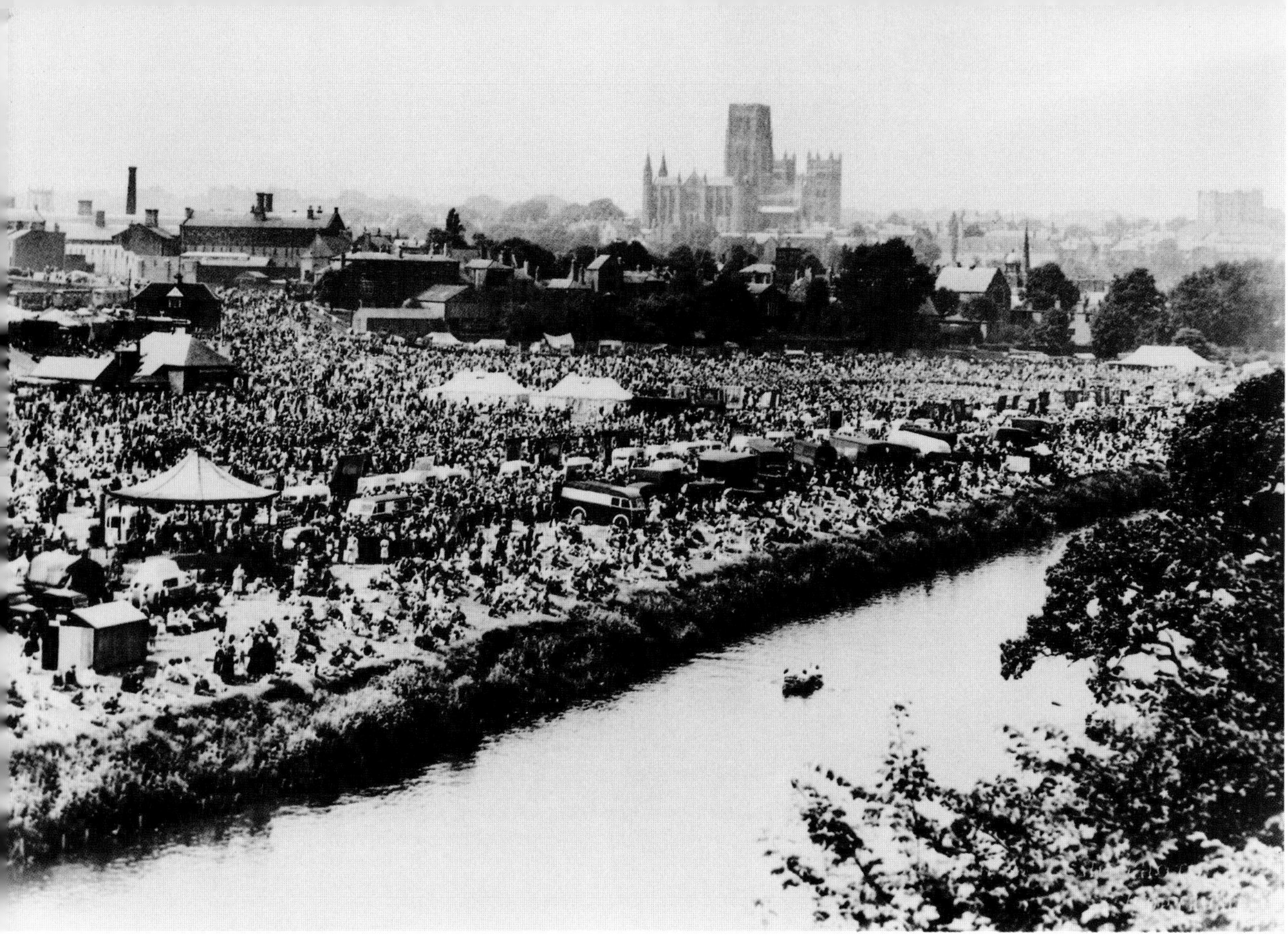

Durham Miners' Gala - the banners, the fun of the fair and the joy of friendship, in the shadow of Durham Cathedral, circa 1950.
Cat No: WPG045 Ref: H9142

Durham Cathedral.
Cat No: WPG047 Ref: B336

Barnard Castle and the River Tees.
Cat No: WPG046 Ref: M4764

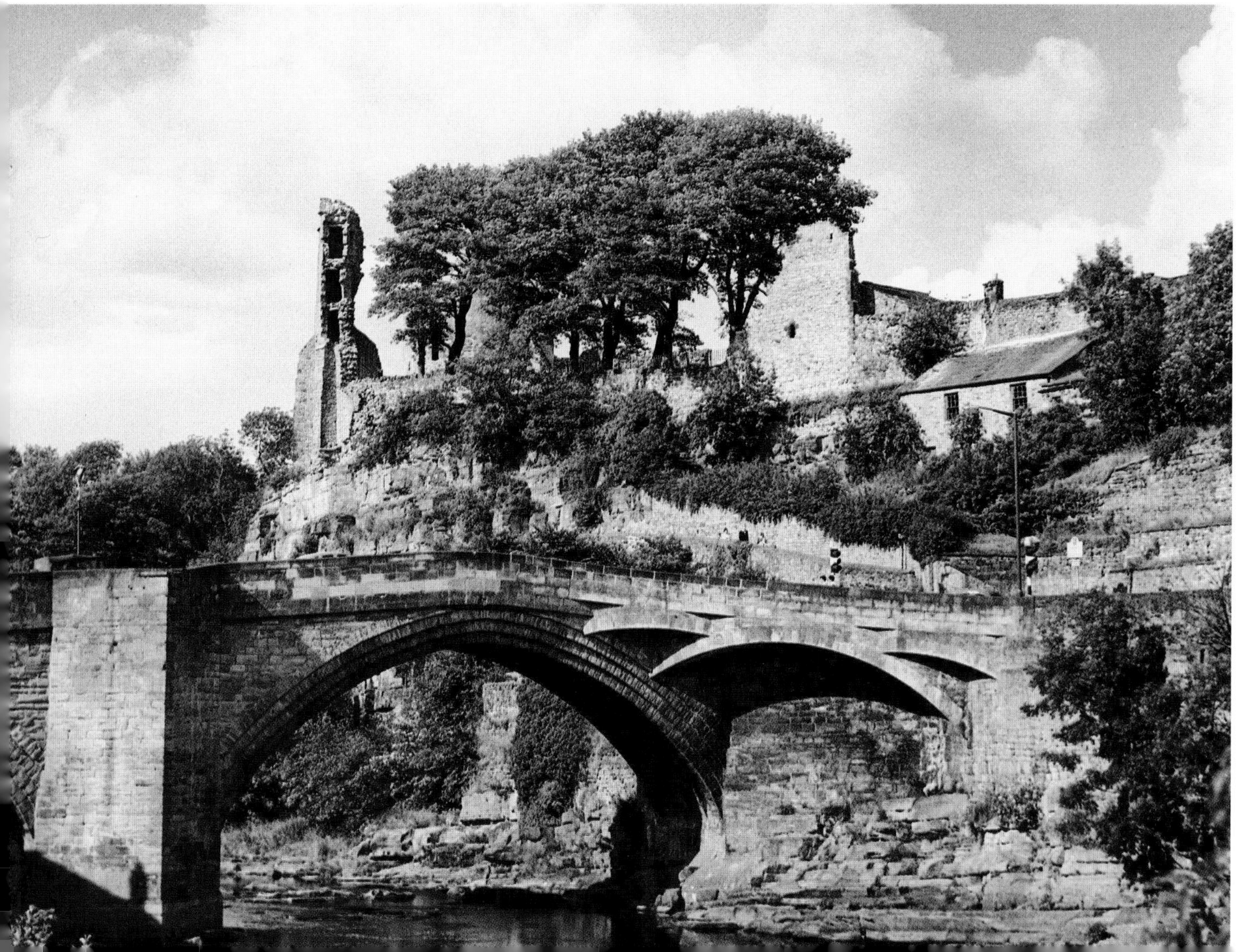

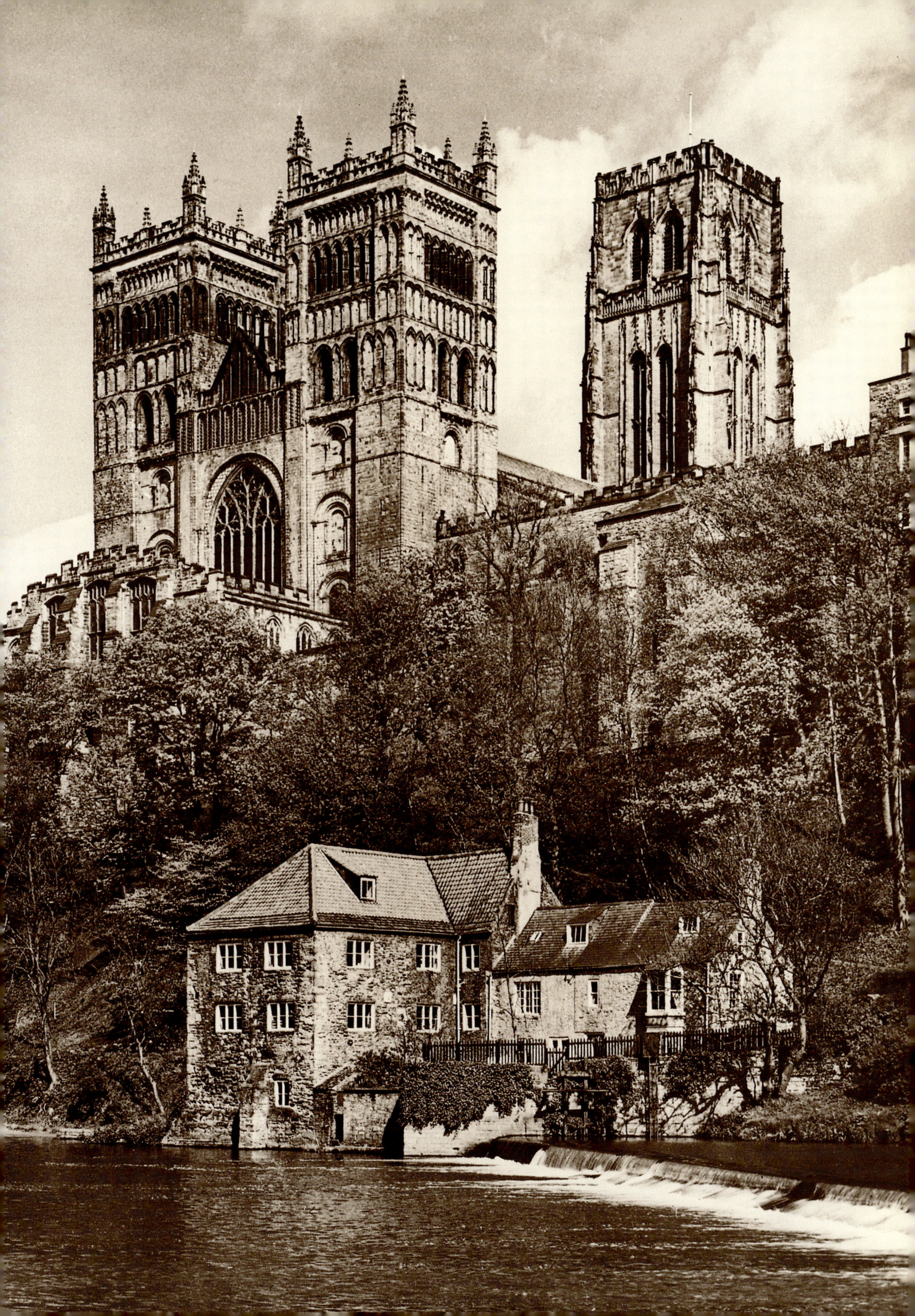

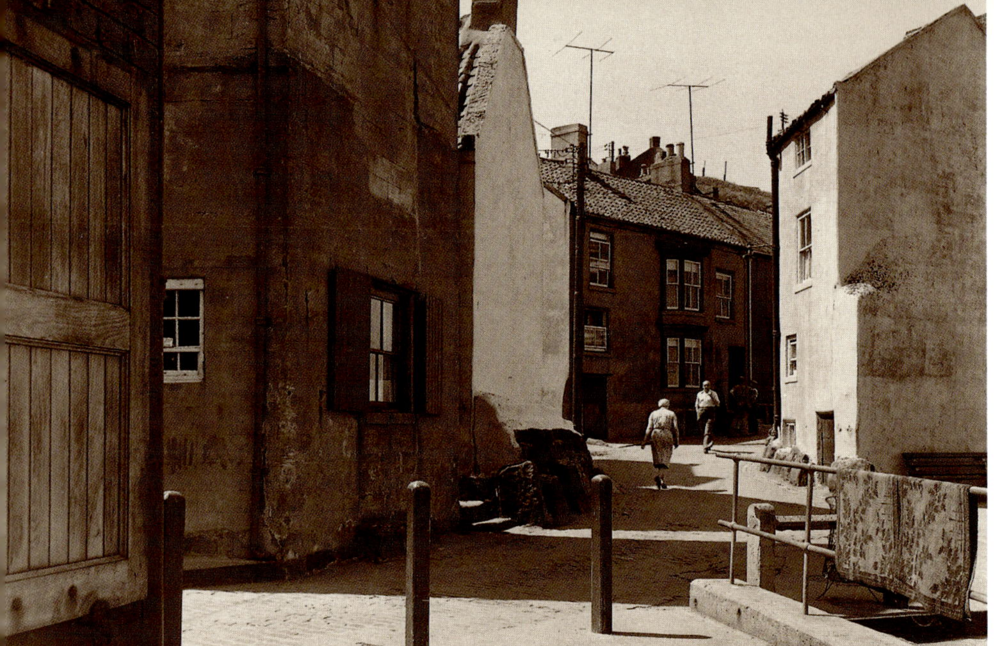

Staithes, North Riding of Yorkshire, 1957.
Cat No: A192 Ref: G2478

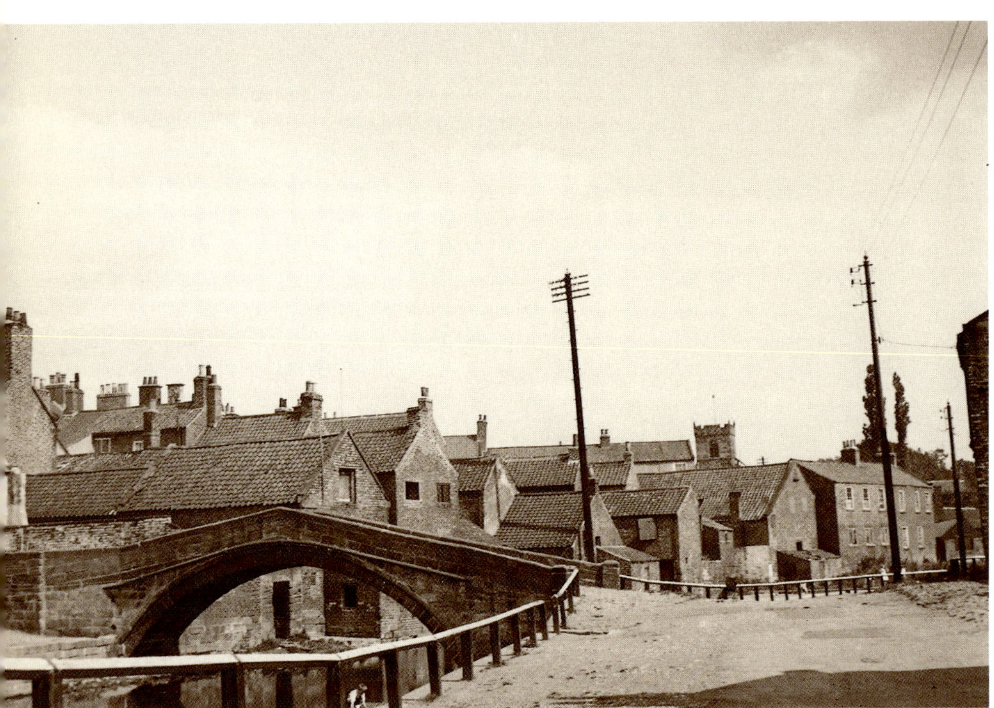

Just at play in Stokesley, North Yorkshire.
Cat No: A193 Ref: H9141

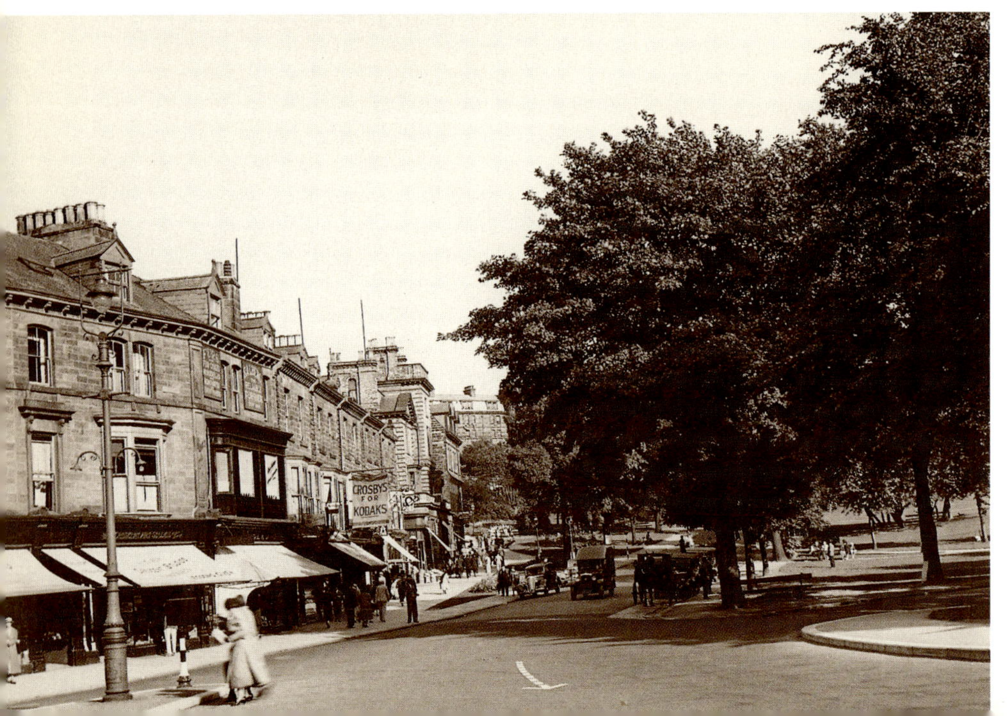

A quiet day in Swainby, Yorkshire.
Cat No: A194 Ref: H9175

Sorting the nets and passing the day at Staithes, North Riding of Yorkshire, 1957.
Cat No: A195 Ref: G2474

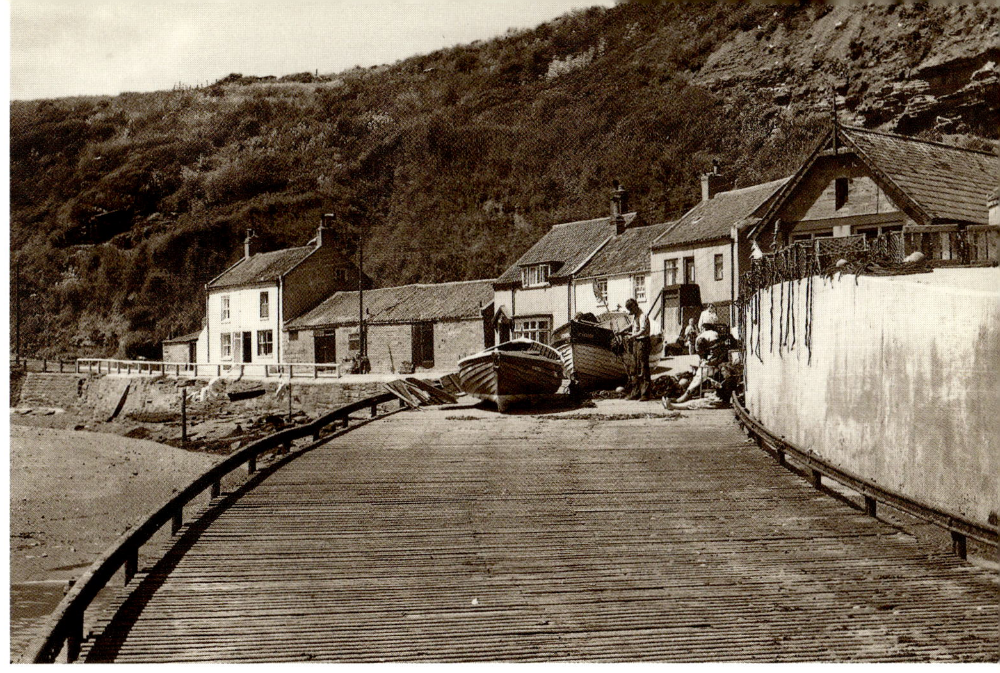

A busy day on the beach, by the pier at Saltburn, Yorkshire
Cat No: A196 Ref: K3333

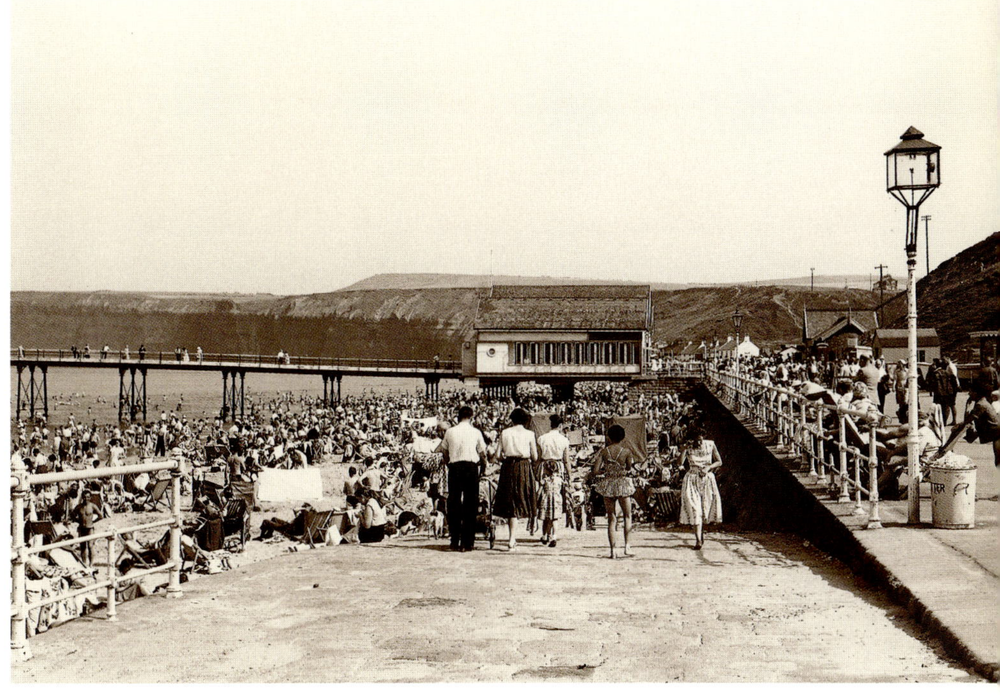

Boat trips and fun for all at the south beach and fairground, Saltburn, Yorkshire.
Cat No: A197 Ref: K3342

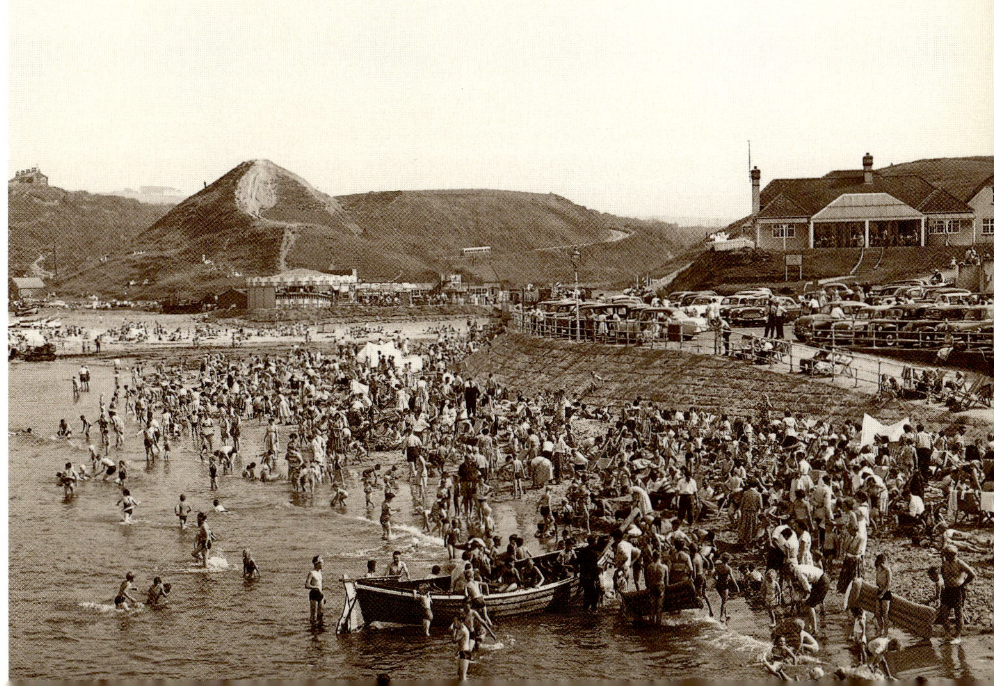

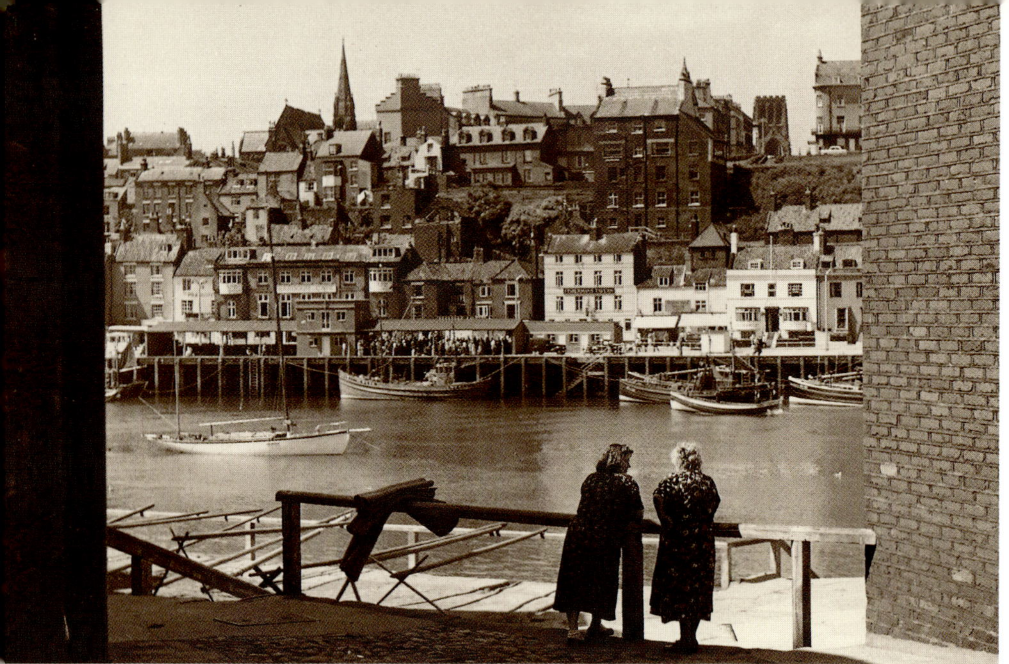

A neighbourly chat and a glimpse of the harbour, Whitby, Yorkshire.
Cat No: A198 Ref: J2536

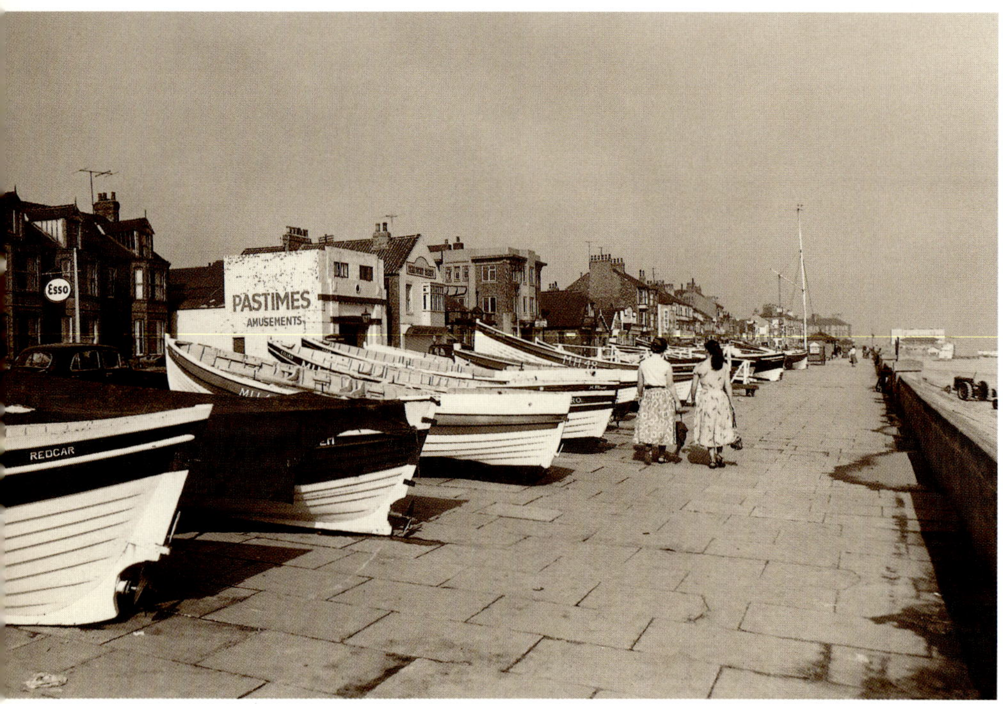

On the esplanade - the fishing boats of Redcar, Yorkshire 1957.
Cat No: A199 Ref: G2468

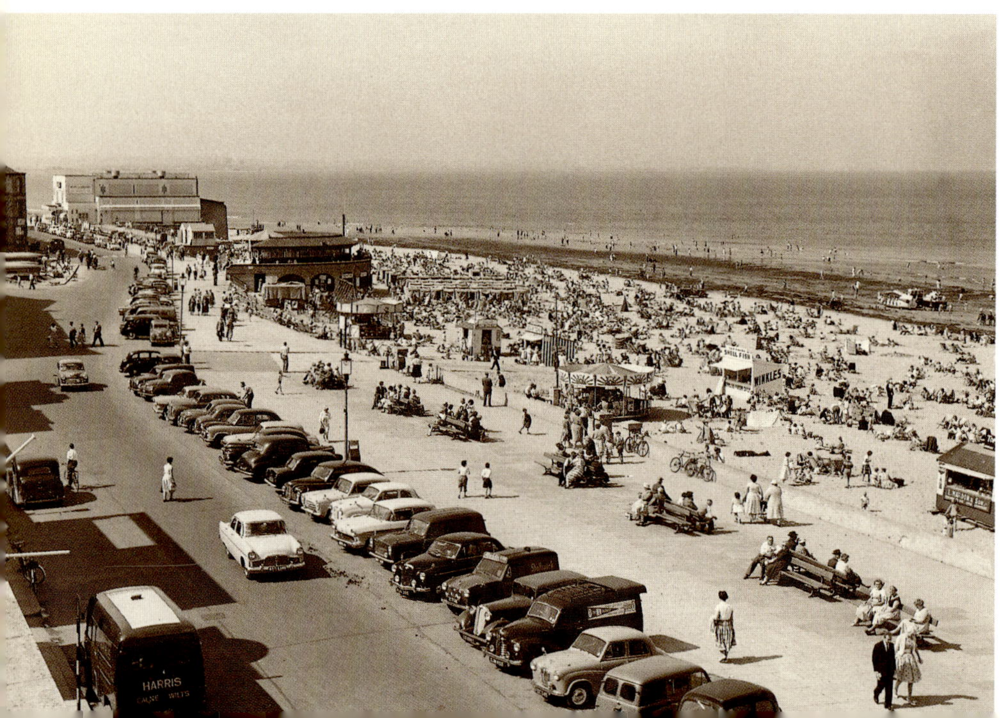

Sand, sea and shellfish - a sunny day on the esplanade and beach at Redcar, Yorkshire.
Cat No: A200 Ref: K3312

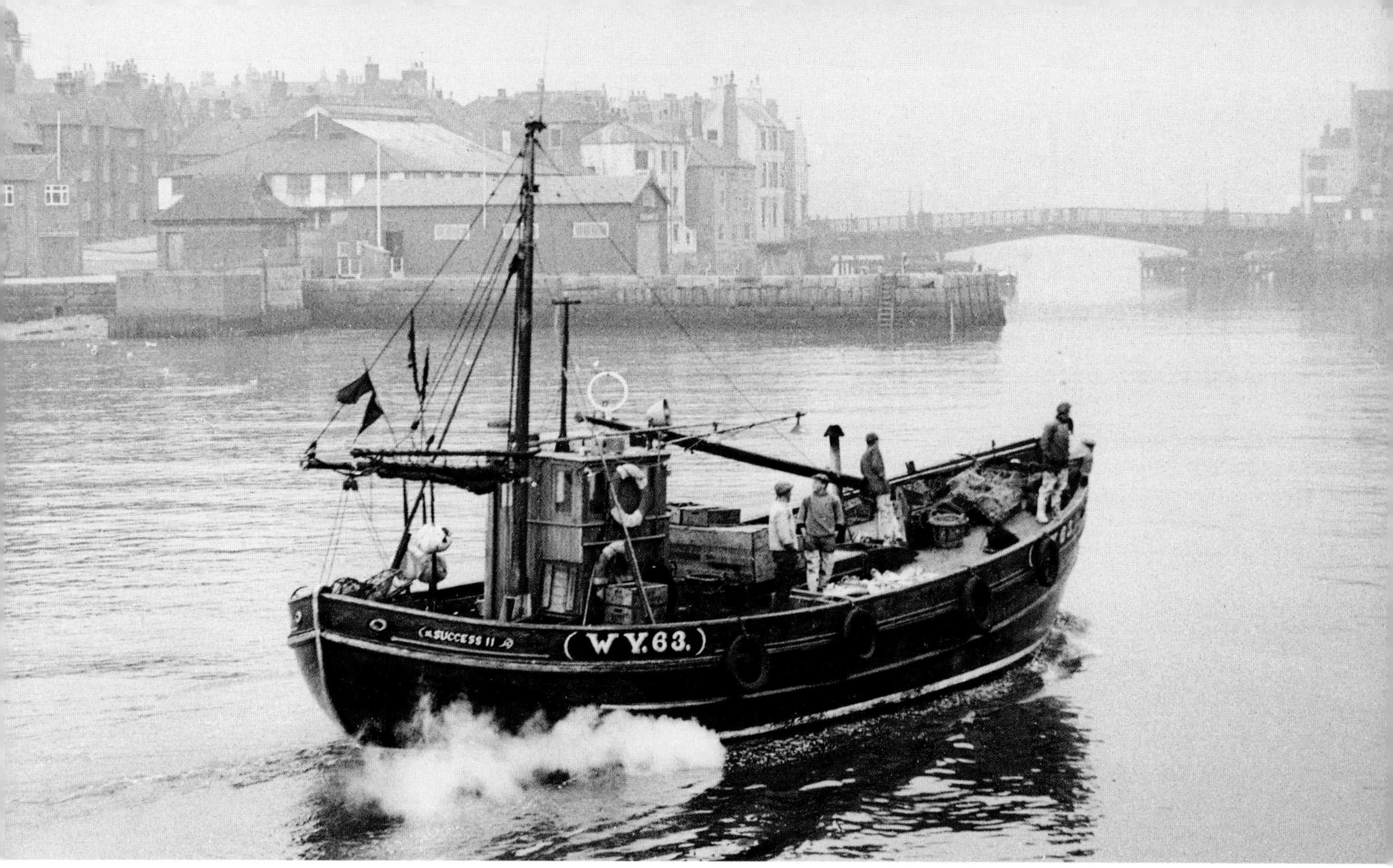

'Success II' sails back into Whitby Harbour.
Cat No: WPG048 Ref: F3548

Whitby Harbour. 'Venus', 'Falcon', 'Joan'n'Eric' and 'Whitby Lass' - fishing boats taking a well-earned rest.
Cat No: WPG049 Ref: J2532

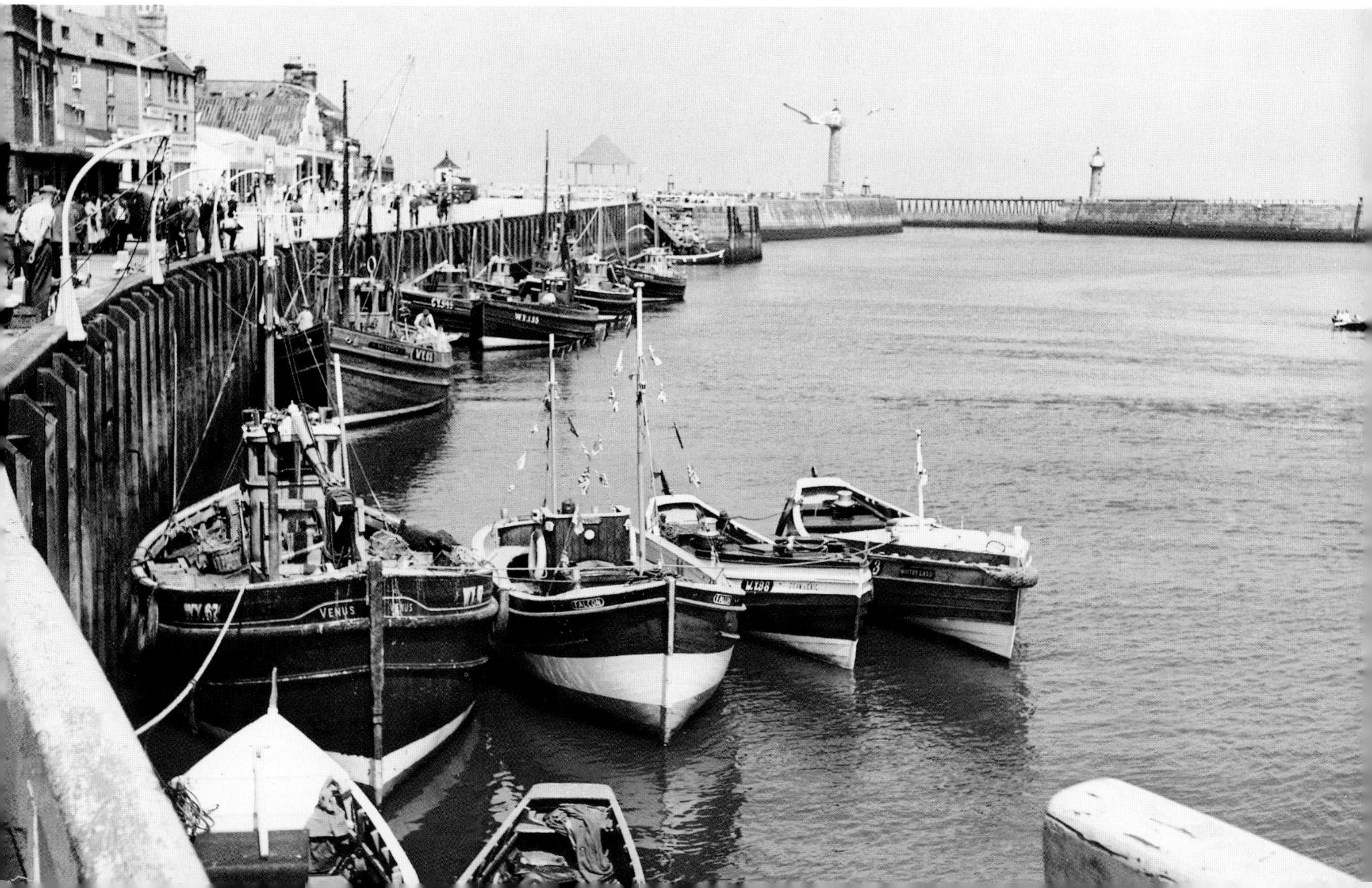

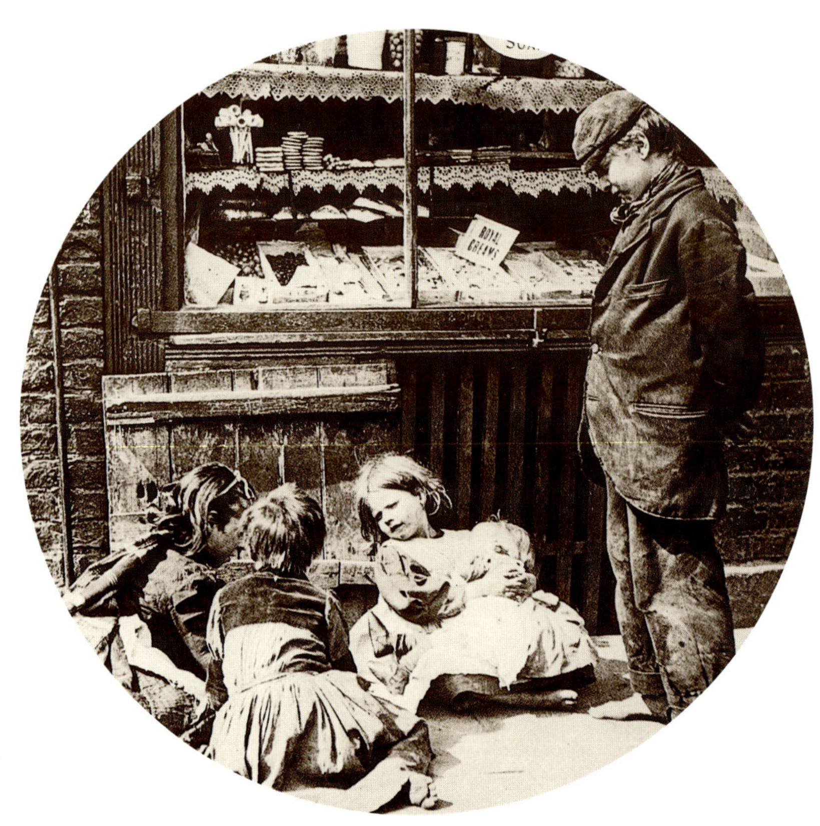

Its fun to play the children's way, while big brother looks on. From an original glass photographic plate.
Cat No: WPG041 Ref: X1577